Crime and Law Enforcement in the Colony of New York 1691–1776

Crime and Law Enforcement in the Colony of New York 1691-1776

DOUGLAS GREENBERG

Cornell University Press ITHACA AND LONDON

Winner, first New York State Historical Association
Manuscript Award, 1974

First published 1976 by Cornell University Press.
Published in the United Kingdom by Cornell University Press Ltd.,
2–4 Brook Street, London W1Y 1AA.

International Standard Book Number 0-8014-1020-7
Library of Congress Catalog Card Number 76-13658
Printed in the United States of America by York Composition Co., Inc.
Librarians: Library of Congress cataloging information appears on the last page of the book.

For My Parents

Contents

Tables

Preface

Crime and law enforcement are universal problems. While all societies establish codes of conduct which they conceive to be essential to their continued existence and stability, the nature of deviant behavior in society and the manner in which it is punished have been of special interest to sociologists and anthropologists because these topics speak so directly to a society's particular values. Thus, the manner in which crime is defined as well as the way in which it is treated are often issues of intense controversy in a society precisely because they so directly reflect that society's implicit world view.

Recently, crime and law enforcement have also attracted considerable attention among historians of early modern Europe. We now have available excellent studies of crime, criminals, and courts in a wide range of European societies from the medieval period into the last quarter of the twentieth century.[1] Historians of

[1] See, for example, the following representative works: John H. Langbein, *Prosecuting Crime in the Renaissance* (Cambridge, Mass., 1974); Werner L. Gundesheimer, "Crime and Punishment in Ferrara," in Lauro Martines, ed., *Violence and Civil Disorder in Italian Cities, 1200–1500* (Los Angeles, 1972); John Bellamy, *Crime and Public Order in England in the Later Middle Ages* (Toronto, 1973); Joel B. Samaha, *Law and Order in Historical Perspective: The Case of Elizabethan Essex* (New York, 1974); John M. Beattie, "Towards a Study of Crime in Eighteenth-Century England: A Note on Indictments," in Paul Fritz and David Williams, eds., *The Triumph of Culture: Eighteenth-Century Perspectives* (Toronto, 1972); Beattie, "The Pattern of Crime in England, 1660–1800," *Past and Present,* 62 (Feb., 1974), 47–95; J. S. Cockburn, *A History of English Assizes, 1558–1714* (Cambridge, England, 1972); J. J. Tobias, *Crime and Industrial Society in*

early America have not yet followed the lead of their Europeanist colleagues. Although there are many excellent studies of the development of law in colonial America, few historians have attempted the sort of sustained, comprehensive, and in-depth analysis of crime and law enforcement which has been emerging in studies of early modern European societies.[2] It is difficult to understand why this should be so. For indeed, crime and law enforcement were central experiences for early Americans, and the ways in which they dealt with these problems have much to tell us about their view of the world in which they lived.

Scholars who have undertaken the study of early American crime and law enforcement have often failed to appreciate the wider significance of their research findings, leaving us, instead, with a catalogue of cases and curiosities that need to be placed in a broader analytical framework. One classic exception to this discouraging pattern is *Law Enforcement in Colonial New York,* a massive volume of almost 900 pages by Julius N. Goebel and T. Raymond Naughton.[3] A highly specialized work written from the lawyer's point of view (the authors warn the reader at the outset that they are skeptical, even contemptuous, of legal history written by scholars without legal training[4]), *Law Enforcement in Colonial New York* is scholarship of the highest calibre, and provides a detailed and exhaustive analysis of the legal records of the colony of

---

the Nineteenth Century (London, 1967); Douglas Hay, *et al., Albion's Fatal Tree: Crime and Society in Eighteenth-Century England* (London, 1976); and the six essays which comprise the Summer, 1975, issue of the *Journal of Social History*.

[2] One exception, though in some ways a problematic one, is Kai T. Erikson, *Wayward Puritans: A Study in the Sociology of Deviance* (New York, 1966). For an examination of this and other works touching on early American crime and law enforcement, see Douglas Greenberg, " 'Persons of Evil Name and Fame': Crime and Law Enforcement in the Colony of New York" (Ph.D. diss., Cornell University, 1974), ch. 1.

[3] Julius N. Goebel and T. Raymond Naughton, *Law Enforcement in Colonial New York: A Study in Criminal Procedure, 1664–1776* (New York, 1944; reprinted: Montclair, N.J., 1970).

[4] *Ibid.*, xxxiv–xxxv.

New York between 1664 and 1776. The major thrust of Goebel's and Naughton's interpretation was to dispute the claim that the frontier experience of life in the New World had seriously altered the legal institutions and traditions of England. They offered convincing evidence to support their contention that legal practice in New York mirrored the English common-law tradition which had been its inspiration. The structure of legal institutions, the roles of attorneys, prosecutors, and justices of the peace, the form and wording of writs, warrants, and other legal documents—indeed, almost every aspect of criminal procedure in colonial New York—had, according to Goebel and Naughton, virtually duplicated that currently in use in England.[5] Thirty years after the publication of *Law Enforcement in Colonial New York,* there is little reason to question the essential validity of this interpretation. The forms and procedures of English criminal law are everywhere apparent in the legal records of the colony, and there can be no doubt that, especially after 1691 when the colony's court structure was thoroughly reorganized, the legal traditions of Britain exercised a powerful influence even in the polyglot colony of New York, more than three thousand miles from the Inns of Court and the Palace of Westminster.

As a history of the law and the courts, then, the book sets a standard to which other scholars can aspire; yet historians interested in what James Willard Hurst has called "the social history of law" will perhaps be less enthusiastic about it. Goebel and Naughton focused too narrowly upon legal problems as such, and often failed to consider them as reflections of more fundamental processes and developments. The system of criminal justice in New York was not as explicitly shaped by a peculiar set of values as those of Massachusetts and Pennsylvania. Nevertheless, a study of the system may provide a number of indices of disguised social phenomena which Goebel and Naughton either chose to ignore or treated as subjects of marginal importance. There is reason to

[5] *Ibid.* See esp. xxi, xxviii–xxix, 760.

think that despite the book's voluminous documentation and elaborate structure it fails in important ways to answer or even raise some of the most significant questions about the history of law and legal institutions in early New York. The almost compulsive attention of Goebel and Naughton to matters of form, precedent, and procedure has tended to obscure a variety of issues that modern legal and social historians may wish to explore. I agree with the observation of George Haskins that "the task of the historian of law is not merely one of recounting the growth and jurisdiction of courts and legislatures or of detailing legal rules and doctrines. It is essential that these matters be related to the political and social environments of particular times and places."[6]

Thus, this work is not intended to revise Goebel's and Naughton's study or to attack their conclusions on matters of law. My differences with them are general and methodological more than they are particular and substantive. For too long the court records of colonial New York have been consigned to scholars who believe that "social historians . . . function in a pleasant anarchic world of their own."[7] I do not believe that social historians need to be intimidated by such polemics, nor should they be dissuaded by what Haskins calls "the traditional isolation of the law from other disciplines."[8] Rather, the time has come to discard Goebel's and Naughton's distinction between legal and social history and use court records not only to analyze the social history of law, but also to illuminate the history of society itself. The point is simply that contemporary historians may wish to cast a wider net and ask other questions of the criminal court records that Goebel and Naughton mined so effectively. In light of the extensive—and excellent—scholarship which has appeared on colonial New York since their book was published in 1944, and given the wide variety of methodological advances that have been made in recent years,

[6] George Lee Haskins, *Law and Authority in Early Massachusetts: A Study in Tradition and Design* (New York, 1960), vii.

[7] Goebel and Naughton, *Law Enforcement,* xxxv.

[8] Haskins, *Law and Authority,* vii.

we have an obligation to examine the court records of colonial New York from another perspective, a perspective that will shed light not only on the courts themselves, but on the many citizens of the colony who stood before them in criminal proceedings.

But how ought such an examination proceed? Historians of early American crime have no established paradigm of analysis, nor do they enjoy the luxury af applying an established methodological framework to a familiar body of evidence. Moreover, the recent studies of early modern European crime provide only marginal assistance, since the local eccentricities of court records often govern the direction of research and mode of inquiry. Sociologists, of course, have been concerned with crime and law enforcement, and some have even speculated about the historical development of these problems.[9] But the sociologist's approach is finally too idiosyncratic to be of much use to the historian—the "pitfalls of ahistorical social science" which Stephan Thernstrom has noted in studies of social mobility are also apparent in the sociological scholarship on crime, law, and deviant behavior.[10] Therefore, since this study of crime and law enforcement in eighteenth-century New York enters what might be called a scholarly vacuum, there may be some value in being very explicit at the outset about the sorts of questions it addresses and the methods it uses to answer those questions.

My purpose is to use a select sample of the population of colonial New York—defendants in its criminal courts—to illuminate some of the larger issues of the colony's social history. I have assumed throughout that the patterns I have identified in the court

[9] See, for example, Marshall B. Clinard, "The Process of Urbanization and Criminal Behavior," *American Journal of Sociology,* 43 (1942), 202–213; Mabel A. Elliott, "Crime and Frontier Mores," *American Sociological Review,* 9 (1944), 185–192; Marshall B. Clinard, *Crime in Developing Countries: A Comparative Perspective* (New York, 1973); Richard Quinney, *The Social Reality of Crime* (Boston, 1970); and Nigel Walker, *Crime and Punishment in Britain* (Edinburgh, 1965).

[10] See Stephan Thernstrom, *Poverty and Progress: Social Mobility in a Nineteenth-century City* (New York, 1969), 225–239.

records are not random or accidental, but rather reflect underlying issues that require our attention if we are to understand the significance of growth and change in New York in the hundred years or so preceding the American Revolution. With this goal in mind, I have sought to probe two fundamental issues: Who were New York's criminal defendants? What happened to them once they began to move through the colony's system of criminal justice? To be sure, questions like these often prompt other queries that will be dealt with along the way, but these two central concerns—the population of criminal defendants and their treatment—inform much of the analysis.

A word or two about methodology may also be in order. Much of the evidence in these pages is quantitatively expressed. Crime is a historical phenomenon peculiarly suited to counting, and readers will find a variety of tables in this volume. I do not, however, regard this work as being primarily an exercise in quantitative history. By most "cliometric" standards, the measures employed are crude—this was necessitated by the incomplete and partial nature of the data—and, perhaps more important, the quantitative data are only one part of the evidentiary apparatus. Virtually none of the figures in this study can be sensibly understood without explicit reference to other, more impressionistic, source materials. This study was "computer assisted," but I have no pretension to being "scientific" or "objective," since the book is ultimately based upon records that are, of necessity, chronologically and geographically incomplete. I shall have more to say about these problems in Chapter 2, but readers should be aware that the quantitative data impart a deceptively straightforward texture to materials that are often complex and ambiguous.

This study was aided and abetted by many people and institutions. I take great pleasure in acknowledging my debts to those who have helped me along the way.

The records that form the documentary basis of this volume were difficult to locate, since most of them were stored in county courthouses. Without exception, county clerks responded thoughtfully to my inquiries and were more than generous when I asked to see records which had been so infrequently examined that often no one knew exactly where they were stored. County courthouses are not geared to historical research; they are noisy, crowded, and, in the summer, very hot. But everywhere I went county officials found a relatively quiet spot with a desk where I could work without interruption. In the counties of New York, Richmond, Queens, Westchester, Dutchess, Orange, Albany, and Suffolk, I was treated with great courtesy. To officials in each of them, I owe thanks for help well beyond the call of duty. The court records of Ulster and Kings counties for the eighteenth century are no longer in the county archives, but the clerks of both counties were helpful in locating the materials I required, and I am grateful for their assistance.

In addition I wish to thank the staffs of the New-York Historical Society, the New York State Library in Albany, and the Library of the Association of the Bar of New York for providing access to several collections of important documents. James A. Owre, Archivist of Queens College Historical Documents Collection, was most helpful when I visited the Collection, and he later provided microfilm copies of court records that I had been unable to locate in manuscript. Arthur Konop, Archivist and Dean of Continuing Education at St. Francis College, generously allowed me to spend several days examining the Kings County records, which were in his care, and lightened the burden of research with his stories of the bureaucratic bungling of city government. All these people were vital to the completion of this study, and I very much appreciate their efforts in my behalf.

The Graduate School and History Department of Cornell University supported this study by providing a generous fellowship during my years in Ithaca. The Faculty Research Council at Cornell also provided a grant that helped to defray my travel expenses during the summer of 1972. Joel Silbey not only gave me some good advice about computerized historical research, but also offered me History Department funds to help pay for computer time. The John Anson Kittredge Educational Fund, whose Board of Control is chaired by Walter Muir Whitehill, was kind enough to furnish me with a very generous grant that allowed me to complete the computer phase of my work. Lawrence University was also generous in providing funds for research assistance and for the purchase of microfilms.

For permission to draw upon earlier versions of chapters of this book published in their journals, my thanks go to the editors of *New York History* and the *American Journal of Legal History*. One of my deepest debts is to the New York State Historical Association and its prize committee, which awarded an earlier version of this book its first Manuscript Award in 1974. The Association and its staff—especially Wendell Tripp—have helped in a variety of ways to guide the manuscript through revision and publication. I am grateful for their patience, advice, and support.

My most warmly felt thanks are also due to the many colleagues and friends who have been so generous with their time and energy during the years of this book's gestation. Sidney Bremer, Richard D. Brown, Thomas J. Davis, Kai Erikson, Michael Hindus, Herbert Johnson, Milton Klein, Sung Bok Kim, William Nelson, Kathryn Preyer, Roy Ritchie, Bruce Wilkenfeld, and L. Kinvin Wroth read either part or all of the manuscript, and I have benefited enormously from their comments and criticisms. The book is better than it would have been without their help, but perhaps not as good as it would have been if I had been less stubborn and always followed their advice. Special thanks are due to David Flaherty, who read and commented extensively upon an earlier version of the book and encouraged me to revise it for publication. In addition, he generously shared the results of his own pioneering work on crime in eighteenth-century Massachusetts and allowed me to use some of his material for comparative purposes. Similarly, John Beattie shared with me some of his research on crime in eighteenth-century England; I appreciate his assistance. Several of my colleagues at Lawrence also read parts of the manuscript: Peter Fritzell, Chong-Do Hah, and Charles Simpkins offered insights of literature, political science, and sociology respectively, and I thank them for their help. Other debts of both a personal and professional nature are owed to my friends Lanny Wright and Bill Bremer, whose contributions have been at once intangible and essential.

No set of acknowledgments would be complete without an expression of gratitude to the teachers who have put up with me over the years. Theirs was the most direct contribution to this book, for it would never have been written without their interest and encouragement. Philip J. Greven, Jr., of Rutgers University first prompted my interest in early American social history. This book incorporates many ideas that I first developed under the stimulating influence of his undergraduate lecture courses and seminars. It was his example as a teacher and scholar that shaped my decision to choose history as a career and it is an example that continues to inspire me. Clive Holmes, Daniel Baugh, and Fred Somkin of Cornell all helped in various ways, providing perceptive criticism and advice, and Mary Beth Norton has also, as both teacher and friend, done much to make this a better book.

The single most important influence upon my personal and professional growth has been Michael Kammen. My debt to him is the greatest and the most difficult to acknowledge fully. He was always available when I was writing the book, and he listened patiently, even when my ideas were imprecise and my thinking muddled. Most of all, his exemplary scholarship, concerned teaching, and warm friendship have improved my work and enriched my life. I would like to think that my own students benefit from his influence.

I rescrve my last and especial thanks for Margee, who helped in innumerable ways. The special grace with which she leads her life helped me to put this book and all my work in perspective. For that, and for so many other things, she has my love and my gratitude.

DOUGLAS GREENBERG

Appleton, Wisconsin

Abbreviations

A.C.S. "Minutes of the Court of General Sessions of the Peace," Albany County, 1717–1723; 1763–1782 (Albany County Clerk's Office, Albany, N.Y.).

C.M. "Minutes of the Coroner's Proceedings in the City and County of New York," 1747–1758 (Columbia University Library, Rare Book Room, New York, N.Y.).

Cal. Hist. Mss. Edmund B. O'Callaghan, ed. *Calendar of Historical Manuscripts in the Office of the Secretary of State, Part II, English Manuscripts* (Albany, N.Y., 1866). This volume is a calendar of N.Y.S.L. Mss.

Circuit "Minutes of the Circuit Court of Oyer and Terminer and General Gaol Delivery," 1721–1749 (Library of the Association of the Bar of the City of New York, N.Y.).

Col. Laws N.Y. *The Colonial Laws of New York from the Year 1664 to the Revolution,* 5 vols. (Albany, N.Y., 1894).

D.C.S. "Minutes of Dutchess County Court of Common Pleas and General Sessions of the Peace," 1721–1775 (Dutchess County Clerk's Office, Poughkeepsie, N.Y.).

Doc. Hist. N.Y. Edmund B. O'Callaghan, ed. *The Documentary History of the State of New York,* 4 vols. (Albany, N.Y., 1849–1851).

Fox, ed., W.C.S. Dixon Ryan Fox, ed. "Minutes of the Court of Sessions (1657–1696), Westchester County" in *Publications of the Westchester Historical Society,* II (White Plains, N.Y., 1924).

Journal Leg. Council *Journal of the Legislative Council of the Colony of New York,* 2 vols. (Albany, N.Y., 1861).

K.C.S. "Court and Road Records Mss., Kings County," 1668–1776 (St. Francis College Archives, Brooklyn, N.Y.).

Kempe Papers Kempe Family Papers, Manuscript Collections of the New-York Historical Society, New York, N.Y.

M.C.C. Herbert L. Osgood, *et al.*, eds. *Minutes of the Common Council of the City of New York, 1675–1776,* 8 vols. (New York, N.Y., 1905).

Mayor and Aldermen "Minutes of the Mayor, Deputy Mayor, and Aldermen of New York City," 1733–1742 (Queens College Historical Documents Collection; microfilm; roll MC27).

N.Y. Col. Docs. Edmund B. O'Callaghan, ed. *Documents Relative to the Colonial History of the State of New York,* 15 vols. (Albany, N.Y., 1853–1887).

N.Y.G.S. "Minutes of the Court of General Sessions of the Peace for the City and County of New York," 1691–1776 (Queens College Historical Documents Collection; microfilm; rolls CMS1-CMS2).

N.Y.S.L. Mss. One hundred and one volumes of miscellaneous original documents relative to New York's colonial history (Manuscript Collections of the New York State Library, Albany, N.Y.).

O.C.S. "Minutes of the Orange County Court of General Sessions of the Peace," 1727–1779 (Orange County Clerk's Office, Goshen, N.Y.).

Q.C.S. "Minutes of the Courts of General Sessions and Common Pleas," 1722–1787 (Queens County Clerk's Office, Jamaica, N.Y.).

R.C.S. "Minutes of the Court of General Sessions and Common Pleas," 1711–1745, 1745–1812 (Richmond County Clerk's Office, St. George, Staten Island, N.Y.).

S.C. (1912) "Minutes of the Supreme Court of Judicature," 1693–1701 (*Collections of the New-York Historical Society,* vol. 45, New York, N.Y., 1912).

S.C. (1946) *Supreme Court of Judicature of the Province of New York, 1691–1704: The Minutes, Annotated,* Paul H. Hamlin and Charles E. Baker, eds. (*Collections of the New-York Historical Society,* vol. 79, New York, N.Y., 1946).

S.C.M. "Minute Books of the Supreme Court of Judicature of the Colony of New York," 1704–1740, 1750–1781 (Queens College Historical Documents Collection; microfilm; rolls SC1-SC8).

S.C.S. "Minutes of the Suffolk County Court of General Sessions of the Peace," 1723–1751, 1760–1775 (Suffolk County Clerk's Office, Riverhead, N.Y.).

U.C.S. "Minutes of the Court of General Sessions of the Peace," Ulster County, 1711–1720 (New York State Library, Albany, N.Y.); 1731–1750 (Queens College Historical Documents Collection; microfilm; roll UC50).

W.C.S. "Minutes of the Court of General Sessions and Common Pleas," 1710–1723 (Liber D of Deeds, Westchester County Clerk's Office, White Plains, N.Y.).

Crime and Law Enforcement in the Colony of New York 1691–1776

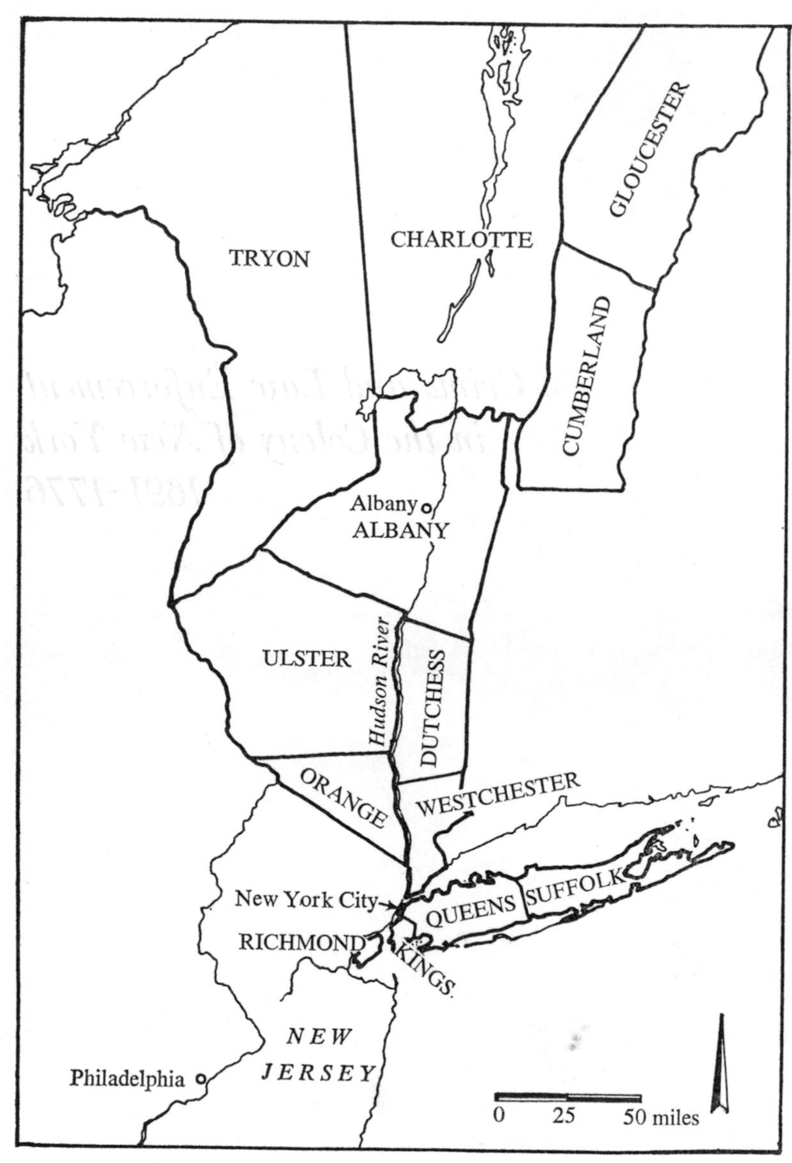

The counties of the colony of New York in 1770

CHAPTER 1

Introduction: Law and Society in Colonial New York

New York was, in many ways, unique among the British colonies in North America. It had not been subjected to the kind of religious experiences that influenced the development of Massachusetts and Pennsylvania. Its systems of local government and land distribution differed significantly from those of the Chesapeake colonies, as did the nature of its agriculture and its utilization of enslaved African labor. It contained, as did no other colony, two urban centers—at New York and Albany—each with a distinct social character. Its politics were among the most turbulent of all the colonies, and its early history was marked by several changes in government. But as Milton Klein has recently observed, "the central fact of the colony's history . . . is the heterogeneity of its population."[1] In none of the other colonies, save Pennsylvania, was ethnic and religious diversity so characteristic of the texture of provincial life. In addition to English Protestants of several stripes, significant numbers of people of Dutch, German, French, Jewish, Scots-Irish and Irish extraction made New York their home.

This demographic complexity was as carefully noted by contemporaries as it has been by later historians, for it shaped every aspect of life in the province. In no forum did the many groups appear in closer proximity or sharper contrast than in the colony's criminal courts. The tensions and antagonisms that so animated life in colonial New York were often reflected in the proceedings

[1] Milton M. Klein, "New York in the American Colonies: A New Look," *New York History*, 53 (1972), 140.

of those tribunals, thus providing the historian with a microcosmic view of the larger society. The next two chapters are devoted to an exploration of the microcosm of New York's criminal courts as it related to the one constant factor of the colony's eighteenth-century history—its religious and ethnic diversity. To be properly understood, however, such an exploration must be made within the context of the broad characteristics of New York society of that day and the legal institutions which were that society's method of dealing with the very serious problems of crime and law enforcement.

I

From the earliest years of English tenure in New York, officials reporting to the imperial administration in London were quick to note the extraordinary heterogeneity of the colony's population. In February of 1687, for example, Governor Thomas Dongan wrote to the Committee on Trade:

> Here bee not many of the Church of England; few Roman Catholicks; abundance of Quakers preachers men and women especially; Singing Quakers, Ranting Quakers; Sabbatarians; Antisabbatarians; Some Anabaptists; some Independents; some Jews; in short of all opinions there are some, and the most part none at all.[2]

In the same message, Dongan noted that the most prevalent opinion was that of the Dutch Calvinists—this in an English and, ostensibly, high-Anglican colony.[3] The diversity of population of which Dongan wrote was a continuing fact of life in New York and indeed, even in the prerevolutionary decade, it was estimated that the population of the province was only half English, "making New York the most polygenetic of all the British dependencies in North America."[4] But estimates varied; in 1765, for example, Lord Adam Gordon estimated that "two-thirds of the Inhabitants,

[2] *Doc. Hist. N.Y.*, I, 186.

[3] *Ibid.*

[4] Klein, "New York in the Colonies," 141.

as well in the Province as in the Town, are Descended of the Dutch and the Germans."[5]

The diverse mix of New York's population was described with a mixture of pride and trepidation by Englishmen who visited the colony. Andrew Burnaby noted the similarity between New Yorkers and their Pennsylvania neighbors and observed that "more than half of them are Dutch, and almost all traders; they are therefore habitually frugal, industrious and parsimonious. Being, however of different nations, different languages, and different religions, it is almost impossible to give them any precise or determinate character."[6] In 1712, the Reverend John Sharpe commented effusively about the advantages of this ethnic heterogeneity. It encouraged Englishmen to learn both Dutch and French, "which are very useful accomplishments," and it also made it possible "to learn Hebrew here as well as in Europe, there being a Synagogue of Jews, and many ingenious men of that nation from Poland, Hungary, Germany, &c."[7]

Not everyone was so sanguine as Burnaby and Sharpe. In the same letter to the Committee on Trade and Plantations which so pungently described the religious groupings of the province, Governor Dongan expressed some concern about the ethnic composition of the population:

> I believe for these seven years last past, there has not come over into this province twenty English, Scotch, or Irish familyes. . . . But of French there have since my coming here several familyes come both from St. Christophers & England & a great many more are expected. Alsoe from Holland are come several Dutch familyes which is another great argument of the necessity of adding to this Government the neighboring English colonyes that a more equall ballance may be kept

[5] Newton D. Mereness, ed., *Travels in the American Colonies* (New York, 1916), 414.

[6] The Reverend Andrew Burnaby, *Travels through the Middle Settlements in North-America in the Years 1759 and 1760: With Observations upon the State of the Colonies* (reprinted: Ithaca, N.Y., 1960), 80.

[7] "Rev. John Sharpe's Proposals, Etc.," in *Collections of the New-York Historical Society for the Year 1880* (New York, 1880), 343.

here between his Majestye's naturall born subjects and foreigners which latter are the most prevailing part of this Government.[8]

Nor was Dongan the first to express his doubts. As early as 1670, the Dutch presence had been a cause of considerable concern. In that year Captain John Barker was sent to Albany "for the well-regulating of the militia and other affairs." The following advice was included in his instructions: "Lett not you eares bee abused with private storyes of ye Dutch being disaffected with ye English, for generally wee cannot expect they love us."[9] Apparently, imperial officials were also concerned lest the Dutch be alienated by unfair treatment from their English conquerors, for among Governor Edmund Andros' instructions in 1674 was the following caution: "As to the Course of Justice you are to take care that it may be administered with all possible equallity without regard to Dutch or English . . . it being my desire as much as may be, that such as live under your government may have as much satisfaction in their condicion as is possible."[10]

Thus, while the creation of the Dominion of New England certainly grew from a variety of larger imperial considerations, it is also fair to speculate that one of the motivations was to protect the English in New York by limiting the impact of the large contingent of Dutchmen in the province. But these concerns were not limited to the period immediately following the English conquest in 1664. In later years, English travelers were to be no more generous in their assessment of the Dutch. One wrote during the Bellomont years that "[the Dutch] are a Boorish sorte of people, and If oppertunity presents would sacrifice the English."[11] As late as 1765, Lord Gordon wrote that the Dutch in Albany had all the traits of

[8] *Doc. Hist. N.Y.*, I, 161–162.

[9] Joel Munsell, ed., *The Annals of Albany* (Albany, 1850–1859), VII, 99.

[10] *N.Y. Col. Docs.*, III, 218.

[11] Margaret Kincaid, ed., "John Usher's Report on the Northern Colonies, 1698," *William and Mary Quarterly*, Ser. 3, 7 (1950), 101. Richard Coote, Earl of Bellomont (1636–1701) was the governor of New York from 1698 to 1701.

native Netherlanders: "an unwearied attention to their own and particular Interests, and abhorrence to all superiour powers.—I have been told it was found necessary in 1765 to Send a Captains Command there to prevent the entire and total Destruction of all the buildings and stores belonging to the King, which was but too well effected before their Arrival."[12]

Aside from the English, the Dutch were the most numerous ethnic group in the province, but they were not the only object of English apprehension. By contemporary estimate, there were more black slaves in New York than in any colony north of Maryland.[13] From the beginning, they were a source of problems for white New Yorkers who realized that the presence of a large and enslaved population of African laborers posed very special dilemmas for their society. Governor William Cosby recognized some of these difficulties in an address to the colony's Legislative Council in April of 1734:

> I see with Concern that whilst the neighbouring provinces are filled with honest usefull & laborious white people, the truest riches and surest strength of a Country; This province seems regardless of the vast advantage which such acquisition might bring and of the disadvantages that attend this too great Importation of Negroes and Convicts, These things are worthy of your Consideration and require your speedy attention, as the greatest good is to be expected from one and the greatest evill to be apprehended from the other.[14]

Cosby echoed sentiments that royal governors of New York had often expressed. For example, after the slave conspiracy of 1712, Governor Robert Hunter suggested in an address to the Legislative Council that New Yorkers should make every effort to discourage the continued importation of black slaves. Instead, he argued, all efforts should be made to bring white servants to New York.[15] In the midst of an economic crisis in 1737, Lieutenant Governor

[12] Mereness, ed., *Travels,* 416.
[13] *Ibid.,* 414.
[14] *Journal Leg. Council,* I, 631.
[15] *Ibid.,* 333.

Clarke added still another objection to the presence of so many slaves: "The artificers complain and with too much reason of the pernicious custom of breeding slaves to trades whereby the honest and industrious tradesmen are reduced to poverty."[16]

Cosby, Hunter, and Clarke, each for his own reasons, reflected a belief then general in the colonies, that slaves might not be worth the aggravation they caused. Aside from the possibility of revolt and the threat of competition with white labor, many New Yorkers believed that the presence of large numbers of heathen and morally inferior Africans had a deleterious effect upon the laboring whites in the population, since the lewd and promiscuous behavior of the slaves brought to the surface similar tendencies previously buried in the population as a whole.

Indeed, ethnic diversity was only one part of the problem of heterogeneity. As Cosby pointed out, and as many other New Yorkers frequently observed, the transportation of British convicts to the colonies was an alarming proposition. The problem was not simply that so many "aliens" had chosen to settle in New York. There was a larger and, in the long run, perhaps even more worrisome question at stake: the moral character of those citizens who were Englishmen. In the early years, officials were inclined to ascribe the unruliness of the population to the Leisler period and its resultant turmoil. A proclamation against profanity, issued in September of 1692 for example, asserted that "the Inhabitants of this Province by reason of the late Confusions are much degenerated having Suffered great obscenities & prophanities to Creep in amongst them whereby the Christian religion is scandalized their Majesties Government lessened and the peace and Concord which ought to be among them [is] disturbed."[17]

[16] Quoted by Samuel McKee, *Labor in Colonial New York, 1664–1776* (New York, 1935), 126. See also similar sentiments expressed in 1731 by Cadwallader Colden, "Cadwallader Colden Papers," in *Collections of the New-York Historical Society for the year 1918,* 32.

[17] N.Y.S.L. Mss., 194. See *Cal. Hist. Mss.,* 228. See also Proclamations on Sept. 30, 1691, and Sept. 1, 1692, which voice almost identical senti-

In 1708, during the administration of Lord Cornbury (who was not one of New York's more able or popular governors), the General Assembly passed "An Act for Suppressing Immorality." It is difficult to know what specific events prompted the Assembly in this case. Cornbury himself may even have been their target. But there can be little question that the Assembly was seriously concerned with the character of the populace and set upon a vigorous course of encouraging virtuous behavior. The preamble of the act argued that profanity and immorality had abounded in the colony and that this was cause for grief among the upstanding citizens of New York. It went on to provide stiff penalities for drunkenness and profanity.[18] Indeed, while not all New Yorkers would have concurred with Governor Bellomont's judgment in 1699 that "the English in New York are so profligate that I can not find a man fit to be trusted," many would have agreed that theirs was a citizenry which was very unruly and most difficult to control.[19]

After a parliamentary act of 1717 regularized the transportation of convicts to the colonies, the causes of vice were more easily identified. *The Independent Reflector,* in its issue of March 15, 1753, echoed sentiments voiced in other colonies. The author of the piece, William Smith, Jr., derided the policy of transporting convicted felons to the colony. He characterized the convicts as "a Herd of the most flagitious Banditti upon Earth" and persuasively argued that although the policy of transportation had originally been designed for the "better peopling of the colonies," it had been calamitous in its real effects.[20] Smith's argument reflected deep and

---

ments. N.Y.S.L. Mss., XXXVIII, 8, 174. Jacob Leisler led a rebellion in New York in 1689. The rebellion now bears his name and created antagonisms which were to fragment New York society and politics for the next twenty years. The best recent evaluation of Leisler and the movement he headed is Thomas Archdeacon's *New York City, 1664–1710: Conquest and Change* (Ithaca, N.Y., 1976). See esp. ch. 5.

[18] *Col. Laws N.Y.,* I, 617–618.

[19] *N.Y. Col. Docs.,* IV, 520.

[20] William Livingston, *et al., The Independent Reflector . . . By William Livingston and Others,* Milton M. Klein, ed. (Cambridge, Mass., 1963),

long-standing anxieties about the character of the people of New York—anxieties that remained current throughout the century. It is in some ways a measure of the strength of those anxieties that Smith's analysis of transportation policy reflected a misperception of events. Transport of English convicts to the colony of New York did occur, but not on nearly the scale which Smith and other New Yorkers believed it did. Approximately 30,000 felons were transported to America in the eighteenth-century. Of these, slightly more than 20,000 were sent to Virginia and Maryland, with none of the other colonies receiving more than a small fraction of that number.[21] Smith thus perceived the problem to be more acute than in fact it was, yet it was perceptions like his that shaped New Yorkers' view of themselves and their neighbors. And it was also these perceptions which shaped the way New Yorkers behaved when it came to law enforcement.

While New York was a heterogeneous society of the first order, it was also a society uncomfortable with its pluralism, for pluralism had not yet achieved the hallowed status it would later obtain on these shores. Despite a rapid growth of social diversity in all the colonies, and especially in New York, most colonials continued to adhere to the time-honored and tradition-bound notions of social hierarchy and order which had guided the societies of Europe for centuries. New York, then, was an extraordinarily heterogeneous society in an environment which held heterogeneity to be politically disruptive, socially untenable, and potentially revolutionary. In short, the structure of society in New York differed radically from that which most men and women believed was necessary for continued stability and growth. As Charles Lodwick wrote to the

---

164–170; for the authorship of the piece, see Klein's appendix, "The Problem of Authorship of the Independent Reflector," 446–449. See also Michael G. Kammen, ed., *The History of the Province of New York* by William Smith, Jr. (Cambridge, Mass., 1972), I, 222–228.

[21] Abbot E. Smith, *Colonists in Bondage: White Servitude and Convict Labor in America, 1607–1776* (Durham, N.C., 1947), 117, 119. See also McKee, *Labor*, 90.

Royal Society in 1692, "our chiefest unhappyness here is too great a mixture of Nations, and English ye least part."[22] In some ways, it could be said that "cultural lag" was New York's most serious problem.

Any understanding of crime and criminals in colonial New York must, therefore, begin with the essential knowledge that this was a society at odds with its own self-image, a society facing problems which, according to all contemporary opinion, were insoluble almost by definition. Here was a society being torn from all the familiar foundations of life by processes it could neither control nor understand. But such a perception, central as it is, should be tempered by the knowledge that there was at least one constant in the equation. The first stirrings of modernization were more trying for New York than for other colonies precisely because the social reality of diversity preceded by so many years any institutional arrangements designed to deal with it effectively.

The unique characteristics of New York society in the eighteenth century did not breed a unique set of legal institutions suited to New York's peculiar problems. The court system of New York took as its model the criminal justice system of England. Certain modifications were made, of course, to suit the New World situation, but, for the most part, English legal practice was preserved intact in New York.[23] The court system which was to survive until the American Revolution was first created in 1691 during the brief tenure of Governor Henry Sloughter. Sloughter, who had secured the province in the wake of Leisler's Rebellion, was authorized to call a legislature. In its turn, the Assembly was granted the power

[22] Quoted in Bayrd Still, *Mirror for Gotham* (New York, 1956), 10.

[23] The details of the New York court system in this and the paragraphs which follow are drawn from Robert Summers, "Law in Colonial New York: The Legal System of 1691," *Harvard Law Review*, 80 (1967), 1757–1772, and Julius N. Goebel and T. Raymond Naughton, *Law Enforcement in Colonial New York: A Study in Criminal Procedure, 1664–1776* (New York, 1944), ch. 1, esp. 26–30. See also two briefer treatments by Goebel, "The Courts and the Law in Colonial New York" and "Law Enforcement in Colonial New York" in David H. Flaherty, ed., *Essays in the History of Early American Law* (Chapel Hill, N.C., 1969), 245–277, 367–391.

to create a court system, and it did so with the Judiciary Act of 1691. This act represented an attempt to escape the chaos that had prevailed in New York law since the surrender of New Amsterdam in 1664 and that had been especially rife during the tumultuous 1680's.

At the center of this new court system was the Justice of the Peace. Long the bulwark of the English legal system, the J.P. was to serve a very similar function in New York. The Justices of the Peace in the various counties of New York were to come together at regular intervals to hold court sessions. Ordinarily these court sessions were held semiannually, but in the more populous counties of New York and Albany sessions were held on a quarterly and triannual basis respectively. There was considerable power attached to the office of J.P. In addition to trying serious criminal matters when they sat in sessions, the justices were also granted wide civil jurisdiction and the power to investigate and try minor criminal matters alone and without the presence of a jury. Despite these very substantial powers, however, the J.P. was usually no more than a leading citizen in his community. As Robert Summers has noted, although the J.P.'s "were the embodiment of the law to the ordinary man, they were themselves lay persons not formally trained in the law."[24] As we shall see in a later chapter, this was a factor with significant consequences for law enforcement in the colony.

In any event, the sessions courts were the central instrument of criminal justice, and most criminal cases were brought before them as the result of a grand jury indictment. But the law also permitted the courts to hear cases resulting from a personal complaint or an information brought by one of the justices. A jury trial was guaranteed to all defendants before the county courts, but many persons accused of misdemeanors waived this privilege and permitted the court to decide a case without the aid of "twelve good men and true."

[24] Summers, "Law in Colonial New York," 1762.

There were very few limits on the powers of the sessions courts, but they were, however, prohibited from trying persons accused of capital crimes. Such cases appeared instead before the Supreme Court of Judicature, which also handled appeals from sessions. The Supreme Court was the highest tribunal in the colony, and it usually met in New York City. Once a year, however, the justices also went on the circuit to hear serious cases in the counties. In addition, a special court of Oyer and Terminer might sometimes be appointed when a crime was so serious that it would be imprudent to wait for the next meeting of the Supreme Court.

The system of criminal justice in New York was, therefore, not nearly so complex as the society it protected. It was decentralized, and it granted extensive powers to local J.P.'s who were free to function without supervision from the provincial authorities in New York City. The system was designed to move defendants from initial complaint to ultimate acquittal or conviction with reasonable speed and limited expense to both the defendant and the state. As we shall see, however, this system did not always work either as effectively or as efficiently as its designers had hoped. The simplicity of New York's criminal justice system belied the underlying complexity of the society it served. Ironically, that complexity appears most sharply when we examine the actual proceedings of the courts that were established by the Judiciary Act of 1691. Indeed, patterns of criminal prosecution mirrored contemporary descriptions of the society at large: both were confusing, complex, and unpredictable. They defy, as does the colony itself, any simple or one-dimensional elucidation. The purpose here is not so much to draw a composite picture of criminal behavior in colonial New York as it is to demonstrate that the fragmented and heterogeneous nature of New York society was reflected in the records of its criminal courts.

Criminal prosecution was as multifaceted as the colony itself. Patterns of prosecution differed widely from one part of the colony to another. Particular categories of crime appeared more frequently in some areas and among some groups than among others. Convictions were more frequent among some ethnic groups than among others. Certain sorts of crime were more frequently brought to the courts than others. In short, the complex social situation which so alarmed contemporaries bred an equally intricate pattern of interrelated phenomena in the criminal courts, a pattern which defies, as did the people of colonial New York, facile analysis or interpretation.

My object in the following pages, therefore, is more to highlight the salient variations than to offer sweeping generalizations. The analysis provided in the next chapter and the one which follows may strike some readers as excessively diffuse and lacking in chronological precision. For the most part, I have quite consciously excluded attention to chronology here. Periodization will be attended to in a later section specifically devoted to shifting patterns over the course of the century. For the moment, the next two chapters will introduce readers to the major figures of the "story": the defendants who stood before the criminal courts of the colony. What follows then, is an attempt to break down New York's population of criminal defendants into its component parts and explore the extent to which the structure of society is revealed in the prosecution of crime.

CHAPTER 2

The Demography of Crime: The Accused

Several problems inhere in the use of quantitative methods to analyze the criminal court records of colonial New York. Of these, the most serious is that only a portion of the court minutes have survived; there are, for example, no extant court records for the counties of Cumberland, Gloucester, and Tryon. Table 1 provides a brief summary of the surviving records from which I have been able to transcribe 5,297 cases. But as is readily apparent, this represents only a portion of all the cases that actually came before the courts. A serious problem of chronological comparability is thereby built into this study, since there is no period for which there are surviving records for every court. This need not concern us for purposes of the present chapter, but another problem created by the unavailability of complete materials merits some attention.

The sample of court cases upon which much of this study depends is not a random one. It is heavily biased in favor of New York City, for which I was able to obtain a complete run of General Sessions records. Generalizations for the entire colony over the total period, therefore, are less than definitive; nevertheless, I have introduced geographic distinctions where they seemed useful in an attempt to check the biases created by the disproportion of New York City materials. In any event, these 5,297 cases are, insofar as I have been able to determine, all that still survive. Readers should realize, however, that discussions of the "population of criminal defendants" refer *only* to the 5,297 cases I have been able

Table 1. Extant court records for eighteenth-century New York*

Court	Years of extant records
Supreme Court	1691–1739, 1750–1776
Court of Oyer and Terminer	1716–1717, 1721–1749
New York General Sessions	1691–1775
New York Court of Mayor and Aldermen	1733–1743
Richmond County Sessions	1711–1745, 1745–1776
Suffolk County Sessions	1723–1751, 1760–1775
Kings County Sessions	1692–1710
Queens County Sessions	1722–1776
Westchester County Sessions	1691–1696, 1710–1723
Dutchess County Sessions	1721–1776
Albany County Sessions	1717–1723, 1763–1776
Ulster County Sessions	1693–1698, 1703–1705, 1711–1720, 1737–1750
Orange County Sessions	1703–1708, 1727–1779
Charlotte County Sessions	1774–1776

* There are no surviving court records for the counties of Gloucester, Cumberland, and Tryon, all of which counties were created in the early 1770's.

to gather rather than to the full population of defendants who may actually have appeared in the criminal courts of New York.

Indeed, even if complete record sets had survived for all the county sessions courts, the sample would still be incomplete. No records of the justices' courts (which dealt with the most minor offenses) have survived, and there is evidence to indicate that there were a variety of informal criminal procedures as well. Drunkenness, for example, was a relatively common offense, especially in New York City, which suffered from a paucity of potable water.[1] But drunkenness was prosecuted relatively infrequently in the sessions courts. Yet there are signs that it was a vexing and common problem. The following incident was recorded by the chronicler John F. Watson in the early nineteenth century, based upon an eye-witness account:

[1] See, for example, Adolph B. Benson, ed., *Peter Kalm's Travels in North America: The English Version of 1770* (New York, 1937), I, 133; and *Patrick M'Robert, A Tour through Part of the North Provinces of America* (New York, 1968), 4.

1772. Montonny's negro man, a drunkard, who had been sent to the Bridewell to receive the usual punishment was found dead the same night! The punishment in such cases was a plentiful dose of warm water (three quarts) and salt enough to operate as an emetic; with a portion of lamp oil to act as a purge.[2]

Among the 5,297 cases I was able to collect, not one suggests a penalty that even resembles this one, and yet a contemporary observer described it as the usual punishment for drunkenness.

There are, as well, additional indications of the incompleteness of the extant court records. Watson recorded the case of "two women named Fuller and Knight, who were placed one hour in the pillory for keeping bawdy houses."[3] Yet no such case appears in the records. There was a dunking stool in New York City which, so far as the court records indicate, was never used. This seems most improbable; why would it have been built if there was no intention or necessity of using it?[4] In addition, a variety of orders to repair stocks and pillories may be found.[5] But the court records would suggest that these instruments of punishment were very rarely used. Finally, there is the issue of reporting. In New York, as in other societies, there were undoubtedly many offenses for which complaints were never filed. Court records measure only those offenses cognizable in judicial tribunals. They fail to record unreported crime, and they are silent as well when a crime was committed but no arrest was made and no trial ever held. Given these facts, I believe it is fair to assume that a large body of both criminal behavior and criminal prosecution in colonial New York has permanently escaped the historian's grasp.

[2] John F. Watson, comp., *Annals of New York . . .* (Philadelphia, 1846), 286.

[3] *Ibid.*, 298.

[4] *M.C.C.*, I, 253 (Oct. 20, 1691).

[5] See, for example, W.C.S. (Dec. 5, 1710); Cuyler Reynolds, comp., *Albany Chronicles: A History of the City . . . from the Earliest Settlement to the Present Time* (Albany, 1906), 229 (April 11, 1743); K.C.S. (Nov., 1692 and Nov., 1707); *M.C.C.*, III, 221 (Feb. 19, 1720); O.C.S. (Nov., 1769).

A final caution relates to the manner in which quantitative data should be interpreted. Court records are not altogether objective sources. They may be more indicative of the attitudes of prosecutors than of the behavior of the prosecuted. They reflect a society's perception of itself, and this perception may seriously distort modern interpretations of social realities by forcing the historian to view them through a complex lens of contemporary cultural assumptions. In some cases, literary evidence may buttress an interpretation that emphasizes the impact of changing attitudes; but, even then, there is no way to assess the *degree* of distortion such attitudes introduce. Quantification of court records is a tricky business, since it gives an aura of objectivity to what may be severely skewed source materials. Therefore, I have emphasized interpretations that consider the quantified data more as cultural artifacts than as unbiased descriptions of social reality, and I have offered explicit alternatives to interpretations that rely on the court records as objective sources of behavioral patterns. I believe this is the most conservative course, since it makes it impossible to demand more from the sources than they can legitimately provide.

I

The population of criminal defendants was predominantly male, white, and English. Of the 5,297 prosecutions tabulated, 4,770 (90.1%) were against men and 527 (9.9%) were against women. Only 388 (7.4%) of the defendants were blacks, and of these, 353 (90.9%) were slaves. As Table 2 indicates, persons of English descent composed by far the greatest proportion of defendants. Each of the other groups accounted for less than 15% of the total, and only the Dutch accounted for more than 10%.

Partly because of the imbalance in the available records, the majority of defendants reported on were tried in New York City (see Table 3). There are reasons, of course, why so many prosecutions took place in the city. Even a cursory comparison of the New York sessions records with those of any of the counties indicates that the city court was much busier. First, crime was probably

Table 2. Ethnic distribution of criminal cases

Ethnic group	Number accused	Percent of all accusations	Cumulative frequency (percent)
English	3889	73.4	73.4
Dutch	693	13.1	86.5
Jewish	44	0.8	87.3
Other whites	252	4.8	92.1
Slaves	353	6.7	98.8
Free blacks	35	0.7	99.4
Indians	31	0.6	100.0
Total	5297	100%	100%

Table 3. Geographic distribution of criminal cases

Location	Number accused	Percent of all accusations	Cumulative frequency (percent)
Albany	506	9.6	9.6
New York	2707	51.1	60.7
Dutchess	484	9.1	69.8
Kings	103	1.9	71.7
Orange	233	4.4	76.1
Queens	140	2.6	78.8
Richmond	169	3.2	82.0
Suffolk	486	9.2	91.1
Ulster	230	4.3	95.5
Charlotte	37	0.7	96.2
Westchester	202	3.8	100.0
Total	5297	100%	100%

more frequent in the urban environment than in outlying areas: the opportunities and the motives for such behavior were certainly greater in an expanding port city than in isolated fur trading and agrarian communities. Further, crime was more quickly reported in the city, and suspects were more rapidly apprehended. In the rural counties the population was often spread over many miles, making both reporting and apprehension more difficult tasks than they would have been in the city.

Thus, it is a reasonable inference that members of the very same groups that held the major responsibility for governing colonial New York—white, male, English, city residents—were also responsible for the largest share of the province's crime. This would not be surprising if it could be shown that these groups had, in fact, also accounted for the largest share of New York's population. Unfortunately, although census data for New York is among the best available for any colony, it is broken down only by sex and race. But some comparisons are possible.

Throughout the century, there were only slightly greater numbers of men than women in the population of the colony. Women, however, were infrequently prosecuted in the criminal courts. Their lives were narrowly circumscribed, and, just as women were excluded from opportunities to control the institutions of society, so too were they prevented from threatening those institutions. Only in the city of New York did women account for a greater percentage of prosecutions (16.3%) than they did in the colony as a whole. In part, this difference may be explained by New York's position as a port city where the inducements for prostitution were increased by the presence of sailors seeking the companionship of women after long weeks and months at sea. Moreover, single women, whose freedom was less limited by the responsibilities of family life, were more likely to live in the city. Settlements in outlying areas were usually agrarian, and although we do not, as yet, have firm data on the subject, it is reasonable to surmise that people were more likely to live in family units in the countryside.[6] Surely there could have been few employment opportunities for single women in the farmlands, and single women could hardly have been welcome in the family-centered communities of Long Island and the Hudson River Valley.

Blacks, like women, were responsible for a smaller percentage

[6] Support for this assertion may be found in Jessica K. Ehrlich, "A Town Study in Colonial New York: Newtown, Queens County (1642–1790)" (Ph.D. diss., University of Michigan, 1974); and Jean B. Peyer, "Jamaica, Long Island 1656–1776: A Study of the Roots of American Urbanism" (Ph.D. diss., City University of New York, 1974).

of criminal cases than their numbers in the population at large would seem to warrant. Blacks were never less than 11.5% of the colony's population, and for much of the period were as high as 15%.[7] Yet they account for only 7.4% of the criminal cases dealt with in this study. An obvious interpretation would be that blacks were, after all, an oppressed people in colonial New York and therefore unlikely to risk their masters' anger by the commission of criminal acts. It might be argued that the demands of survival made it necessary for slaves to be docile and unthreatening.[8] Although it cannot be denied that slavery was a brutal institution whose psychological effects might often have been debilitating, there are alternate explanations for the relatively infrequent presence of blacks in the criminal courts. In the rural counties of New York, unlike the plantation areas of the Chesapeake, most slaves worked not in gangs but as domestic servants. Thus cut off from the supportive environment of others of their race, and under the constant surveillance of their masters, slaves might have found it difficult indeed to commit a crime—even if the opportunity presented itself. Punishment would be swift and brutal and escape improbable, since the offender was so clearly marked by his complexion. In addition, it is likely that when a slave stole from his

[7] Computed from Evarts B. Greene and Virginia D. Harrington, *American Population before the Federal Census of 1790* (New York, 1932; reprinted: New York, 1966), 88–105.

[8] There is, of course, a plentitude of literature on this subject. Interested readers are referred to Stanley Elkins, *Slavery: A Problem in American Institutional and Intellectual Life* (New York, 1959), for the most articulate example of the so-called "Sambo thesis." Elkins' work has inspired a wealth of critical literature. Especially relevant in the present context is Gerald W. Mullin, *Flight and Rebellion: Slave Resistance in Eighteenth-Century Virginia* (New York, 1972). See also James M. McPherson *et al.*, eds. *Blacks in America: Bibliographical Essays* (New York, 1971), esp. Parts II and III; Eugene Genovese, *Roll, Jordan, Roll: The World the Slaves Made* (New York, 1974); Robert W. Fogel and Stanley C. Engerman, *Time on the Cross: The Economics of American Negro Slavery*, 2 vols. (Boston, 1974); and Peter H. Wood, *Black Majority: Negroes in Colonial South Carolina from 1670 through the Stono Rebellion* (New York, 1974).

master, for example, the offense would never be reported to the courts, since the master would usually punish the offender himself. Moreover, the master was the most likely target of slave crime and, therefore, faulty reporting was probably more likely for crimes committed by slaves than for offenses by members of other groups.

In the city of New York, on the other hand, where slaves did have access to each other and where identification and, therefore, capture would be more difficult, other factors came into play. Consequently, slave crime was more frequent in the city. In New York, slaves accounted for a larger proportion (10.7%) of prosecutions than they did in the colony as a whole, but this was still smaller than their relative position in the population. These figures can, of course, be interpreted in several ways. But there are several factors that I believe most persuasively explain the discrepancies between the frequency of crime by blacks and their numbers in the population.

First, whites throughout the colony engaged in a comprehensive attempt to control what they believed was a restive slave population. Blacks were prevented by law from buying liquor, holding funerals after dark, going out at night without a candle or lantern, assembling in groups of more than three, belonging to the militia, or carrying a gun or other weapon of any kind, leaving their masters' houses on the sabbath, or even training a dog. In addition, several laws were passed by the Assembly under the general rubric of preventing conspiracies and insurrections by slaves. Further, in the city proper the House of Correction was made available to masters with "unruly and ungovernable" slaves.[9] Every effort was

[9] The following citations are illustrative rather than comprehensive. Restrictions on slave behavior were promulgated by every governmental body from the Assembly right down to local grand juries. The examples which follow are drawn from a variety of sources, but regulations of this type were current throughout the century in every county. On buying liquor, see K.C.S. (Nov., 1698); Munsell, ed., *Annals of Albany,* V, 202 (Dec. 9, 1709). On funerals, see *M.C.C.,* III, 296 (Oct. 3, 1722); *N.Y. Col. Docs.* VI, 117; and John W. Blassingame, *The Slave Community: Plantation Life in the Ante-Bellum South* (New York, 1972), 33–34, on the significance of 

made by slave owners to limit the opportunities for their bondsmen to engage in criminal behavior.

A second, and perhaps more important, factor that accounts for the apparently small volume of slave crime is that prosecutions for what was probably the most common and, from the master's point of view, the most costly of slave crimes—running away—appear very infrequently in the records, since slave runaways were seldom captured. There is copious evidence to indicate that runaway slaves were a constant source of difficulty to white New Yorkers. One may pick up almost any issue of the newspapers of colonial New York and find advertisements for runaway slaves.[10] The slaveholders of Albany, for example, often complained that their slaves were running away to the French in Canada.[11] In June, 1705, the Albany Justices of the Peace petitioned the Assembly to protect the rights of masters whose slaves were disappearing into Canada. The Assembly responded by passing an Act in August "to prevent the running away of Negro slaves out of the City and County of

---

slave burial rites. On going out after dark, see *M.C.C.*, III (Feb. 28, 1713); Reynolds, comp., *Albany Chronicles,* 219 (Nov. 5, 1753). In regard to illegal assemblies, see Mss. Conveyances Kings County, Liber III, p. 70 (in St. Francis College Archives, Brooklyn, N.Y.); U.C.S. (Sept., 1694); *Cal. Hist. Mss.,* 626 (Feb. 5, 1755). A prohibition against blacks joining the militia may be found in *Col. Laws N.Y.,* III, 394 (Sept. 21, 1744). Regulations regarding weapons appear in Munsell, ed., *Annals of Albany,* IX, 14–15 (Nov. 10, 1726); Fox, ed., W.C.S., 66–67 (June 8, 1692). Insofar as slaves leaving their masters' houses on the Sabbath is concerned, see *Cal. Hist. Mss.,* 334 (Feb. 6, 1705); K.C.S. (Oct., 1698). The stricture against walking a dog may be found in Fox, ed., W.C.S., 66–67 (June 8, 1692). For comprehensive attempts at colony-wide regulation of slave behavior, see *Cal. Hist. Mss.,* 338, 626 (Aug., 1705; Feb., 1755); and *Col. Laws N.Y.,* II, 679–688 (Oct. 29, 1730). On the New York House of Correction, see *M.C.C.,* IV, 310 (March 3, 1736).

10 For example, the following advertisement appeared in Weyman's *New York Gazette* on May 7, 1759: "Ran Away Last Friday from Elizabeth Carpender, a negro man named Venture, about five foot high, walks shambling or loose-kneed; with striped upper jacket, and red under ditto, leather britches and red cap." See also "Eighteenth Century Slaves as Advertised by their Masters," *Journal of Negro History,* 1 (April, 1916), 163–216.

11 See, for example, *Cal. Hist. Mss.,* 677 (April 15, 1757).

Albany." While the act provided for the death penalty and was renewed in July, 1715, there is no evidence that any slave was ever executed under its provisions.[12]

In 1745, as conflict with the French again became a problem, another act of similar intent was passed.[13] Despite the severity of the penalities, these measures could not have been very effective. The resources of the government were simply not adequate to the task. Constables and sheriffs had many duties and were overworked. There were too few officers for them to spend very much time as slave catchers—especially in time of war when such duties could be very dangerous. And Albany was not the only county where runaways were a problem. In other parts of the Hudson River Valley and on Long Island, as well as in New York and Albany, masters often petitioned government officials to assist them in returning their slaves.[14] Thus, the figures for blacks in Table 2 are somewhat skewed, mainly because runaway slaves were so rarely prosecuted.

Finally, we come to the most troublesome figure in Table 2—the percentage of Dutch citizens appearing in the criminal courts. As I have already observed, the lowest contemporary estimates placed the Dutch proportion of New York's population at one-half

[12] Reynolds, comp. *Albany Chronicles,* 172 (June 5, 1705); N.Y.S.L. Mss., L, 85–86. See *Cal. Hist. Mss.,* 336 (June 5, 1705); *Col. Laws N.Y.,* I, 582–584 (Aug. 4, 1705); *ibid.,* 880 (July 21, 1715). In *N.Y. Col. Docs.,* V, 418, a letter appears from Governor Hunter to the Lords of Trade which describes the act.

[13] *Col. Laws N.Y.,* III, 448.

[14] See the following examples: a letter from a group of Ulster slaveholders complaining that their slaves run away to the Minisinks and intermarry with Indian women, in N.Y.S.L. Mss., LX, 165. See *Cal. Hist. Mss.,* 433 (May 10, 1717); and a petition from Samuel Denton of Hempstead asking the arrest of his slave "who has been run off and concealed in Westchester" and the accompanying return from the sheriff of Westchester stating that he has been unable to find her, in N.Y.S.L. Mss., XLVII, 18. See *Cal. Hist. Mss.,* 305 (Jan. 14, 1703); and a warrant issued by one of the Westchester J.P.'s for the arrest of two runaway negro boys in N.Y.S.L. Mss., XC, 138. See *Cal. Hist. Mss.,* 732 (Oct. 7, 1761).

of the total, even at the very end of the colonial period.[15] Unfortunately, New York's eighteenth-century censuses were not broken down by national origin, so there is no way to be absolutely sure. But we can surmise that the amateur demographers of the 1760's were probably not off by as much as 35%, which is approximately the difference between their estimate of the Dutch proportion of the population and the percentage of prosecutions against persons of Dutch descent. Although there are no reliable figures, few historians of colonial New York would estimate that the Dutch were as low as 15% of the population. How then can the relatively meager percentage of 13.1% of the criminal defendants be explained?

One source of this imbalance is that, aside from an occasional positive identification in the court minutes, the only way for the historian to recognize Dutch New Yorkers is by their last names. Thus, people who anglicized their names after the English conquest, and Dutch women who married Englishmen, have been unavoidably excluded. The computed percentage of 13.1%, therefore, is almost certainly lower than the actual proportion of Dutchmen appearing in the courts. But while it is true that these calculations fail to include all Dutch defendants, the discrepancy is still too large to be explained by any weakness in my methods of identification. Not *that* many of the Dutch changed their names, and one might even argue that such persons ought not to be considered "culturally" Dutch in any case. Women, as I have observed, constituted a very small proportion of the defendants; certainly their numbers were not so great as to skew the ethnic distribution very severely. Therefore, although a number of Dutch defendants have probably escaped recognition, I am persuaded that a real discrepancy exists between the percentage of Dutch persons in the

[15] One estimate made by Howard F. Barker and Marcus N. Hansen in 1931 and based on family names placed the percentage of Dutch persons in the population of New York in 1790 at 17.5%. Presumably, the percentage was much higher for the better part of the eighteenth century. *Historical Statistics of the United States: Colonial Times to 1957,* Series Z (Washington, 1960), 756.

population and among criminal defendants, and that the question requires further examination.

One place to seek an explanation is in the records themselves. Again, there are no entirely reliable figures, but it is generally agreed that most of the colony's Dutch citizens lived in the rural counties of Kings, Ulster, Orange, Dutchess, and Albany.[16] Of these five counties, only in Albany and Dutchess have records for a substantial number of cases survived. But even if we examine the figures for just these counties, the dilemma cannot be resolved. Indeed, only Kings seems to approach the figure we might have predicted on the basis of population estimates, and even this is distorted by the fact that 71.8% of the surviving cases for Kings County occurred before 1710—a period during which the population of the county was, in all likelihood, far more than 50% Dutch. As for the other counties, the figures are certainly more in line with the ethnic parameters of their populations but not nearly what one might say they "ought" to be.

The biases created by the incompleteness of the records, therefore, offer no solution. We are left with two choices: either contemporary population estimates were wildly inaccurate, or persons of Dutch descent were less likely to be objects of criminal prosecution than their proportion of the population would warrant. The former is no alternative at all since, in effect, it dismisses the problem; but the latter explanation is difficult to account for. It is true, for example, that as the Dutch became a diminishing percentage of the population over the course of the century, they also accounted for a smaller percentage of criminal prosecutions. There were fluctuations, but the long-term trend was certainly downward. In this sense, at least, trends in the defendant population reflected tendencies in the population as a whole. This is encouraging, of course, since it does seem to indicate that despite the biases created by the absence of complete records, the available sample is, in

[16] Beverly McAnear, "Politics in Provincial New York, 1689–1761" (Ph.D. diss., Stanford University, 1935), 24–50.

some cases at least, fairly representative. Still, there are no explanations for the more general discrepancies noted above, and for the moment I can only say that the Dutch were less likely to appear in the criminal courts than population estimates might have led me to believe. Perhaps English officials were overzealous in enforcing Governor Andros' instruction to treat the conquered Dutch fairly, or perhaps the Dutch really were less given to committing crimes. As we shall see in a moment, there is good reason to believe that the Dutch committed certain frequently prosecuted crimes less often than other New Yorkers. Still, there is no way to know for certain why the Dutch seem to have appeared so infrequently as criminal defendants in colonial New York.

II

Generalizations regarding the prosecution of particular groups (determined by sex, race, or geography) may be refined by an analysis of the specific categories of crime that were most likely to bring members of those groups to the courts. Such an analysis may proceed in two ways. First, it is possible to compare the percentage of a particular group prosecuted for a given crime to the percentage of all prosecutions accounted for by that crime. Second, one may compare the percentage of prosecutions for a given crime accounted for by members of a particular group to the percentage of the entire defendant population accounted for by that group. In the first case, for example, the percentage of blacks who were accused of theft would be compared to the percentage of all defendants who were accused of theft. In the second case, we would compare the percentage of thieves who were black to the percentage of all defendants who were black. On the one hand, an assessment may be made of the relative frequency of a specific category of offense within one group. On the other hand, the analysis emphasizes the extent to which the pattern found in one group differs from the patterns recognizable in the defendant population as a whole.

Table 4 summarizes distributions by sex for eight frequently

Table 4. Distribution of major categories of crime (by sex)

Crime	Men			Women			Total	
	N	Row %	Column %	*N*	Row %	Column %	*N*	Percent of defendant population
Crimes of violence against persons, not resulting in death	1076	94.4	22.6	64	5.6	12.1	1140	21.5
Thefts	537	73.9	11.3	190	26.1	36.1	727	13.7
Contempt of authority	296	94.9	6.2	16	5.1	3.0	312	5.9
Crimes by public officials	198	99.5	4.2	1	0.5	0.2	199	3.8
Illegal relations with slaves	69	67.6	1.4	33	32.4	6.3	102	1.9
Disorderly houses	115	59.6	2.4	78	40.4	14.8	193	3.6
Violations of public order	964	96.7	20.2	33	3.3	6.3	997	18.8
Frauds	93	90.3	1.9	10	9.7	1.9	103	1.9

prosecuted offenses. Among men, these eight accounted for 70.2% of all prosecutions, and among women for 80.7% of all prosecutions. But as can be readily observed, for each of the sexes these crimes were prosecuted with differing frequency. The offenses most frequently committed by men were crimes of personal violence, violations of public order, and thefts. Among women, however, violations of public order were relatively infrequent, while prosecutions for keeping disorderly houses accounted for 14.8% of the total. This is hardly remarkable, since women were far more likely to be running taverns and bawdy houses than to be engaged in full-scale rioting. It is important to note, though, that contemporaries viewed these two crimes with equal distaste, since they posed, though in different ways, precisely the same problem for society at large—the maintenance of a stable social order.

Turning now to a comparison of the distribution for each crime (by sex) to the distribution in the population at large (by sex), several striking patterns emerge. Of these, the most impressive is that thefts were so much greater a cause of prosecution among women than among men. Remembering that in the defendant population as a whole women accounted for only 9.9% of all prosecutions, the fact that women were involved in 26.1% of all prosecutions for theft is especially noteworthy. Combine this observation with the fact that thefts constituted 36.1% of all prosecutions against women and only 13.7% in the defendant population as a whole, and the conclusion that women were far more likely to be prosecuted for theft is inescapable.

Similar, if less dramatic, patterns may be noted for two other categories of crime. Referring again to Table 4, it is apparent that prosecutions for keeping disorderly houses and "illegal relations with slaves" (this usually refers to the sale of liquor) accounted for a greater percentage of prosecutions against women than against men. Moreover, the distribution by sex of prosecutions for these two offenses is at variance with the distribution by sex of all prosecutions. Women were prosecuted in 32.4% of all cases involving illegal relations with slaves and 40.4% of all cases involving disorderly houses, but constituted only 9.9% of the defendant population. Why should the figures for these crimes suggest a pattern so strikingly different from that for other crimes?

The first observation which ought to be made is that precisely because the lives of women were so circumscribed, we would not expect the statistics to indicate that they were frequently accused of "public" crimes like riots, assaults, and contempt of authority. Of necessity, women would be accused of crimes which the social boundaries of the society made available to them: offenses committed in private or by stealth. Each of these three offenses—theft, illegal relations with slaves, and keeping of disorderly houses—may be so described. But there is an underlying connection among these three categories of crime that must not be ignored: disorderly houses were regarded as the well from which the fountain of criminality flowed; thievery, in particular, was thought to be grounded in the corrupt atmosphere of the bawdy house and tavern;[17] accordingly, eighteenth-century New Yorkers were especially concerned that their slaves not have access to alcoholic beverages, consumption of which was believed to be the first step to sin and, ultimately, to rebelliousness.

That there is a connection between thievery and slave conspiracies and the keeping of a disorderly house is revealed by the number of women appearing in the courts under indictment for theft and illegal relations with slaves who were also charged with running disorderly houses. For example, Catharine Johnson, who was tried and convicted for theft in 1766, appeared again in 1773 for keeping a bawdy house.[18] Likewise, in 1714 Mary Wakonn was

[17] See, for example, the two most famous English tracts on the subject: Daniel Defoe, *An Effectual Scheme for the Immediate Preventing of Street Robberies . . .* (London, 1731); and Henry Fielding, *An Enquiry into the Late Increase in Robbers* (London, 1751). The preambles of several acts to suppress disorderly houses expressed similar sentiments. See *Col. Laws N.Y.*, III, 194 (Nov. 27, 1741); 460 (Nov. 29, 1745); V, 100 (Jan. 27, 1770); and 583 (March 8, 1773).

[18] S.C.M. (Jan. 25, 1766, and Oct. 27, 1773). See also King *vs.* Elizabeth Steward in S.C.M. (April 27, 1773) for Petty Larceny; and King *vs.* Elizabeth Steward in N.Y.G.S. (May 3, 1764) for Disorderly House.

simultaneously indicted for running a disorderly house and selling liquor to slaves.[19] A presentment against Catharine O'Neill in November, 1747, embodies the attitude of public officials toward disorderly houses as sources of vice and dishonesty. The presentment charged that

> Catharine O'Neill alias Tregow late of the Out Ward of the City . . . Did keep and maintain a certain common and ill-governed and disorderly house; and then and . . . there for her own lucre and gain, unlawfully and willfully did cause and procure certain evil and ill disposed persons as well men as women of evil name and fame and of dishonest conversation to frequent and come together . . . and that the said persons remained in the house . . . drinking, thieving, tippling, quarrelling, fighting, whoring and misbehaving themselves to the great damage and Common Nuisance of all.[20]

Whatever the relationship between thefts, disorderly houses, and illegal relations with slaves may or may not tell us about the behavior of criminals, it does demonstrate the extent to which contemporary theory (or commonly held opinion) about the social sources of criminality was confirmed in patterns of prosecution. To some degree, of course, the connections delineated here may have been the result of a self-fulfilling prophecy. After all, the records of the courts do provide the precise pattern the theorists would have predicted. Whether the pattern gave rise to the theory or *vice versa* is a question that defies definitive resolution. For now, it will be enough to note the striking confluence of social ideas and legal realities.

III

Table 5 summarizes the geographic distribution of several major categories of crime. The six offenses in the table accounted for 62.9% of the prosecutions in New York City, 72% of the prosecutions in the rural counties, and 67.3% of the prosecutions in the

[19] N.Y.G.S. (Aug. 3, 1714). See also King *vs.* Hannah Bond in N.Y.G.S. (Aug. 7, 1739) wherein she was indicted for keeping a disorderly house and selling liquor to slaves.

[20] New York City, Misc. Mss., Box 43, Manuscript Collections of the New-York Historical Society, New York, New York.

Table 5. Geographic distribution of major categories of crime

	New York City			*Counties*			*Total*	
Crime	*N*	Row %	Column %	*N*	Row %	Column %	*N*	Percent of defendant population
Crimes of violence against persons, not resulting in death	570	50.0	20.9	570	50.0	22.1	1140	21.5
Thefts	570	78.4	20.9	157	21.6	6.1	727	13.7
Contempt of authority	143	45.8	5.3	169	54.2	6.6	312	5.9
Crimes by public officials	60	30.1	2.2	139	69.8	5.4	199	3.8
Disorderly houses	167	86.5	6.1	26	13.5	1.0	193	3.6
Violations of public order	205	20.6	7.5	792	79.4	30.8	997	18.8

colony as a whole. The figures suggest several conclusions about the nature of life in colonial New York. One cannot help but be struck, for example, by the absolute numerical equality of prosecutions for acts of personal violence. Remembering that city residents account for 51.1% of the cases under study, it must be concluded that the imperatives for personal violence and its prosecution were as strong in the city as in the country. In both locations slightly more than one-fifth of all prosecutions fell within this category.

These observations bear directly upon Michael Zuckerman's recent and arresting argument that the towns of eighteenth-century New England were "peaceable kingdoms" undisturbed by personal rancor and political discord.[21] They relate, as well, to John Demos' suggestion that living conditions in the New World reoriented aggressive behavior in socially acceptable directions.[22] Neither author has expanded his argument beyond Puritan Massachusetts, but the evidence set forth in Table 5 certainly indicates that any such generalizations about life in the small communities of New York would be open to serious question. To be sure, New York lacked many of the ideological imperatives to which both Zuckerman and Demos attach such great importance, and the nature of New York's diverse population and politics was certainly not without effect. Still, Puritan social ideas were not entirely *sui generis;* they were shared by many men of the seventeenth and eighteenth centuries. In any case, a substantial number of people who settled in New York, on Long Island and in the Hudson Valley were transplanted New Englanders.[23] The point is simply

[21] See Michael Zuckerman, *Peaceable Kingdoms: New England Towns in the Eighteenth Century* (New York, 1970).

[22] See John Demos, *A Little Commonwealth: Family Life in Plymouth Colony* (New York, 1970); and "Underlying Themes in the Witchcraft of Seventeenth Century New England," *American Historical Review,* 75 (1970), 1311–1326.

[23] On this point it ought to be noted that Suffolk County, which was settled almost entirely by New England Puritans, was anything but a "peaceable kingdom." Acts of personal violence and violations of public order (mostly breaches of the peace) accounted for 80.6% of all prosecutions—

that the court records indicate that neither New York City nor the rural counties were composed of "consensual communities" where aggressiveness was limited by social stricture.

Reservations about the stability of social life in New York are buttressed by other calculations in Table 5 as well. Violations of public order were the second most common source of criminal prosecution in colonial New York. What is especially significant, however, is the extent to which such offenses were largely a rural phenomenon. That almost 80% of the prosecutions took place in the counties and that more than 30% of all prosecutions in the counties were for riots, breaches of the peace, and the like seems especially remarkable to members of a society like our own which regards such acts as primarily urban phenomena. New York experienced a variety of land and tenant riots over the course of the century, and the figures here reflect those disturbances.[24] What is surprising, though, is not that violations of public order were so frequent in the countryside, but that such prosecutions were so infrequent in the city. New York City underwent phenomenal growth in the 1700's. Its population burgeoned from 4,937 in 1698 to 21,863 in 1771, and the city was not without its share of economic crises.[25] Yet the urban rioting about which so much recent historical literature has centered was not nearly as significant a phenomenon in New York as in London, for example.[26]

---

more than any other county. But this argument cannot be pushed too far. This extraordinary percentage may simply result from a characteristic overzealous vigilance by the Puritan Justices of Long Island. Second, it may be that the very fact of their migration from New England "selected out" individuals and families who could not or would not follow the New England way, as Zuckerman and Demos have described it.

[24] See Irving Mark, *Agrarian Conflicts in Colonial New York, 1711–1775* (New York, 1940); and Patricia U. Bonomi, *A Factious People: Politics and Society in Colonial New York* (New York, 1971), esp. 200–224. Bonomi's argument provides additional, though indirect, refutation of the "consensual community" theory, since it demonstrates that many of the rioters were transplanted New England Puritans. See also Ehrlich, "A Town Study," and Peyer, "Jamaica, Long Island."

[25] Greene and Harrington, *American Population,* 92, 102.

[26] The literature on this subject is of high quality and expanding. Two of

The fact that violations of public order comprised only 7.5% of all prosecutions in New York City is remarkable and suggests that we must look elsewhere to discover a category of crime that was characteristically urban.

Thefts were as significant in the city as violations of public order were in the countryside. Compare, for a moment, the figures in Table 5 for these two crimes. Seventy-eight and four-tenths percent of all prosecutions for theft occurred in New York City; 21.6% occurred in the country. Turning to violations of public order, it is apparent that the proportions are reversed. Similarly, although the parallel is not nearly so dramatic, thefts constituted 6.1% of all prosecutions in the country and 20.9% of those in the city, while violations of public order were 7.5% of the cases in the city and 30.8% of those in the country. If acts of personal violence were present throughout the colony in about equal balance, and violations of public order were primarily rural, there can be no question that thefts were equally inherent in the urban setting.

In addition, the figures for cases involving the keeping of disorderly houses demonstrate once again that the presumed relationship with thievery noted earlier is evident here as well. Fully 86.5% of all prosecutions for disorderly houses occurred in the city—many of them against individuals who also appear in actions for theft. For example, John and Elizabeth Dowers, who ran a tavern at the corner of Broadway and Robinson Street, appeared in the courts no fewer than seven times for a variety of offenses, including several indictments for keeping a disorderly house and various forms of thievery.[27] Theft and disorderly houses were con-

---

the most thoughtful contributors have been E. P. Thompson and George Rudé. See Thompson's "The Moral Economy of the English Crowd in the Eighteenth Century," *Past and Present,* 50 (1971), 76–136; and Rudé's *Hanoverian London, 1714–1808* (Los Angeles, 1971), esp. chs. 5, 9, 10 and 11. In *The Crowd in History, 1730–1848* (New York, 1964), Professor Rudé has offered some useful distinctions between country and city riots. See esp. chs. 2 and 3.

[27] S.C.M. (June 19, 1765; Jan. 24, 1766; April 28, 1767; and June 19, 1765); N.Y.G.S. (Aug. 4, 1763; Feb. 5, 1765; and March 8, 1766).

Table 6. Ethnic distribution of major categories of crime

Crime	Ethnic groups (percent of sample)						Total	
	English (73.4)*	Dutch (13.1)*	Jews (0.8)*	Other whites (4.8)*	Blacks (7.4)*	Indians (.6)*	*N*	Percent of defendant population
Crimes of violence†								
Number	871	156	27	65	18	3	1140	21.5
Row percent	76.4	13.7	2.4	5.7	1.6	0.3		
Column percent	22.4	22.5	61.4	25.8	4.6	9.7		
Thefts								
Number	585	30	4	19	86	3	727	12.7
Row percent	80.5	4.1	0.6	2.6	11.8	0.4		
Column percent	15.0	4.3	9.1	7.5	22.1	9.7		
Contempt of authority								
Number	221	79	1	10	1	0	312	5.9
Row percent	70.8	25.3	0.3	3.2	0.3	–		
Column percent	5.7	11.4	2.3	4.0	0.02	–		
Crimes by public officials								
Number	137	47	0	15	0	0	199	3.8
Row percent	68.8	23.6	–	7.5	–	–		
Column percent	3.5	6.8	–	6.0	–	–		
Disorderly houses								
Number	163	17	0	10	3	0	193	3.6
Row percent	84.5	8.8	–	5.2	1.6	–		
Column percent	4.2	2.5	–	4.0	0.07	–		
Violations of public order								
Number	795	135	6	48	7	6	997	18.8
Row percent	79.7	13.5	0.6	4.8	0.7	0.6		
Column percent	20.4	19.5	13.6	19.0	1.8	19.4		
Crimes against masters‡								
Number	3	0	0	0	217	8	228	4.3
Row percent	1.3	–	–	–	95.2	3.5		
Column percent	0.1	–	–	–	58.7	25.8		

* Percent of all accusations (see Table 2). † Against persons, not resulting in death. ‡ By servants or slaves.

nected not only by popular opinion but also in the number of actual prosecutions; both offenses were, at least in the colony of New York, more frequently prosecuted in the urban areas, which afforded greater opportunities for the criminal to commit the crime and for the courts to apprehend the criminal.[28] These facts help to explain why women accounted for a larger percentage of prosecutions in the city (16.3%) than in the colony as a whole (9.9%).

One final difference between the city and the country may be inferred from Table 5. The figures for cases involving contempt of authority and crimes by public officials are indicative of two significant trends. First, the comparable proportion of contempt cases between city and country may be paralleled by those found for acts of personal violence. Contempt of authority was clearly a problem found consistently throughout the colony. Even if most communities were stable and peaceful, it is undeniable that some people in every area refused to submit to authority. Second, the high proportion of crimes by public officials in the countryside bears directly on the question of effective law enforcement, and it will be taken up in detail in a later chapter. But it should still be noted at this point that it was apparently very difficult to find competent public officials outside the city of New York and that almost 70% of all prosecutions for neglect of duty and related offenses took place in the countryside.

IV

Distinctions among the identifiable ethnic groups in the defendant population are no less dramatic than those among groups identified by sex and geography. Table 6 tabulates the ethnic

[28] Moreover, there were specific neighborhoods in New York City which were more prone to this sort of offense than others. See *Patrick M'Robert, A Tour . . .*, 3; and Alexander Hamilton, *Gentlemen's Progress: The Itinerarium of Dr. Alexander Hamilton, 1744,* Carl Bridenbaugh, ed. (Chapel Hill, 1948), 46. See Carl Abbott, "The Neighborhoods of New York City, 1760–1775," *New York History,* 55 (1974), 35–54, for some penetrating suggestions on this topic.

breakdown of several of the most frequently committed offenses. The seven categories of crime in Table 6 account for 71.6% of all the cases under study—a total of 3,796 out of 5,297.[29]

Acts of personal violence serve as controls here, as in Table 5. Like the cases showing distribution by geographic groups, cases involving each of the ethnic groups occur with approximately the same frequency in this category of crime as within the defendant population as a whole. The three exceptions are blacks, Jews, and Indians. The actual numbers of Jews and Indians are so small that the addition or subtraction of even one case will cause a radical alteration of the percentage values. As for blacks, the fact that they account for only 1.6% of the acts of personal violence is related to the way in which the data for this study was coded. All acts of violence by blacks against whites have been coded as crimes against masters and, for that reason, appear under that category. Thus, the figures demonstrate that acts of personal violence were not specific to any particular group. All groups committed such acts, and especially among the Dutch and the English the proportions were remarkably close to figures for the defendant population as a whole. The English were involved in 73.4% of all cases and were accused of 76.4% of the acts of personal violence. The Dutch were 13.1% of the defendant population as a whole and appeared as defendants in 13.7% of the cases involving acts of personal violence. Similarly, 21.5% of all defendants were accused of acts of personal violence, and among the English and Dutch defendants the percentages were 22.4% and 22.5% respectively—within one percentage point of the pattern for the defendant population as a whole. For the English and Dutch in

[29] It will be noted that although the tabulation includes six groups only three of those groups are discussed in the pages which follow. This is because Jews, "other whites," and Indians were really too small numerically to permit firm generalizations. Moreover, the "other whites" category is very vague, since it merely includes individuals who could be positively identified in no other way. The six categories are therefore included in the table only for reasons of completeness. At the moment, I do not believe any valid generalizations can be made for Jews, "other whites," and Indians.

particular, there can be no question that ethnic background had no effect on the figures for prosecutions of acts of personal violence. For other crimes, however, the pattern is less clear and sheds considerable light on the position of each of the respective groups in New York society.

English and black New Yorkers both accounted for a greater share of actions for theft than they did respectively for all prosecutions. But within the English group, thefts were not a much larger percentage of prosecutions than they were in the defendant population as a whole. Prosecutions for theft were almost twice as frequent among blacks as in the defendant population at large. This figure is a function both of the "real" position of blacks in the eighteenth century and prevailing ideas *about* blacks. On the one hand, slaves stole because they were deprived, and on the other, they were deprived because people believed them inherently sinful. In 1716 an eighteen-year-old slave woman named Hannah confessed to stealing "as much Bristol Stuff as would make her a Gown and Pettycoat," but she added that "she stole the goods because she was almost naked and her mistress would give her no clothes."[30]

On the other hand, blacks were sometimes imprisoned summarily without formal charges, as in the case of two free blacks, Josepho Antonio Fialo [?] and Alexandro Josepho de la Torres, who wrote to Attorney-General William Kempe in November of 1753 asking that he intercede in their behalf to permit their return to Spain. They wrote again to Kempe later in the month expressing their concern over the coming winter and once again begged for his aid. Finally, Kempe drafted a petition to Lieutenant-Governor Delancey explaining the situation and asking that he release the two men. Unfortunately, we have no record of Delancey's response or the final disposition of the case.[31] But it should be clear that no

[30] N.Y.S.L. Mss., LX, 117. See *Cal. Hist. Mss.*, 431 (July 13, 1716).

[31] Kempe Papers, Box IV, William Kempe Letters, "Davenport-Hood." One of the letters is in Spanish addressed to "S^{n}. D^{n}. Gyyermo Cuempo" and is accompanied by an English translation. The other, in the same hand

ultimate distinction can be made in the court records between the response of blacks to their condition and the ideological preconceptions of their masters. The most that can be said with assurance is that blacks were prosecuted for theft almost twice as often as they were prosecuted for other crimes and that this fact can be explained both by the pressures of the institution of slavery upon slaves and by the tendency of whites to use the courts as a vehicle for reinforcing deeply felt anxieties and fears about their bondsmen.

If blacks were more likely to appear for theft than for other crimes, persons of Dutch descent exhibited exactly the opposite pattern. They were infrequently tried for theft. Actions for theft were almost three times as frequent in the defendant population as a whole (13.7% of all prosecutions) as among the Dutch (4.3%). Moreover, although the Dutch accounted for 13.1% of all criminal defendants, they comprised only 4.1% of those prosecuted for theft. These figures are even more dramatically highlighted when compared to those for blacks. Blacks accounted for almost three times as many prosecutions for theft as the Dutch, although they were only about half as numerous in the defendant population. Clearly, these seemingly anomalous calculations require some explanation. A brief review of New York's early history is necessary to understand this seeming ambiguity.

New York, it will be remembered, was "discovered" in 1609 by Henry Hudson, an Englishman in Dutch employ. The first permanent European settlement in New York was located at Fort Orange in 1624. The Dutch province of New Netherland was conquered by the English in 1664 and thereupon became New York. After a brief return by the Dutch in 1673, the English regained control and maintained it, with varying degrees of success, until the end of the American Revolution. Few Dutchmen settled in New York

---

as the translation of the first, appears only in English. The petition is in Kempe's hand and is undated. See also a similar petition from Juaquin Beneto and his son on May 22, 1755. Kempe Papers, Box IV, William Kempe letters to his son John Tabor Kempe, J. Bendt and son concerning slaves [mislabeled file].

after it was lost by their native land. Thus, most Dutch residents of eighteenth-century New York were members of families that had been in the colony for several generations and could be traced to the New Netherland period. Many of them were substantial landowners, merchants, and traders, and although there is no hard data, it is reasonable to assume that few of them were destitute.

English settlers were a more diverse lot: many were originally indentured servants and, over the course of the years, their numbers grew through substantial immigration, as well as through natural increase, while Dutch immigration had virtually ceased by 1700. Thus, there was a large group of New Yorkers of English origin who had come to the New World to make their fortunes. Not all of them succeeded and, unlike their Dutch neighbors, many of these people had no roots in New York and no family ties to rely on in times of stress. They were probably less secure economically and, perhaps, more likely to commit theft. New Yorkers of Dutch descent were generally well established and, in New York City especially, a greater proportion of them were men of substance.

It may fairly be argued, then, that the low percentage of actions for theft against persons of Dutch lineage reflects the position and social history of the Dutch population of the colony. More Englishmen were likely to be accused of theft, because more Englishmen were likely to find it necessary to steal. Of course, this line of argument is speculative, since it does not rely on anything more substantial than a few commonplace facts and several undocumented, if reasonable, suppositions. But the statistical evidence is only descriptive and demands interpretation. I am persuaded that the basis for such an interpretation lies in New York's demographic history. The lines of that story are already being drawn.[32] But until

[32] See Alice P. Kenney's series on "Patricians and Plebeians in Colonial Albany," in *de Halve Maen;* "Part I—Historical Demography and the Hudson Valley Dutch," 45 (April, 1970), 7–8, 14; "Part II—Aggregation," 45 (July, 1970), 9–11, 13; "Part III—Family Reconstitution," 45 (Oct., 1970), 14–15; "Part IV—Community Analysis," 45 (Jan., 1971), 13–14; and "Part V—The Silent Tradition," 46 (April, 1971), 13–15. A recent

we have firmer notions of the social structure of the colony, we shall have to be satisfied with sketchy interpretations based upon presently available evidence.

If the Dutch were under-represented in prosecutions for theft, they were over-represented in cases involving contempt of authority and abuse of public office. The percentages of English citizens involved in such prosecutions are slightly less than the proportion of Englishmen in the defendant population. Likewise, Englishmen were tried for these offenses slightly less often than other defendants. For the Dutch, however, the figures are strikingly different. Whereas contempt and neglect of duty comprised 5.9% and 3.8% respectively of all prosecutions, they accounted for 11.4% and 6.8% of prosecutions against persons of Dutch lineage. Similarly, although the Dutch were only 13.1% of the entire group of defendants under study, they accounted for 25.3% of all actions for contempt and 23.6% of all prosecutions against public officials. Therefore, they were approximately twice as likely to be tried for these crimes as we might have expected on the basis of their numbers in the population of defendants and the frequency of the two crimes in the sample. For an explanation of these figures we must again turn to New York's seventeenth-century history.

The English towns of New York had enjoyed, in the New Netherland period, a peculiar independence. Anxious to attract settlers, the Dutch had granted to the English towns liberal charters which afforded them considerable local autonomy. Local officials in the Dutch towns, on the other hand, often found themselves locked in a battle for power with central authorities. Moreover, English communities were more cohesive since they were often settled by groups of people with pre-established connections to

---

article and a book by Thomas Archdeacon would seem to contradict my interpretation to some extent. See Archdeacon, "The Age of Leisler—New York City, 1689–1710: A Social and Demographic Interpretation," in Jacob Judd and Irwin H. Polishook, eds., *Aspects of Early New York Society and Politics* (Tarrytown, N.Y., 1974), 63–82; and *New York City, 1664–1710.*

each other. In contrast, the Dutch settlers often lacked any sense of community and "separated themselves from one another, and settled far in the interior of the Country, the better to trade with the Indians."[33] They often settled as individuals and were less inclined to accept the legitimacy of central authority. The cavalier treatment which the Dutch received at the hands of their own countrymen had taught them to distrust all authority. On the one hand, the Dutch towns had pressed for greater independence in the years prior to 1664; but on the other, they had seldom obtained it, and, when the colony changed hands, they had neither tradition nor concrete experience to guide them. Moreover, they were a conquered people not likely to trust the usurping English and were unaccustomed, as well, to English legalism.[34] The Dutch legal tradition was grounded in Roman Law, and the Anglo-Saxon tradition of English common law was most unfamiliar.

When viewed in this light, the propensity of the courts to prosecute Dutch residents for contempt of authority and neglect of duty is somewhat less mystifying. Highly individualistic and traditionally suspicious of established authority, Dutch settlers often expressed their contempt for local and provincial officials. For example, in November of 1692, Hendrick Mattyse Smack, a Dutch resident of Kings County was taken into custody for contempt of authority. His offense was that he "did impudently and in a riotous manner declare these mutinous, scandalous and seditious words, viz. that what the justices of this Court did act was by force and not according to law." Thus, Smack had directly challenged the legitimacy of local officials appointed, in this case, by English

[33] Quoted in Langdon G. Wright, "Local Government and Central Authority in New Netherland," *New-York Historical Society Quarterly,* 57 (1973), 15.

[34] These details of the history of local government in New York are drawn from the Wright article cited above. In his dissertation Mr. Wright finds that this disparity between Dutch and English towns continued in the English period. See Langdon G. Wright, "Local Government in Colonial New York, 1640–1710" (Ph.D. diss., Cornell University, 1974).

authorities in the city.[35] Of course, contempt for authority could be considerably more blunt, as in the case of Petrus Chock of Westchester who declared that Governor Benjamin Fletcher was the "worst Governor that Ever was in New York."[36] Blunter still was the case of Jacobus Cosyne, who was indicted in 1735 for beating the sheriff of Kings County and his assistant and for setting fire to the county jail.[37]

Further, many public officials of Dutch descent found themselves working in an administrative system with which they were not familiar and to which they had little loyalty. Thus, Hendrick Wyckoff was fined thirty shillings for refusing to be sworn in as a constable in 1707. Similarly, when he was re-elected against his wishes the following year, he refused once again—despite the fact that his fine was increased to five pounds.[38] But some officials were more concrete in their failure to do their duty. Citizens of Dutchess County complained that a J.P. named Van Wyck had abused a number of local people and had said that he "Valued no English Law no more than a Turd," thus combining abuse of his office with contempt of authority.[39]

Finally, since incompetent officials were more likely to inspire abuse, and, concomitantly, communities with reputations for rancorous treatment of governmental officers were the least likely to attract vigorous and skillful government, these two offenses were related in a more general way. A dialectic was thereby established that isolated Dutch communities and helped to maintain the behavior patterns of the seventeenth century well into the eighteenth century. Moreover, there can be no question but that the very act of conquest itself encouraged contempt of authority and abuse of public office among the Dutch. People with no traditional loyalty

[35] K.C.S. (Nov., 1692).

[36] Fox, ed., W.C.S., 102–103 (June 4–5, 1695).

[37] S.C.M. (Oct. 20, 1735).

[38] K.C.S. (Nov., 1707).

[39] Kempe Papers, Box IV, William Kempe Letters, "Davenport-Flood."

to a system of law are neither likely to admit its legitimacy nor administer it efficiently.

There is literary evidence to support this view as well. Lord Adam Gordon's suggestion that the Dutch had an "abhorrence to all superiour power" certainly makes sense when viewed from the perspective of the evidence presented here.[40] Sir William Johnson also distrusted the Dutch and said, in commenting in 1761 on the quality of Dutch judges, "there is no justice to be expected by any Englishman in this country, nor never will, whilst the bench of judges and justices is entirely Dutch, who pride themselves in the appellation, which alone, in my opinion, should render them odious to every Briton."[41]

Persuasive as this line of argument may be, a caveat should be entered. As the quotations from Gordon and Johnson demonstrate, the English analysis of the situation was much the same as the one outlined here. Conquerors are always suspicious of the conquered. As Captain Barker was warned in 1670, "wee can not expect they [the Dutch] love us."[42] The English expected the Dutch to be contemptuous, and they could hardly have believed that the Dutch would make faithful public servants. Therefore, if the Dutch were frequently tried for contempt of authority and abuse of office, it was not simply because the English perception of the situation was correct, but also because governments, like historians, are very much prone to find what they look for.

As in the case of thefts, Dutch New Yorkers were under-represented in prosecutions for keeping disorderly houses. If the connection between the two crimes is assumed correct, this is precisely the pattern we would predict. English New Yorkers accounted for an even greater percentage of actions against disorderly houses than against thefts, while blacks were responsible for a very small percentage of such prosecutions. Only the figures for blacks are

[40] Mereness, ed., *Travels,* 416.
[41] Quoted in McAnear, "Politics in Provincial New York," 557.
[42] Munsell, ed., *Annals of Albany,* VII, 99.

strikingly different from calculations for theft prosecutions, and this may be easily explained. Blacks, after all, were seldom property owners; and although they may have been suspected of patronizing disorderly houses, it would have been very difficult indeed to try a slave for a crime that depended upon the ownership of property. With this single exception, the computations for cases against disorderly houses support my earlier contention that such prosecutions were connected to thievery and that, for reasons of geography and social structure, English New Yorkers were more likely to appear in the courts for both of these offenses.

Distribution patterns for cases involving violations of public order, which differ so dramatically from overall distribution patterns determined by sex and geography, are strikingly parallel to the general distribution of prosecutions among ethnic groups. There were some differences of course. English and Dutch New Yorkers appeared somewhat more frequently for this crime than their percentile place in the general defendant pool would indicate, and these offenses did account for a slightly larger percentage of prosecutions against the Dutch and English than in the defendant population generally. But these are relatively minor differences. This is especially true if one considers that coding decisions placed many similar offenses by blacks in a different category—"crimes against masters." Thus, we could expect the proportions to differ slightly and, in fact, the "slack" left by the partial removal of blacks from this category is almost exactly taken up by corresponding increases in the Dutch and English percentages.[43] Cases involving violation of public order were, then, about equally distributed among the ethnic groups in much the same way—and for many of the same reasons—as cases involving acts of personal violence.

[43] That is to say, the difference between the percentage of blacks in the total defendant population and the percentage of blacks in the category of violations of public order is about equal to the sum of the differences between the percentages of English and Dutch in the general population and in this category or (7.4 – 0.7) = (79.7 – 73.4) + (13.5 – 13.1).

General patterns of prosecution in colonial New York were as varied and complex as was the colony itself. Specific interpretations must often be tentative, and general conclusions must be even more cautiously tendered, but some things can be said with assurance. The court records confirmed a variety of notions about crime and the people of New York: blacks were thieves; the Dutch were tendentious and antipathetic to authority, but highly individualistic and economically secure; many English residents of New York, men and women alike, were transported felons who continued their thieving ways on the shores of the New World; women who ran taverns were usually prostitutes, and their activities could be clearly associated with theft; invariably, cities bred disorderly houses and disorderly houses bred crime; and finally, New York society was unstable and subject to a variety of difficult social problems directly attributable to the composition of the population.

All of these ideas found credence in the pattern of the proceedings of the criminal courts. Whether these perceptions of society were more prescriptive than descriptive we shall probably never know, for in the criminal courts of the province of New York theory and reality converged to create a rich and complex series of intersecting social phenomena. The extent to which these phenomena reflected social expectations more than social realities is necessarily beyond our grasp. Criminal statistics, however, as sociologists have often pointed out, are always suspect; even more so when those statistics are gathered 200 years after the fact and are unavoidably incomplete. The vagaries of time play strange tricks on us all. What can be said is that eighteenth-century New York was not a peaceable kingdom. The social antagonisms of the society, no matter what their origin, revealed themselves in the prosecution of crime.

CHAPTER 3

The Demography of Crime: The Judged

The demographic complexity of eighteenth-century New York is everywhere apparent in any examination of the colony's criminal court records. Discussion has thus far been concerned with the different patterns of prosecution among the many groups who made New York their home. Here the emphasis will be upon the ultimate results of those prosecutions—convictions and acquittals.

Preliminary to a demographic analysis of verdict patterns in the courts of colonial New York, several methodological points ought to be raised. Primary among these is the difference between accusations and convictions as modes of historical evidence. We have already seen that any discussion of criminal prosecution must account for social theory as well as social reality. Convictions are a better gauge of actual behavior than accusations, and to some extent this ameliorates the problem of separating a society's presuppositions from actual events. Since an analysis of convictions selects out—almost by definition—some cases of unjustified accusation, somewhat more confidence may be placed in conclusions that emphasize the behavior of the criminal rather than the attitudes of the prosecutor. Nonetheless, I have offered in this chapter, as in the last, interpretations that account both for the cultural prejudice of the judicial system and for the behavior of those persons tried under its aegis.

The most important reason for continuing to exercise such caution is that there is some reason to believe that many defendants who pleaded or were found guilty may actually have been innocent. Defendants frequently preferred to plead guilty to charges and accept a fine. This was especially true in cases involving less serious offenses, since a trial—even if it resulted in acquittal—might cause a defendant greater inconvenience than a small fine.[1] As a result, conviction figures might be misleading if relied upon as absolute indices of behavioral patterns. There is no question that such figures more accurately reflect the nature of criminal activity *per se* than accusations do. But the extent of that accuracy is open to question and must be accounted for in any analysis of judgment patterns.

A second problem relates to the connection between percentage figures for convictions and similar calculations for acquittals. Of the 5,297 cases under study, 2,538 (47.9%) resulted in a guilty verdict. In other words, only about one-half of those individuals accused were actually convicted and sentenced. On the face of it, these figures appear low and suggest that a large share of the courts' time was wasted trying innocent people. But conviction statistics are not mirrored by those for acquittals. In fact, only 15% of those accused of crime were found innocent. But if 47.9% were convicted and 15% were acquitted, we still have not accounted for a large percentage of those accused. The missing 37% of the 5,297 cases were never resolved at all. That is to say, almost two-fifths of all criminal actions resulted in neither conviction nor acquittal. They simply disappear from the records entirely before a verdict is recorded. This is an essential point to be kept in mind. The problem of being unable to bring cases from indictment through to a final judgment, a problem which plagued New Yorkers throughout the eighteenth century, was directly related to the effectiveness of law enforcement and will be discussed in detail in a later chapter. For the moment, it need only be re-emphasized

[1] The form of such pleas was usually: "The defendant professed his innocence, but rather than contend with Our Lord the King pleads guilty and prays to be admitted to a fine." For a complete discussion of this type of plea, including citations of relevant cases, see Julius N. Goebel, Jr., and T. Raymond Naughton, *Law Enforcement in Colonial New York,* 591–597.

that the seemingly low percentage figures for convictions that appear in the following pages should not be interpreted without careful attention to the parallel figures for acquittals that appear in the tables accompanying the text.

I

As might be expected, the general demographic profile of the convicted defendants parallels that for the defendant population as a whole: they were predominantly white, male, and residents of New York City. Table 7 summarizes the breakdown of convictions and acquittals among the various ethnic groups.[2] It will be readily observed that the proportions of the several frequency distributions for convictions are much the same as those for accusations. Among the ethnic groups the only dramatic disparity is among slaves, who accounted for 9.5% of all convictions but only 6.7% of all accusations. Further, 68.6% of all slaves accused of crime were convicted—a figure almost 20 percentage points greater than that for the group with the next highest rate of conviction. This difference is refined, and to some degree explained, by Table 8, which compiles conviction statistics for the four crimes most frequently committed by slaves.

The four crimes in Table 8 accounted for 95.9% of all slave convictions. It will be observed that for each of the four crimes, the percentage of slaves convicted exceeds the figure of 47.9% (Table 7) for the defendant population as a whole; and that for every offense but one, the percentage convicted exceeds the 68.6% conviction rate for all cases involving slaves. Clearly, enslaved Africans were more likely to be convicted than members of other groups.

To some extent, the large percentage of convicted slaves may be explained by the imperatives of the institution of slavery itself, as well as by the specific character of that institution in New York.

[2] Once again, I have included calculations for Jews, "Other Whites," free blacks, and Indians; but for reasons discussed in the previous chapter, I have refrained from commenting upon them in the text. See Chapter 2 above.

Table 7. Patterns of judgment for ethnic groups

Ethnic group	Number accused	Percent of all accusations	Number convicted	Percent convicted of those accused	Percent of all convictions	Number acquitted	Percent acquitted of those accused	Percent of all acquittals
English	3889	73.4	1809	46.5	71.3	542	13.9	68.0
Dutch	693	13.1	329	47.5	13.0	118	17.0	14.0
Jews	44	0.8	14	31.8	0.6	16	36.4	2.0
Other whites	252	4.8	115	45.6	4.5	48	19.0	6.0
Slaves	353	6.7	242	68.6	9.5	59	16.7	7.4
Free blacks	35	0.7	13	37.0	0.5	6	17.1	0.8
Indians	31	0.6	16	51.6	0.6	8	25.8	1.0
Total	5297	100.0	2538	47.9	100.0	797	15.0	100.0

Table 8. Conviction patterns for slaves

Crimes by slaves	Number of accusations	Number of convictions	Percent convicted of those accused	Percent of all convictions against slaves
Thefts	69	38	55.1	15.7
Crimes against masters	214	149	69.6	61.6
Crimes against morality (all Sabbath breach)	32	32	100.0	13.2
Crimes of violence, not resulting in death	16	13	81.3	5.4
Total (these crimes)	331	232	71.0	95.9
Total (all cases involving slaves)	*353*	*242*	*68.6*	*100.0*

Slavery required an elaborate system of formal controls. These were wide-ranging and touched every facet of the slave's daily life.[3] But a variety of inchoate, unarticulated controls were also at work. Each time a slave was convicted of a crime it served as an object lesson for other slaves. The principle of punishment-as-deterrent infused eighteenth-century thought on the subject of crime. But that principle was even more powerful when applied to a group like black slaves who, it seemed, could so severely threaten the society. A violation of Sabbath regulations was more seriously regarded when a slave was involved. The symbolic value of such an act was great and heavy with overtones of rebellion and pagan savagery. Acts of violence, whether directly threatening to masters or not, suggested just what slaves might be willing to do to satisfy their longing for freedom. Moreover, New York experienced two major prosecutions of slave conspiracies (in 1712 and 1741), and the psychological climate thereby created could hardly have done

[3] See Chapter 2 above; and Oscar R. Williams, "Blacks and Colonial Legislation in the Middle Colonies" (Ph.D. diss., Ohio State University, 1969).

much to ameliorate white fears.[4] Further, rumors of impending slave uprisings circulated throughout the century in the countryside as well as in the city.[5]

In such an atmosphere, it was not unlikely that blacks would be more frequently convicted than whites. Tried before unsympathetic judges and juries charged with protecting the community from social chaos, ignorant of English law, and without the means to provide an adequate defense, blacks could hardly have expected fair treatment in courts which viewed them with deep apprehension.

But the reasons for the high percentage of convictions among blacks appear to be still more complex. Referring again to Table 8, it is useful to note that the four crimes described are not only those of which blacks were most likely to be accused, but also those which they were most likely to commit. Each of the four

[4] In this connection, see Kenneth Scott, "The Slave Insurrection in New York in 1712," *The New-York Historical Society Quarterly,* 45 (1961), 43–74; and Daniel Horsmanden, *The New York Conspiracy,* Thomas J. Davis, ed. (reprinted: Boston, 1971).

[5] See, for example, the following: an order from the New York Common Council in April of 1760 offering a reward to any "white person" who discovers the "person or persons lately concerned in attempting to set fire to Several Dwelling Houses. . . ." (*M.C.C.,* VI, 210; see also N.Y.S.L. Mss., LXXXVIII, 14, and *Cal. Hist. Mss.,* 707, April 1 and 3, 1760); an Ulster County inquiry into a "meeting of Negroes" six months after the trials of 1741 in the city (Miscellaneous Court Papers, Ulster County, nos. 7460–7473, New York State Library, Albany, December 29, 1741); a message from the Common Council of Albany to [Governor Cosby?] in August of 1732 informing him of a plot involving "a Negro Man belonging to Captain Henry Hillard" to blow up the powder house (Joel Munsell, ed., *Annals of Albany,* X, 25); an order from the New York Common Council in April of 1721 "to pay Elias Chardovine Junior . . . the sum of one pound twelve shillings and four pence half penny . . . being Expenses in Enquiring into the Report and Taking Examinations of A supposed designed Insurrection of the Negroes of this City" (*M.C.C.,* III, 254, April 18, 1721); a trial of two slaves of Abraham Kip in Albany in July 1722 relating to a series of fires in the city (A.C.S., July, 1722); and a letter from Cadwallader Colden to General Gage on July 8, 1765, asking protection of the fort "sufficient to secure it against the Negroes or a mob" (Cadwallader Colden, "The Colden Letter Books, 1760–1775," in *Collections of the New-York Historical Society for the year 1877,* 23).

inhered in the slave's situation. Frequently deprived of food and clothing, slaves stole. Sometimes mistreated or galvanized into rebellion by their condition, they responded with violence. Left on their own as they were not during the rest of the week and perhaps not entirely understanding the religion of their masters, slaves frequently violated the Sabbath. Treated violently and oppressed by a vicious institution, it is not unthinkable that the slave responded in kind.

In short, if it is true that whites had powerful motivations for securing convictions, it is also true that slaves had equal reason to commit "criminal" acts. Indeed, whether such behavior may be legitimately considered criminal at all is open to question. Some scholars would probably argue that the crimes were, instead, "political" in nature.[6] I am not entirely prepared to do so. But I do believe that frightened though white New Yorkers may have been, the high rate of conviction among slaves cannot be explained solely by the paranoia of their masters. Indeed, this was not paranoia at all, but a justifiable fear of the reaction of an enslaved people to their plight. A dialectic was thus established in colonial New York in which white expectations and black behavior were mutually reinforcing. It is impossible to distinguish clearly between the two, but there can be no question that both contributed to a higher rate of conviction among blacks than among other groups in the population of the province of New York.

II

An examination of Table 9 suggests that men and women were about as likely to be convicted as they were to be accused. Men accounted for 90.1% of all accusations and 90.3% of all convictions, while women comprised 9.9% of accusations and 9.7% of convictions—a negligible difference of 0.2%. The striking difference here is not in convictions but in acquittals. Several factors

[6] See John W. Blassingame, *The Slave Community;* and Sterling Stuckey, "Through the Prism of Negro Folklore: The Black Ethos of Slavery," *The Massachusetts Review,* 9 (1968), 417–437.

Table 9. Patterns of judgment (by sex)

Sex	Number accused	Percent of all accusations	Number convicted	Percent convicted of those accused	Percent of all convictions	Number acquitted	Percent acquitted of those accused	Percent of all acquittals
Men	4770	90.1	2293	48.1	90.3	683	14.3	85.7
Women	527	9.9	245	46.5	9.7	114	21.6	14.3
Total	5297	100.0	2538	47.9	100.0	797	15.0	100.0

suggest that women were far more likely to be found innocent than men. Not only was a smaller percentage of women (46.5%) than of men (48.1%) actually found guilty, but a larger percentage was found innocent (21.6% for women as opposed to 19.3% for men). Moreover, although women accounted for 9.9% of all accusations and 9.7% of all convictions, they comprised 14.3% of all acquittals. There is no question, therefore, that women were more likely to be exonerated than men.

How can this clear disparity between men and women be explained? I am not entirely sure that it can be; but let us consider, for a moment, the following line of reasoning. One way to explain the difference is to examine the geographic distribution of prosecutions between the sexes, since geography might be a factor governing the frequency of acquittals. Eighty-four and four-tenths percent of all actions against women occurred in the city of New York. Acquittals were more frequent in the city than elsewhere, constituting 18.8% of all prosecutions as opposed to a figure of 15% for the colony as a whole. The reason, therefore, that women were so frequently acquitted may be simply that the vast majority of them were prosecuted in the city where acquittal was more likely to be the end result of a trial.

On the face of it, such an interpretation seems relatively straightforward and persuasive, but it is probably misleading. If, for example, we look again at Table 9 and note that the percentage of women found innocent (21.6%) is, in fact, greater than the percentage of city residents exonerated (18.8%), our earlier reliance upon geographic differences appears somewhat less justified. Moreover, an examination of Table 10 demonstrates that women were

Table 10. Geographic breakdown of distribution of acquittals (by sex)

	Percent of women acquitted	Percent of men acquitted
City	22.2	18.1
Counties	18.3	10.9
Colony-wide	21.6	14.3

more frequently acquitted than men in the counties as well as in New York City. These figures seem to suggest, in fact, that the disparity between the sexes was even greater in the countryside than in the city. In any case, it is clear that although the proportions differ slightly, courts in rural as well as urban New York were more inclined to acquit women than men.

An interpretation that emphasizes geography clearly will not do here. How then are we to explain the high rate of acquittal among women? There can be no firm answers, but I would suggest two possible solutions to this riddle. First, it should be noted that the crime of which women were most frequently accused—theft—was also a crime with one of the highest rates of acquittal. Twenty-one and two-tenths percent of all prosecutions for theft ended with the defendant being found innocent, and 36.1% of all prosecutions against women were for theft. Thus, a large number of women were concentrated in a category of crime where an innocent judgment was more likely. Indeed, the disparity in rates of acquittal between men and women is not nearly so great for thefts as it is for crimes generally. Men were acquitted in 20.7% of actions for theft, while women were found innocent in 22.6% of such cases. Furthermore, thefts accounted for 37.7% of all acquittals among women, while they constituted 36.1% of all accusations. Similarly, thefts comprised 16.3% of all innocent verdicts in cases involving men, but only 11.3% of all accusations. Therefore, it can reasonably be asserted that regardless of the defendant's sex, theft was a more significant source of acquittal than accusation. These figures certainly suggest that acquittals were more frequent among persons accused of theft (regardless of their sex) than among defendants generally. Thus, one might expect women, who were brought to trial for theft about three times as often as men, to be acquitted more commonly than their male counterparts.

To some degree, then, the high rate of acquittal among women may be explained simply by the high percentage of acquittals in cases of theft—the crime for which women most often appeared as defendants. But if the high rate of acquittal among women also seems to indicate that women in general were more likely to be unjustly accused than men, some further explanation is required. Such an explanation may be found in the marital status of most of the women who were tried in New York's criminal courts.

Eighty-seven and three-tenths percent of the women appearing as defendants were unmarried. As single women, these individuals occupied an ambiguous position. A married woman conformed to the standards of behavior set for her sex: she had a husband who provided for her, as well as for their children, and she, in turn, was expected to accept his authority in the home as though it had the force of law. The "rules of the game" were clear, even if not always to the woman's advantage. Similarly, married men were bound by certain clear, though somewhat more flexible, responsibilities and duties to their wives. Single men, on the other hand, were unconstrained by the obligations of family life. It was generally acknowledged, however, that some men required the freedom an unmarried status allowed. In any case, men were *expected* to be occasionally base and corrupt in their behavior. Indeed, that was what the courts were for.

But single women were neither controlled nor protected by the formal social code that bound married women. Unlike single men, they often had no legitimate means of supporting themselves. Moreover, they seemed to pose a threat to the stability of family life, since they might seduce husbands from the home and hearth to the tavern and bawdy house. In short, the single woman was more likely than others of her sex to be an object of suspicion and antagonism—the natural social pariah.[7] Sometimes such suspicions may have been justified, if only because the available options were so few for women without husbands. But there can be no question that single women were often victimized by social circumstances.

An excellent example of the dynamics of this principle at work

[7] For some speculations on this subject in another context, see Demos, "Underlying Themes," 1311–1326.

in colonial New York occurred in August of 1755. William Kempe, attorney-general of the colony, received a letter from Alderman John Bryant of the city of New York. One of Bryant's constituents, Daniel Waldron, had complained that "he and his families Rest was very much Obstructed and Disturbed by one Elizabeth Collier Single Woman who leads a Base and very Lewd Life as a Common Bawd and Harbored also some of the worst Strumpets and Vile Adultermen." Bryant described Collier's exploits in considerable detail, claiming that she and another woman, "Jew Nell," had engaged in fighting, stealing, and general disturbance of the peace. He went on to condemn Kempe for not being sufficiently vigorous in prosecuting Collier:

> [I suppose] she has not much Imposed upon your Goodness as to occation you so much trouble and pain. For my part I have no Rest Night or Day from the manifold Complaints those creatures make which are a trouble to Mankind in general and More so Especially to the Magistrats of this City. And I fear it will be much worse if they can find men of the Law that will Espose their cause.[8]

Bryant's letter contained all the traditional suspicions harbored against single women: disturbance of family life, prostitution, encouraging adultery, stealing, and using their sex to circumvent the law. Bryant kept after Kempe, writing him twice more about Elizabeth Collier. In the meantime, Kempe received a letter from an unidentified man who seems to have been Collier's lawyer, claiming that she was being harassed by Waldron and a constable named Nelson because she refused to pay an exorbitant rent. Petitioned from both sides, Kempe's reply to Bryant was soon forthcoming.

Kempe began by explaining that his job required him to provide "all the equal Justice I am able to Procure for His [Majesty's] injured Subjects, as well the poor as the Rich without any favor or affection or any other corrupt Bias." This was characteristic of

[8] Details of this case may be found in William Kempe to Alderman John Bryant, Kempe Papers, Box IV, William Kempe Letters, "Armstrong-Correy."

Kempe's scrupulous nature. He often forewarned complainants that he would not be influenced by any consideration but firm evidence. "You say this single Woman is as bad as Strawberry," he continued. "As to Mary Anderson for I Suppose she it is you mean by Strawberry, I am convinced, and I believe most of the better and more sober thinking people judge she was injured and scandalously injured, too."[9] Apparently, Kempe recognized that Elizabeth Collier was not the first single woman to be the object of such accusations, and he went on to lecture Bryant for improperly searching Collier's quarters. After reprimanding Bryant again for presuming to tell him how to do his job, Kempe succinctly summarized his own view of the case: *"I have always* looked upon Justice and the Object of it as two different Things . . . God has called his Son to save the just and the unjust equally alike and the Rays of Justice ought to be equally diffusive. I value your friendship greatly, but I value the cause of Justice more."

Kempe never did prosecute Elizabeth Collier; but his handling of the case indicates that he was conscious of a prejudice against single women—especially those in low circumstances. Single women were a natural target in a society that placed such a high value on family life and its relation to social stability. Although this particular case never came to trial, it is fair to assume that similar cases did. The high percentage of acquittals among women, therefore, is less mystifying if one takes into account the disproportionately high percentage of single women accused of crime, and the strong possibility that some of those accusations were unwarranted by the facts and closely related to the social anxieties of

[9] Mary Anderson was "a loose and profligate witch" from Philadelphia who was whipped for theft in 1754. "She afforded some Diversion while at the post to the Mob as she was very obstinate and resisting, causing several to try the Sharpness of her Teeth, others to feel the weight of her Hand, a Third got Kicked by her." Carl Bridenbaugh, *Cities in Revolt: Urban Life in America, 1743–1776* (New York, 1955; reprinted: New York, 1964), 113. It is interesting to note, moreover, that this case never appears in any of the surviving court records—another indication that mine is but a partial sampling of criminal defendants.

eighteenth-century life. To be sure, not all acquittals resulted from a fair and impartial weighing of evidence, and it is probably a mistake to assume that acquittal is necessarily an indication of innocence. But we can not ignore the facts that the percentage of single women acquitted was so high and that the social position of single women was so clearly adverse. That women were more frequently acquitted than men is incontrovertible; and I believe that, speculative though it may be, an interpretation that emphasizes the marital status of the accused provides the most persuasive available explanation of this striking difference.

III

Ethnic and sex differences are clearly reflected in acquittal and conviction statistics for the various groups living in colonial New York. Even more dramatic are the wide variations among the different regions of the colony. Table 11 summarizes judgment statistics for the major geographic divisions. Even a casual examination of the table immediately suggests that patterns differed widely from one area to another. Despite these disparities, a coherent pattern emerges, reflecting the differing character of each area.

The primary generalization that may be drawn from Table 11 is that conviction and acquittal rates differed radically between the city of New York and the rest of the colony. Apparently, convictions were more difficult to obtain in the city, where 42.6% of those accused were convicted, than in the countryside, where 53.5% were found guilty. Equally impressive is the fact that although the city accounted for 51.3% of all accusations, it comprised only 45.7% of all convictions. Predictably, similar calculations for the counties indicate a contrary trend—48.6% of all accusations were in the counties, but 54.2% of all convictions were rural in origin. Moreover, computations for "not guilty" verdicts also suggest discrepancies between New York City and the outlying counties. In New York, 18.8% of all defendants were acquitted, while in the counties the rate was 11.1%. New York

Table 11. Patterns of judgment among the geographic regions

Location	Number accused	Percent of all accusations	Number convicted	Percent convicted of those accused	Percent of all convictions	Number acquitted	Percent acquitted of those accused	Percent of all acquittals
New York	2722	51.3	1160	42.6	45.7	511	18.8	64.1
Counties	2575	48.6	1378	53.5	54.2	286	11.1	35.9
Richmond, Queens, Kings, Westchester (borough counties)	618	11.7	351	56.8	13.8	87	14.1	10.9
Suffolk	486	9.1	361	74.3	14.2	31	6.4	3.8
Ulster, Dutchess, Orange (river counties)	939	17.7	487	51.9	19.1	130	13.8	16.3
Albany, Charlotte	532	10.0	179	33.6	7.0	38	7.1	4.8
Total (colony-wide)	5297	100.0	2538	47.9	100.0	797	15.0	100.0

also accounted for a disproportionate 64.1% of all acquittals (as compared to 51.3% of all accusations), while acquittals in the counties comprised only 35.9% of the total.

These differences between the city and the counties are striking and appear in even sharper relief if they are refined somewhat by a more precise regional breakdown. Generally speaking, the pattern of conviction and acquittal rates held true for all the regions but one—Albany-Charlotte. The precise proportions differ, but in each of the other regions there were contrasts with the city which were consistent with more general colony-wide trends.

Conviction and acquittal rates in the Hudson Valley counties and those immediately adjacent to New York City were most closely parallel to the average for all the counties, with convictions somewhat more frequent and acquittals slightly less so in the "river" counties than in those closer to the city. In Ulster, Dutchess, and Orange counties, 51.9% of those accused were convicted, while in the "borough" counties and Westchester the rate was 56.8%. Similarly, acquittals were more frequent in the Hudson Valley than near the city.

In both Suffolk and Albany-Charlotte, however, strikingly different patterns are evident. In Puritan Suffolk convictions were more frequent than in any other area, occurring in 74.5% of all cases; and similarly, acquittals were *less* frequent there than in any other county—accounting for only 6.4% of all verdicts. In other words, verdict patterns in Suffolk differed from those of the city in the same way as the other counties, but the discrepancy was even sharper on Long Island than elsewhere.

In Albany-Charlotte, on the other hand, there was a unique pattern of conviction and acquittal. In this northernmost part of New York, only 33.6% of all prosecutions resulted in conviction—a smaller percentage than in any other part of the province. Moreover, acquittals were not, as might be expected, more frequent in Albany than in other areas. Rather, acquittals occurred in only 7.1% of all prosecutions—a smaller percentage than that for any other county except Suffolk where, unlike Albany, a low acquittal rate was paralleled by a high conviction rate.

In sum then, there seem to have been four distinct patterns of judgment among the geographic regions of the colony of New York. In New York City, convictions were relatively low and acquittals relatively high. In the river and borough counties, convictions were more frequent than in New York and acquittals were less so. In Suffolk county, guilty verdicts were more common than in any other area, and innocent judgments were less abundant than elsewhere. Finally, in Albany-Charlotte, both convictions and acquittals were relatively infrequent, with a majority of cases never even reaching a verdict at all. These differences are clear and dramatic and may be explained both by the demographic character of the different areas and by conditions imposed by geography itself.

In New York City, judgment patterns were the result of the dynamics of urban life. Apprehension of suspects was easier in the city than elsewhere, but it was also less likely that those arrested would be guilty. The process of accusation and arrest probably tended to be more arbitrary in New York. Because constables were not required to travel long distances to make arrests, and because individuals were more easily located in the city, law-enforcement officers could be less selective about whom they apprehended than in the rural counties where arrests could be arduous and difficult. In other words, it was less important in New York City to be certain that an individual taken into custody was guilty. In the countryside, law enforcement could be most inconvenient, and constables were not inclined to go to the trouble of making an arrest unless they were relatively certain of a suspect's guilt. Indeed, this pattern might have held for the whole colony had there not been special conditions in Suffolk and Albany which caused a divergence from more general trends.

Suffolk was the most homogeneous county in the colony. Settled by New Englanders, it was solidly English and Puritan in character.[10] The Puritan presence colored law enforcement in a variety of ways, but none was more dramatic than its influence upon rates of conviction and acquittal. Scrupulous about law enforcement and more attentive to matters of morality than other New Yorkers, the Long Island Puritans were probably less inclined to acquit persons accused of crime.[11] As in the other rural counties, it was less likely that Suffolk constables would arrest innocent persons than in the city, but this tendency was even more pronounced because of the characteristic care with which the Long Islanders pursued lawbreakers.[12] If it was true that innocent persons were less likely to be arrested in the rural counties generally, it was equally true that guilty persons were unlikely to escape punishment in the courts of Puritan Suffolk county.

Finally, we come to the most anomalous area of all—Albany and its environs. Here a variety of influences were at work. On the one hand, law enforcement in the city of Albany was almost certainly shaped by forces similar to those at work in New York City. On the other, the constables of Albany County taken as a whole were faced with a larger expanse of territory, a more severe climate than those of any other area in the province, and the intermittent threat of war. The combination of these factors certainly contributed to the unique pattern of judgments in Albany. But the manner in which these variables affected judgment patterns is difficult to as-

[10] Beverly McAnear, "Politics in Provincial New York," 33.

[11] In fact, the Justices of the county complained in 1716 that their powers to suppress "illegal cohabiting and fornication" were insufficient. "Upon using our Endeavors to Suppress these vices," they wrote, "we have been in a great measure obstructed by means of an opinion spread amongst the people that we have no power to inflict any punishment upon such persons as are guilty of the crimes above Named for that they are only cognizable in a Spirituall Court." N.Y.S.L. Mss., LX, 136 (Nov. 1, 1716); see also *Cal. Hist. Mss.*, 432.

[12] For an examination of Puritan attitudes and practice in Massachusetts, see Emil Oberholzer, Jr., *Delinquent Saints: Disciplinary Action in the Early Congregational Churches of Massachusetts* (New York, 1956); and Edwin Powers, ed., *Crime and Punishment in Early Massachusetts, 1620–1692* (Boston, 1966).

certain, since fully 60% of all the cases from Albany and Charlotte counties were never resolved. Comparisons with the other areas of the colony are, therefore, somewhat more difficult to make. But several things can be said with some assurance.

In Albany-Charlotte, convictions outnumbered acquittals by almost 5 to 1—a higher ratio than in any other area save Suffolk. It is not unreasonable to argue that conviction was the most likely outcome of prosecution in Albany—if you were caught. But as we shall see in a later chapter, law enforcement was more precarious and difficult in Albany than elsewhere. The area of the local sessions court's jurisdiction was simply too wide. In fact, the high ratio of convictions to acquittals in Albany probably supports the contention that acquittals were less likely in rural areas because the apprehension of suspects was so much more difficult. This problem was intensified in Albany, and the result was a relatively small percentage of guilty verdicts combined with a high ratio of convictions to acquittals.

IV

Patterns of judgment differed from one geographic group of New Yorkers to another, and they also differed from one crime to another. Table 12 tabulates conviction and acquittal statistics for the six most common categories of crime. These six crimes accounted for 67.3% of the 5,297 cases under study, and the frequency of acquittal and conviction differed radically among them. Generally speaking, however, trials for these six crimes seem to have resulted in conviction more often than was the case for the defendant population at large. Forty-seven and nine-tenths percent of all defendants were convicted, but defendants for these crimes were convicted at a rate of 52%. Similarly, although these crimes accounted for 67.9% of all prosecutions, they composed 73.2% of all convictions. Conviction, therefore, was more likely in cases involving theft, disorderly houses, acts of personal violence, violations of public order, contempt of authority, and crimes by public officials. Conversely, acquittal was less frequently the final verdict

Table 12. Judgment patterns among six major categories of crime

Crime	Number accused	Percent of all accusations	Number convicted	Percent convicted of those accused	Percent of all convictions	Number acquitted	Percent acquitted of those accused	Percent of all acquittals
Thefts	727	13.7	389	53.5	15.3	154	21.2	19.3
Disorderly houses	193	3.6	64	33.2	2.5	21	10.9	2.6
Acts of personal violence	1140	21.5	546	47.9	21.5	78	6.8	9.8
Violations of public order	997	18.8	578	58.0	22.8	74	7.4	9.3
Contempt of authority	312	5.9	178	57.1	7.0	56	17.9	7.0
Crimes by officials	199	3.8	103	51.8	4.1	44	22.1	5.5
Total (these crimes)	3568	67.3	1858	52.0	73.2	427	11.9	53.5
Total (all crimes)	*5297*	*100.0*	*2538*	*47.9*	*100.0*	*797*	*15.0*	*100.0*

for these crimes than for others. Eleven and nine-tenths percent of defendants accused of the six tabulated offenses were found not guilty, while the rate in the defendant population as a whole was 15%. In addition, although these crimes were 67.3% of all accusations and 73.2% of all convictions, they constituted a mere 53.5% of all acquittals. The conclusion is clear, therefore, that when taken as a group, offenders tried for these six crimes were more likely to be convicted and less likely to be acquitted than trends in the defendant population at large would suggest. Yet a crime-by-crime breakdown demonstrates that there was little consistency among the six offenses. Indeed, each had a unique pattern of conviction and acquittal all its own.

The rate of conviction for prosecutions for theft was 53.5%—slightly higher than that for the six tabulated offenses and substantially greater than the rate for all crimes. In addition, thefts accounted for 15.3% of all convictions and only 13.7% of all accusations. The conviction rate for thefts, therefore, was relatively high. On the acquittal side, a similar but even more striking pattern is apparent. Twenty-one and two-tenths percent of all theft cases ended in acquittal, as opposed to rates of 11.9% and 15%, respectively, for the six crimes in the table and for the defendant population as a whole. Furthermore, although thefts accounted for only 13.7% of accusations, they comprised 19.3% of all acquittals. Clearly, both acquittal and conviction were more frequent in theft cases than in the general defendant population.

A pattern similar to that for thefts may be noted for contempt of authority and crimes by public officials. For both these offenses, rates of conviction were higher than the 47.9% computed for the whole population of defendants and, moreover, in each case, these crimes accounted for a greater percentage of convictions than accusations. Similarly, acquittal rates for contempt of authority and offenses by officials were considerably higher than for other crimes. In addition, each of the two offenses accounted for a larger percentage of acquittals than prosecutions. Thus, Table 12 suggests a certain commonality of judgment patterns among thefts, contempt cases, and crimes by officials. In all these cases, conviction and acquittal rates are higher than we might have predicted on the basis of general trends in the defendant population.

Somewhat different patterns may be discerned for the other crimes listed in Table 12. Violations of public order, for example, more frequently resulted in conviction than any other crime in the table. Fifty-eight percent of such prosecutions ended with a guilty verdict; and violations of public order accounted for a significantly larger percentage of convictions than accusations. These conviction figures are not unlike those for thefts, contempt cases, and crimes by officials; but there is a striking difference in the acquittal calculations. Only 7.4% of all cases involving violations of public order ended in acquittal as compared to a parallel figure of 11.9%, for all crimes. Moreover, although these offenses accounted for 18.8% of accusations, they comprised only 9.3% of innocent verdicts.

The data for acts of personal violence exhibit yet another configuration. Here both conviction and acquittal rates were relatively low. Among cases involving acts of personal violence 47.9% resulted in conviction; and precisely the same percentage of all crimes concluded with guilty verdicts. Furthermore, acts of personal violence accounted for exactly the same percentage of convictions as accusations—21.5%. Thus, convictions were as common for assaults and the like as for crimes generally, but less common than for thefts, violations of public order, contempt of authority, and crimes by public officials. Acquittal statistics indicate that "not guilty" verdicts were also relatively infrequent, occurring in only 6.8% of all cases as compared to 11.9% for the six crimes tabulated. Further, although these offenses accounted for only 21.5% of all accusations, they composed only 9.8% of all "not guilty" verdicts. Thus, conviction and acquittal rates for acts of personal violence were extremely low.

Still another pattern of conviction and acquittal calculations is evident for cases involving disorderly houses. Here a very low percentage (33.2%) of the defendants were convicted, and a relatively high percentage (10.9%) were acquitted. What is most striking, however, is that such a very small percentage of these cases were ever resolved at all. Of the 193 prosecutions commenced for keeping disorderly houses, only 84 (44.1%) were actually completed. Therefore, the pattern for disorderly houses differs not only from those for each of the other crimes in Table 12, but from the configuration in the defendant population as a whole.

There were, then, four distinct varieties of judgment patterns among the six major categories of crime in Table 12. Thefts, contempt cases, and crimes by public officials had high rates of conviction and high rates of acquittal. Violations of public order evidenced a very high conviction rate, but a very low acquittal rate. Convictions for acts of personal violence were only as frequent as in the defendant population generally, and "not guilty" verdicts for such offenses were relatively uncommon. Finally, prosecutions for keeping disorderly houses followed a completely atypical pattern—a low rate of conviction combined with a relatively high rate of acquittal and a very small percentage of cases actually resolved. These figures demand explanation. In fact, the varying rates of conviction and acquittal seem directly related to the nature of the particular crimes involved and the manner in which they were viewed in eighteenth-century New York.

The high rates of conviction and acquittal in cases of theft may be attributed to the seriousness with which such crimes were regarded. Theft was considered to be among the most grievous of all offenses against society, and the harshest penalties were reserved for convicted thieves. Because larceny was looked upon as such an odious crime, the courts were especially vigorous in prosecuting it. The high rate of conviction is, therefore, probably an indication of the scrupulousness with which defendants were prosecuted. The frequency of acquittals in actions for theft would seem to be more ambiguous. Convictions are likely if a crime is viewed as a serious threat to society, but why would so many defendants have been found not guilty?

There is a sense in which the high rate of acquittals is merely an additional indication of the zealousness with which larceny was prosecuted. Theft was a most serious crime; and because this was true, cases involving larceny were more likely to be processed through the courts from indictment to judgment. That in 21.2% of these cases the judgment was in the defendant's favor suggests two possible interpretations. Either the defendant was guilty and the evidence was insufficient to obtain a conviction—not an unlikely eventuality in a society which had no regular police force and few effective investigative methods—or the defendant was, in fact, innocent and had been unjustly accused in the first place.

The latter interpretation is buttressed by the fact that 55.8% of these innocent judgments occurred between 1760 and 1775—just the period when New Yorkers were most concerned about theft and most intent upon limiting it. In 1762, for example, John Holt wrote that "such various attempts to rob and so many Robberies actually committed, having of late been very frequent within the circuits of this City, both Day and Night, it is become hazardous for any person to walk in the latter."[13] The situation became so alarming by 1773 that the Common Council ordered the constables of the city to arrest every vagrant "wandering in and about this city."[14] In such an atmosphere, it might be surmised that many individuals suspected of theft were unjustly accused, or at least that the vigor of prosecution often outstripped the ability of law-enforcement officials to gather adequate evidence. Thus, high rates of acquittal and conviction in cases of theft resulted from the zeal with which thieves were pursued and the tenacity of the courts in securing final verdicts in such cases.

If we turn from cases of larceny to the related crimes of contempt for authority and offenses by public officials where rates of conviction and acquittal were similarly high, we can see another variant of the same theme. These two crimes were also viewed

[13] Quoted in Bridenbaugh, *Cities in Revolt,* 302.
[14] *M.C.C.,* VII, 435.

with concern, accounting for almost 10% of all prosecutions between them. Local officials throughout the colony often found themselves in conflict with ordinary citizens. Sometimes these conflicts took the form of an assault on a public official, in which case the result would be a prosecution for contempt of authority; at other times, residents would petition for the removal of a justice or sheriff on grounds of maladministration.[15] It is difficult to know to what extent violations of the law were really involved in these disputes, but one suspects that both sorts of prosecution were liable to be used to advance personal ends. In any case, such accusations, whether spurious or not, could seldom be ignored—the complainants were usually too persistent and, more importantly, these two offenses involved the very heart of a stable social and political order by touching questions of authority which were far too sensitive to disregard.

The courts of colonial New York were, therefore, tenacious in their efforts to secure a final judgment in cases where contempt and abuse of authority were involved. The fact that persons accused of contempt were less frequently acquitted and more frequently convicted than officials brought to courts for abusing their office is significant. It is not surprising that juries were more inclined to believe officials who accused citizens than *vice versa*—we could expect this to be the case in almost any society. But there is, I think, a peculiar eighteenth-century dimension to this problem. Corruption was no surprise to men of affairs. Indeed, they

[15] Examples of such cases were numerous, but see the following example for the manner in which such prosecutions seem to have reflected local antagonisms: a letter from Samuel Gerritson of Kings County to William Kempe in [April ?] of 1753 complaining that he was being mistreated by the local sheriff and clerk. "The Sheriff," he wrote, "is as griedy as a vulture to Extort Exorbitant Fees from the people." As for the rest of the local officials, they were nothing but "a parcel of grasping criminals as have nothing in view but their interests" (Kempe Papers, Box IV, William Kempe Letters, "Gale-Hyatt"). Kempe never prosecuted the accused officials, but a year later, Gerritson, his son, and six other men were tried for abusing authority. After a considerable delay, they were acquitted. S.C.M. (Jan. 17, 1754; Aug. 2, 1755; Oct. 28, 1756; Oct. 26, 1759).

understood all too well that the very basis of English politics was official corruption and patronage. But a rebellious citizen was far more dangerous to society than an incompetent official. An ineffective or arbitrary justice of the peace was, after all, only one man. If he was too ineffective or too arbitrary, he would have to be removed—but not because he violated moral or legal codes. Rather, he was removed because his actions might tend to undermine all legitimate authority. On the other hand, a man accused of contempt of authority might soon find followers, and the disastrous result might be that the entire basis of social order would be eroded. Contempt of authority was, therefore, a crime that demanded swift and effective adjudication, and it is not surprising that juries composed of people with a real stake in the prevailing order were more inclined to convict the citizen accused of rebellion than the official under indictment for corruption.

Of the six offenses appearing in Table 12, the highest rate of conviction was for violations of public order. Contrarily, the rate of acquittal was low. These figures may be traced to the nature of the crime itself. Riots and breaches of the peace were "public" offenses often committed in the presence of witnesses. Positive identification of offenders was considerably easier than in the case of thefts, for example, which were often committed by stealth and under cover of darkness. As a result, convictions were more frequent and acquittals less so. Because acts that violated public order were often widely witnessed, it was unlikely that many people would be unjustly accused of riotous conduct. Similarly, because it was possible to know with some certainty just who was involved in such acts, a high rate of conviction was possible. Indeed, we might well speculate that convictions would have been even more common if it had been possible to apprehend all those accused of violating public order. But 79.4% of all such prosecutions occurred in the rural counties, where apprehension was most difficult, and it is for this reason that such a large percentage of these cases went unresolved. Nonetheless, the rates of conviction and acquittal are a reflection of the nature of the offenses themselves: public acts observed by large numbers of people who could later appear as witnesses and identify offenders.

Acts of personal violence had the lowest rates of both conviction and acquittal of any of the six crimes in Table 12, except for maintaining disorderly houses. This most frequently prosecuted of all categories of crime was among the least likely to be seen through from indictment to final verdict. Again, I believe we must turn to the nature of the crime itself to understand why this was so. Acts of personal violence posed little threat to the society at large. Individuals were injured to be sure, but assaults and the like bore few of the broader implications of social disorder attached to the other crimes we have discussed thus far. More often than not, these were acts that vented personal antagonism and touched only those directly involved. Law-enforcement officers were unlikely to pursue the perpetrator of an assault with the same diligence as a thief, for example. Apprehension and conviction were simply not as important in such cases.

Convictions for acts of personal violence, although less frequent than for some other offenses, were still forthcoming in almost 50% of the cases. This was because positive identification of offenders was usually possible, even though apprehension of the offender was less crucial to society than it was in cases involving violations of public order. Acquittals were uncommon, because such offenses were usually clear-cut, involving an attack by one individual on another. Therefore, the only real grounds for acquittal were either that the attack was justified or that the offender had been mistakenly identified. The figures in Table 12 for cases involving acts of personal violence reflect both the relative unimportance that society attached to such offenses and the likelihood that those individuals whose cases actually did reach final judgment were, in fact, guilty as charged.

Our survey of judgment patterns ends with the most ambiguous set of figures in Table 12—those for disorderly houses. These calculations are unlike any others in the table. All the other conviction rates are within ten percentage points of each other, but the rate for conviction in cases involving disorderly houses is almost fifteen points less than that for the next lowest crime and almost twenty-five points less than the rate for violations of public order —the crime with the highest percentage of convictions. The acquittal rate, on the other hand, is more in keeping with the pattern for other offenses. Why were convictions so difficult to obtain in these cases? There can be no firm answers, but some speculations are possible.

The disorderly house was, as I have already pointed out, a significant cause of concern to eighteenth-century society. The phrase usually referred to a house of prostitution, but its significance was considerably wider. The disorderly house was the concrete realization of some of society's deepest fears and anxieties—a microcosm of a society out of control. A disorderly house was one where lines of authority were indistinct, where hierarchy was disrupted, and immorality was rampant. More than a simple bawdy house or tavern, the disorderly house was a cancer which threatened to consume the body politic. In Daniel Defoe's words, these disorderly houses were the "garrisons" of thieves. "If these Houses of Retreat are once demolished and blown up," he wrote, "the Gangs [of Thieves and Thugs] will be dispers'd and separated and will immediately disappear."[16] Despite such apprehensions, however, the definition of a disorderly house was vague. The depth of social anxiety was such that prosecution was relatively frequent, but the vagueness of the legal definition made conviction very difficult.

The problem prosecutors faced was adequate proof. If a person was found with stolen goods, a conviction for theft was the likely outcome. If witnesses could testify that an individual committed an assault or spoke ill of the King or led a riot, a conviction would not be difficult to obtain. But how did one go about proving that a public house was disorderly? By the character of those frequenting it? Perhaps. By the testimony of neighbors? Maybe. But these were matters of opinion, not of established fact. Prostitution might be the crucial variable, but proof of such a crime is difficult to estab-

[16] Daniel Defoe, *An Effectual Scheme,* 31.

lish. Even in our own time, with the benefit of an enormous police force, convictions are very difficult to obtain in cases of prostitution. In short, the accusation that an individual (or individuals) was keeping a disorderly house was far easier to make than to prove. As a result, not only was the rate of convictions very low, but also only a relatively small percentage of cases ever reached the judgment stage at all.

There was no consistent pattern of judgment in the criminal courts of eighteenth-century New York. No clear or uniform interpretation applies, for the variables involved were at once too numerous and too specific. But in each of the examples discussed in this chapter, patterns of acquittal and conviction seem to have grown from a combination of factors that permit reasonable, if not entirely documented, opportunities for interpretation and explanation. Whether analysis centers upon cases involving slaves, single women, Suffolk County Puritans, or thieves, it is usually possible to isolate some factor inherent in the situation that illuminates not only the dynamics of a given set of specific circumstances, but also the social texture of life.

Lacking specific data, historians have often tended to homogenize groups of people or periods of time into the "Such and Such Class" or the "So and So Age." Although techniques of aggregate data analysis provide the means for limiting that process and are now widely available, we ought not be deceived into believing that we can ever entirely "dehomogenize" history simply by classifying people into smaller and smaller groups, for in the end we must come back to the individual—the true repository of human experience. Numbers can be useful tools; but numbers represent people, and in the next chapter we will meet some of the people who, thus far, have appeared only as numbers. Having reviewed broad patterns of accusation and judgment, it is time that we returned to the experience of individual people; for it is only in the specific context of such experience that the generalizations presented thus far can be properly understood.

CHAPTER 4

Crimes, Criminals, and Courts

The variety of patterns of accusation and judgment in the criminal courts of eighteenth-century New York was very wide indeed. But there is more to understanding the operation of the colony's criminal justice system and the people who appeared before it than a litany of statistical patterns. Despite the significant consistencies of the system, one of its most salient characteristics was the extent to which its procedures were personalized and suited to individual criminals as well as to particular categories of crime. In fact, the variety of crimes and criminals was far wider than the statistics in previous chapters might seem to imply.

I

Criminals, like the poor, have always been with us. Theories about the origins of criminality have been equally universal, but usually the argument has been reduced to a series of assertions about human nature. In our own time, the discussion is cast in pseudoscientific terms. We are told that people are merely "naked apes" bound by a "territorial imperative" which condemns them to aggressive behavior and mutual antagonism.[1] The terminology we use obviously differs from that of the eighteenth century. Indeed, in

[1] These theories have been widely popularized in: Desmond Morris, *The Naked Ape* (New York, 1967); Robert Ardrey, *The Territorial Imperative* (New York, 1966); and Konrad Lorenz, *On Aggression* (New York, 1966). But see Jane Van Lawick-Goodall, *In the Shadow of Man* (Boston, 1971), for an example of the manner in which we may note the similarities between human and animal behavior without conflating the two and thus distorting them.

those "prescientific" times there was very little debate at all. Crime was sin and, in the end, all sin could be traced to Original Sin. Men were ineluctably condemned to damnation rather than to aggression—two very different hells to be sure, but as theoretically unavoidable then as now.

The fundamental sources of crime were never far from the minds of judges and juries in colonial New York. As one Chief Justice said in his charge to the Grand Jury in March of 1727: "We find by almost daily Experience, that in the Conduct of Humane Life, Men let their Appetites and Passions get so far the Superiority that they are almost wholly governed by them. . . . Men daily offend, notwithstanding their having a sufficient Knowledge of their Duty."[2] But despite their certain knowledge that crime resulted from the essentially corrupt nature of the species, men were also conscious that specific circumstances also contributed to the commission of crime. Because this was so, the life stories of condemned prisoners were sometimes published as object lessons for the citizenry. Fortunately, several of these accounts have survived, and they allow us to reconstruct with some precision the social context of "lives of crime" in eighteenth-century New York.

Owen Sullivan was one of the most notorious criminals in colonial America. The acknowledged leader of a gang of counterfeiters operating throughout New England and New York, he had no fewer than six aliases. In March of 1756, after seven years of disrupting the currencies of the northern colonies, Sullivan was arrested in Dutchess County, New York, and convicted in the Supreme Court of the colony. He was sentenced to hang and, after a brief delay, the sentence was carried out.[3] Before he was hanged, Sullivan described the circumstances that brought him to the gallows. His story merits retelling.

[2] *The Charge given by the Chief Justice of the Province of New-York to the Grand Jury of the City of New York, in March term, 1726–7 . . .* (New York, 1727), 4.

[3] See Kenneth Scott, *Counterfeiting in Colonial New York* (New York, 1953), 87–94.

On the gallows awaiting execution, Sullivan claimed that he had been a mischievous and disobedient child born of English parents in the County of Wexford, Ireland. His parents had vainly attempted to correct his behavior by confining him alone in a room and feeding him nothing but bread and water. "Then," he said, "I seemed to humble myself; till again I obtained my Liberty, and after that I was often Times, worse than before." In desperation, Sullivan's parents sent him to a schoolmaster, but he ran away to Limerick where he was placed under a seven-year indenture by a "Gentleman" he met along the road. Unhappy with these new circumstances, he ran away once more—this time to Boston as an indentured servant. In Boston, he married a woman who was "given to take a Cup too much," and he soon enlisted in the army to escape her "Aggravating tongue."

In the army, Sullivan became a silversmith, and it was here that his life of crime began in earnest. Now he had a skill which might be put to dishonest but profitable use. Soon he was caught counterfeiting a Spanish dollar and received a whipping of fifty lashes for his offense. He left the army, going this time to New Hampshire. He became an engraver and began to issue counterfeit New Hampshire currency. He was caught and sentenced to twenty lashes plus two hours in the pillory. He was almost immediately apprehended for the same offense, broke jail, and fled to Rhode Island where, according to his own estimate, he counterfeited another £1100 of money. He was arrested once more and convicted. This time he was branded on both cheeks and had his ears cropped. He was arrested three more times in Connecticut, escaping each time. Finally, he went to New York where he went into hiding with a gang he had gathered in the course of his various exploits.

But Sullivan's career was far from over. "During my stay in Dutchess County," he said, "I made large sums of Rhode-Island Money, of six Assortments, and New-Hampshire Currency ten or twelve thousand pounds . . . and printed off three Thousand Pounds . . . of New-York Currency of four Sorts, and had four different Setts of Accomplices." Eventually, Sullivan was caught and convicted for the last time. As he was awaiting execution, he refused to name his accomplices, but he warned them to destroy "all the Money, Plates and Accoutrements that they have by them and that they may not die on a Tree as I do." Asking the hangman not to pull the rope too tight and God to have mercy on his soul, Owen Sullivan said the Lord's Prayer and was hanged. Thus ended the life of the same little boy whose first punishment had been solitary confinement and a diet of bread and water.[4]

Sullivan's story was hardly unique. Francis Burdet Personel was convicted of murder in July, 1773, at the age of twenty-six, and while awaiting execution he wrote an "Authentic and particular account" of his life. Born in Ireland and raised by "careful and industrious parents," Personel learned a trade at an early age. When his father died, he was left to care for his nagging mother. "Growing weary of her continual admonitions," he "was resolved to get out of her reach" and went to America. He stayed for eighteen months, after which time he returned to Ireland and lived again with his mother, who proceeded to arrange a marriage for him. The marriage was a failure and Personel set out for America once more—this time resolving never to return to Britain.

In America, Personel fell in with a group of revivalists in Annapolis. He soon tired of their preaching and became engaged to a widow, planning to settle down and practice his trade. But he changed his mind, stole a horse, and fled to New York where he married a former prostitute. When he came down with smallpox, his wife returned to her former profession to support them. He found this situation unbearable and, in a fit of rage, killed one of her customers. Thus he "put a stop to the sinful course" he and his wife had followed. After his conviction, he was converted to Christ and wrote a brief autobiography in hopes that he could convince others to repent before it was too late.[5]

[4] Owen Sullivan, *Narrative of the wicked Life and surprising adventures of that notorious money maker and cheat, Owen Sullivan who was hanged in the City of New-York, May 10, 1756. Together with his dying speech at the place of execution* (Boston, 1756).

[5] Francis Burdet Personel, *An Authentic and particular account of the*

Like Sullivan and Personel, John Campbell was a recent immigrant to the colonies. A Scotsman, Campbell took to crime at an early age, "profaning the Sabbath Day, gaming, drinking, whoring and [engaging in] all manner of debauchery." He emigrated to the colonies and became a notorious robber, not only in New York but in the neighboring colonies of New Jersey, Pennsylvania, and Connecticut. He was branded and had his ears cropped at New Haven, after which he resumed his escapades almost immediately. "Once [he] had nearly been Guilty of Murder, by throwing a bottle of water at a Woman . . . which broke her Scull." He appeared in the courts of New York for a variety of offenses in the late 1760's, and finally was sentenced to death in December, 1769, for "robbing Sundry Persons and Vessels."[6]

Crime was not the exclusive province of people from poor families, of course. Men of greater wealth in desperate circumstances were also tried in New York's criminal courts. John Clarkwright was the son of a "great farmer" in England. But he "met with great misfortune in the World which hurt [his] estate much." He was forced to go to London where he was "conscripted into the army." The army proved his undoing, for it was a "school of vice for drinking, gaming, whoring, thievery, etc. and everything that was bad." His hitch in the army brought Clarkwright in 1756 to the colonies, where he was captured by the French. At the end of the war he was released in England, and in 1768 he returned to America, going first to Maryland and then to New England. Clarkwright could find no employment and soon was starving. He turned to crime in order to feed himself, and was arrested for horse theft. Tried and convicted, he was executed on the twentieth of July, 1770, at Poughkeepsie.[7]

---

life of Francis Burdet Personel written by himself, Who was executed at New-York, Sept. 10th, 1773, in the twenty-sixth year of his age, for the murder of Robert White (New York, 1773).

[6] John Campbell, *A Short Account of the Life and Character of John Campbell. Now Under Sentence of Death, for Robbery and to be Executed this 29th of December 1769* (New York, 1769).

[7] John Clarkwright, *The Last speech and dying words of John Clark-*

The experience of immigration often played a role in leading people to criminal behavior. Immigrants to the colonies were, by definition, people without firm roots of any kind. They found employment difficult to obtain and frequently had no family to rely on in times of economic distress. Being born in the colonies, however, was hardly a guarantee of a virtuous life. Native-born colonists might also find themselves in trouble with the law. For example, a condemned counterfeiter, John Smith, was born in New Jersey and lived there until he was sixteen. Although he later said that "the circumstances of [his] life [had] been very precarious" and that from his youth he had been "exposed to the hard scenes of life," he did have an older brother who had married into a North Carolina family. Going south to visit his brother, Smith found him "living in great splendor." The example of his brother's wealth determined him to seek "the filthy lucre of gain." After marriage in Boston, he began to counterfeit colonial currency. He was caught and sentenced to be cropped and branded, but he broke jail, went to New York, and again took up his illicit occupation. Caught once more, he was tried in court there and hanged at Albany in 1773.[8]

All of the individuals discussed thus far were relatively young men, and all of them were quite explicit in dating their antisocial behavior to their very earliest years. But some men, like John Jubeart, came to crime late in life. Jubeart was born on Staten Island in 1701. "His parents were industrious Honest People, and gave him as genteel an Education as their circumstances would allow; they early instilled his mind with principles of Virtue and Purity." Jubeart became a blacksmith as well as a skilled watch and clock repairman. He married a New Jersey woman who bore him several children, two of whom died before reaching maturity.

---

wright who was executed at Poughkeepsie, on Friday, the 20th of July instant, for horse stealing . . . (New York, 1770).

[8] John Smith, *The Last speech, confession and dying words of John Smith, who was executed at Albany . . . for counterfeiting the currency of the Province of New-York . . .* (Albany, 1773).

After the marriage of his only surviving child, a daughter, Jubeart's wife took sick and soon died. This event "threw him into a deep melancholy" and marked the beginning of his downfall.

The death of John Jubeart's wife upset the entire structure of his life. From his own description, he seems to have been seized by a profound psychological disturbance. "He found himself unsettled," he said, "and even at Some-times, a little delirious. . . . The uncomfortable ideas with which he was perpetually haunted, he imagined, could only be alleviated by keeping himself in continual agitation of body and by removing himself from one place to another." He became a wanderer, practicing his trade all over New England. After several years of this, he settled at "a place called Quaker-Hill in the Great Nine Partners at which place he heard there was a silver mine." He found a small quantity of silver, melted it down with five Spanish dollars and then forged ten counterfeit ones. He later said that he had no fraudulent intention but was merely trying an "experiment." Soon, however, he found himself low on money and "greatly in need of linen and other necessaries." He attempted to pass the counterfeit dollars he had made and was caught. He was brought to New York where he was tried, convicted, and hanged at the age of 68 on September 6, 1769.[9]

All of these men—young or old, rich or poor, immigrant or American-born—suffered society's ultimate sanction—the death penalty. Each man committed a serious crime, and each was forced to pay with his life for his misdeed. They were not typical criminals, for the crimes they committed and the penalty each suffered were severe. But it is for precisely this reason that we know as much about them as we do and, despite the clear differences among them, the parallels in their several life stories are striking and bear brief examination.

These condemned men shared a common rootlessness. None of them lived in one place for very long. At one time or another, each

[9] John Jubeart, *The Confession and dying statement of John Jubeart, who was executed at New-York, upon Wednesday, the sixth of September, 1769; for coining and passing counterfeit dollars . . .* (New York, 1769).

of them was a vagabond of sorts, moving from one place to another without taking or finding employment. Only Jubeart enjoyed a stable family life, and even he lost several children and a wife in the period just before he became a counterfeiter. All of these men were alienated from the society in which they lived. They formed no permanent attachments and never participated in the public life of the towns and villages where they resided. Their disaffection was perhaps more severe than most, but it was no accident that each of their "dying speeches" referred to family life and its virtues. Nor was it a coincidence that their obligatory references to religion emphasized the social value of Christian fellowship. Living in a society in the process of undergoing significant change, none of these condemned men was able to find a suitable niche for himself.

To some degree, of course, all criminals are alienated from society at large. But it is also true that criminals are disaffected with their specific society, not merely with the abstraction of Human Society. Therefore, a common pattern in the lives and behavior of criminals in a society may reflect something of the nature of the society itself. And indeed, the life stories of these capital offenders suggest some of the most important dimensions of life in the eighteenth-century colonies.

An underlying theme in these autobiographies is the extraordinary physical mobility enjoyed by each of these men. Not only did they travel freely and often between colonies—indeed, none of them was really a permanent resident of New York or any other colony—but also they were able to travel outside the country—to England and back—with relative ease. Historians have long recognized that America afforded unprecedented opportunities for physical mobility by reason of its social and economic institutions as well as the wide availability of land. More recently, students of early America have begun to appreciate the potentially disruptive effects of mobility.[10] But we also need to recognize that the honest

[10] See Philip J. Greven, Jr., *Four Generations: Population, Land, and*

tradesman or farmer as much as the criminal benefited from the possibility of moving easily from one place to another. It might permit a man to escape a nagging wife, as it did for Owen Sullivan; or it might allow him to avoid the payment of debts, as it did for John Clarkwright. Perhaps it would allow him to steal with impunity, as it did for Francis Personel, or to ignore the admonition of punishment, as it did for John Campbell. It might even allow a man to exorcise his own personal devils, as in the case of John Jubeart. But whatever its specific impact, the general effect of physical mobility was to grant the felon a certain freedom from social stricture which made him bolder, and thereby more dangerous to society. Geographic mobility was a mixed blessing in America—not only because it tended to encourage the dissolution of small, stable, open-field villages, but also because it made it possible for persons bent on crime to escape more easily the informal as well as the formal restraints which held in check what one minister called "that Tyranny which the unbridled Lust of abandon'd Sinners exercises over their rational Powers."[11]

The biographical details which condemned prisoners offered on the gallows have great value, but very few such memoirs are extant. As a result we know considerably less (though still something) about most of the other men and women who were tried in New York's criminal courts. It is difficult to reconstruct the lives of most defendants, but it is possible to sketch with some detail the kinds of crimes they committed. There is, moreover, ample evi-

---

Family in Colonial Andover, Massachusetts (Ithaca, 1970); Kenneth A. Lockridge, *A New England Town, The First Hundred Years: Dedham, Massachusetts, 1636–1736* (New York, 1970); Kenneth A. Lockridge, "Land, Population, and the Evolution of New England Society, 1630–1790," *Past and Present,* 39 (1965), 62–80; and Richard L. Bushman, *From Puritan to Yankee: Character and the Social Order in Connecticut, 1690–1765* (Cambridge, 1967).

[11] Chauncey Graham, *God will trouble the troublers of his people. A sermon preached at Poughkeepsie in Dutchess-County, in the Province of New-York, July 14th, 1758. Being the day of the execution of Hugh Gillaspie, for Felony . . . Published at the request of the hearers* (New York, 1759).

dence that defendants were as diverse in background as the crimes they committed, and considerable evidence can also be marshaled to provide some notion of conditions in New York's jails and of the treatment of prisoners as their cases moved through the court system.

II

Men and women were brought to the courts of colonial New York on a variety of criminal charges, as we have seen; but the most common grounds for prosecution were acts of personal violence. Within this category, however, there was considerable diversity, and the nature of such acts varied widely. The courts tried every sort of assault, from overzealous family arguments to rapes and attempted murder. People from all walks of life and all strata of society were tried for these crimes. Several examples may illustrate the wide variety of circumstances from which such prosecutions arose.

One of the most common sources of complaint was servants who besought the courts to relieve them of the severe treatment they received from their masters. For example, Richard Caine wrote to Attorney-General William Kempe that he was "more miserable by the hard usage of my master and mistress than any Negro slave." Caine went on to tell a story of incredible cruelty complete with shackles, a bread and water diet, and solitary confinement.[12] Both William Kempe and his son and successor as Attorney-General, John Tabor Kempe, received a host of similar letters. One man, Andrew Francks, had been sent to the colonies as a convict. He was bound to Stephen Wilkins, a New York City ropemaker, and soon wrote the younger Kempe that Wilkins was attempting to "make a Slave of [him]"; moreover, "the Cruel Usage and Mistreatments" he had received were so great that he could not describe them with words.[13]

[12] Richard Caine to William Kempe (Oct. 23, 1754), Kempe Papers, Box IV, William Kempe Letters, "Armstrong-Correy."

[13] Andrew Francks to John Tabor Kempe (Oct. 4, 1772), Kempe Papers,

Both Cainc and Francks made explicit comparisons to the inferior position of black slaves, clearly indicating that, as white men, they deserved better treatment. Despite the prejudices of the day, however, even slaves could sometimes seek redress in the courts for cruel treatment. Captain John Warren, for example, was tried in Albany for "leaving a negro woman he Lately Bought Run at Large in the Streets of this City so that if she had not been taken care of She would have been frozen in the streets."[14] A similar case occurred in October of 1768 when the court was "informed that a Negro Wench belonging to the Heirs of Hendrick Hardenbeck [was] going about the streets Naked and without any Sustenance."[15]

Such cases did not result in a criminal penalty. Rather, masters would be admonished to be more humane lest their slave or servant be freed from service. On the other hand, the courts seldom hesitated to assess stiff penalties when asked to intervene on behalf of a master as in the case of Patrick Smith, a servant under indenture to John Peck Taylor. Taylor complained to the Court of General Sessions in New York that Smith was a most "Unruly Servant" and requested the aid of the court, which promptly ordered that Smith be "carried to the House of Correction there to receive thirty-one lashes."[16] In cases like these, the courts served as domestic arbitrators adjudicating differences between masters and servants or slaves, but acts of violence were most frequently committed outside of the home, and it was this group of cases which most occupied the courts of New York.[17]

Box I, John Tabor Kempe Letters, "Fisher-Guest." This citation and those which follow in this chapter are not comprehensive. Rather than burden readers with a clumsy scholarly apparatus, I have chosen representative cases to illuminate the issues raised in the text. Additional case citations may be found in Douglas Greenberg, " 'Persons of Evil Name and Fame.' "

14 A.C.S. (Feb., 1722).

15 *Ibid.* (Oct., 1768).

16 N.Y.G.S. (Aug. 2, 1743).

17 For another example of the courts' function as domestic arbitrators, see King *vs.* Richard Hook, S.C.M. (April 27, 1752). Hook was tried for beating his mother, Susannah Hook, in a family argument.

Cases involving acts of personal violence were relatively straightforward: one individual attacked another, and the court assigned an appropriate punishment. But the circumstances under which such attacks might occur varied enormously. It might be a case of one individual posing a singular threat to the community, as in the case of Henry Stringham, who "often threaten'd many honest people . . . with loss of Life and Limb" in Suffolk County and received thirty-nine lashes for his trouble.[18] But usually the circumstances that gave rise to such prosecutions were quite specific. In November of 1710, for example, an Albany innkeeper named Douw Aukers complained in a letter to Governor Hunter that a Captain Fletcher Matthews had stayed at his inn and caused some trouble. Aukers wrote that Matthews had "called for punch but not being Sattisfied with all your petitioner's wife could do for him Called her all the ould Whores and Bitches Imagineable and Shitt in the Room Damaged the bed and bedding. . . . Called your petitioner's wife into the Room and when she came in threw gunpowder in the fire to burn and frighten her." Aukers was understandably upset by this behavior and asked that Hunter secure Matthews for prosecution. By that time, unfortunately, Matthews was nowhere to be found.[19]

Not all such cases ended so unsuccessfully. When the offense was grievous enough, acts of personal violence could be most vigorously prosecuted. In the fall of 1766, for example, John Tabor Kempe received a letter from the mother of a little girl named Catharine Larkings, complaining that one John Domine had attempted to rape her daughter. Domine was immediately indicted, and the jury was presented with the horrifying testimony of the little eight-year-old girl:

Says that John Domine used to Lay in a Bed, near her feet and when she was asleep, he came to her Bed and Lay'd along Side of her and She is Sure altho no Candle was in the Room that She knew him to be

[18] King *vs.* Henry Stringham, S.C.S. (Sept., 1727, and March, 1728).
[19] N.Y.S.L. Mss., LIV, 134 (Nov. 18, 1710). See *Cal. Hist. Mss.*, 376.

John Domine by his voice. And that she did shove him away from her Two or Three Times and Said She would call her Mother when he Retird from her. And when she was Asleep he Came again and put Something between her Leggs behind, As She Lay on her Side. And that he then Took hold of both her Leggs and got between them . . . and did Shove Some Thing to her Private Parts.

Domine pleaded not guilty, but two days after he was indicted a jury convicted him of assault with intent to rape and sentenced him to be "publickly whipt at the Carts Tail and carried round the Town at three several times . . . and that one each of the three several Days the prisoner receive . . . thirty-nine lashes on the bare back."[20]

Thus, if the crime was serious enough the courts would act with alacrity to punish the evildoer. Of course, most crimes of personal violence were not so serious. Most were simple disagreements which had erupted into violence. An argument between friends in a tavern over ale, a dispute between neighbors over the placement of a fence, a duel between enemies could all result in a criminal prosecution. But in colonial New York, people could be tried for their words as well as for their deeds, and the courts did, in fact, often try individuals for saying something that seemed to endanger the body politic.

A very large number of these prosecutions were undertaken in the late 1690's and early 1700's when divisions created by the Leislerian controversy were still current. In April, 1702, Roger Baker was tried in the Supreme Court for saying that King William was "but a nose of wax and is no longer King as we please." Baker was a tavernkeeper and confessed that he was drunk when he said it, but the court was disinclined to show mercy in such a case and fined him 400 pieces of eight.[21]

The very next month Mary Burroughs petitioned for the release of her thirteen-year-old son from prison; the boy's crime had been

[20] Unsigned deposition, Kempe Papers, Lawsuits C-F; and King *vs.* John Domine, S.C.M. (Nov. 1, 1766).

[21] King *vs.* Robert Baker, S.C. (1946), 98, 101, 105 (April 9–10, 1702).

appending the words "and hang John Nanfan" to a proclamation. His mother claimed that her son would never do such a thing unless he was misled. No record has survived of the final disposition of the case, but, as we shall see in a moment, the New York courts tended to be relatively lenient in their treatment of juvenile offenders; in all probability the young man was remanded to the custody of his mother.[22]

Contempt of authority might be expressed in other ways as well. One might, for example, make deleterious remarks about religion, as did Justice Jonathan Whitehead of Queens, who said that "it was his opinion that Religion was only an Inuention of cunning men to get their living by." Apparently, Whitehead was not alone in this opinion: a fellow Queens justice, John Taleman, had said that the Scriptures could not be considered "a rule for men to walk by" since they had been written by sinful men. As a result of these statements, both men found themselves the object of prosecution in the criminal courts, although neither of their cases was ever resolved.[23]

Throughout the century, others were tried for one sort of "scurrilous language" or another. But sometimes such violations were treated with more understanding, as in the case of Gilbert Livingston who was to be tried for Sabbath breach and contempt in September of 1712. Livingston was indicted for driving his wagon on the Sabbath, but the indictment was quashed when the court was informed that Livingston's wife had been ill, and he merely wanted her to get a little fresh air.[24]

If law-enforcement agencies could be understanding about the commission of crime when circumstances warranted it, they were no less understanding when they believed that an individual had been unfairly accused. Isaac Rodrigo [Rodrigues?] Marques was a Jewish merchant who lived in New York. Apparently, he was not

[22] N.Y.S.L. Mss., XLV, 18 (May 13, 1702). See *Cal. Hist. Mss.*, 294.

[23] *Doc. Hist. N.Y.*, III, 199–200 (Jan. 28, 1702, and Feb. 1, 1702).

[24] U.C.S. (Sept., 1712).

well thought of by some of his neighbors, for he found himself the object of several unsubstantiated complaints that he had altered the weigh-house books, and in so doing had defrauded his customers. On several occasions between 1696 and 1701, grand juries offered presentments against Marques. On each occasion, the Attorney-General refused to prosecute. Marques was probably the victim of prevailing prejudices against Jews, and the Attorney-General's reluctance to prosecute indicates that, in his view, the accusations were unjustified by the evidence.[25]

This sort of leniency was manifested in other cases as well. Stephen Herman was tried in 1761 for keeping a gaming house. This was a serious offense, and another man tried with Herman for the same crime received a stiff fine of four pounds. But Herman himself was fined only two shillings. The reason for this indulgence was that the court understood that Herman was an upstanding citizen who "had not made a practice of Suffering Gaming in his House."[26]

There was, then, a meaningful personalization of criminal trial proceedings in colonial New York; and treatment was often tailored more to fit the individual than the crime. But although the courts could be merciful to evildoers, even when their crimes severely violated prevailing standards of behavior, they could also be most severe with people who posed a clear and constant threat to the community, and the prostitute posed just such a threat. Elizabeth Martin was, according to the court records, "a very Low Notorious Wicked Woman of Evil Life Conversation and Behavior and Reputed a Common Whore as with Negro Slaves as to others and a great Disturber of the Peace." Such an obvious danger to the structure of the entire community could not be allowed to remain in the city of New York, and in April of 1738 Elizabeth Martin was ordered out of the city. She refused to leave and received thirty-one

[25] S.C. (1946), 57, 71 (Oct. 11, 1701, and Nov. 29, 1701). Also *Cal. Hist. Mss.*, 254 (Oct. [?], 1696); and S.C. (1912), April 10, 1697.

[26] King *vs.* Stephen Herman, Nehemiah Sermons [?], and Walter Coovert, Q.C.S. (May, 1761; Sept., 1761; and May, 1762).

lashes as a result. She was then immediately banished from the city—this time for good.[27] Such treatment was not uncommon, especially for accused prostitutes suspected of consorting with slaves.

The courts could be very severe in their treatment of the "very low," but they often were no less vigorous in trying persons of established standing in the community. One Francis Pelham, a justice of the peace, discovered that the punishment for abusing his office could be very swift indeed. According to the inhabitants of North-Castle, Pelham was much given to excessive drinking. This in itself was bad enough, but he compounded the crime by being "very Rash In way of Speaking in Liccor," threatening to commit a murder, blaming it on the poor men of the community, and then extorting protection money from them. Pelham was promptly suspended from office, as the people of North-Castle had requested.[28]

Liquor led another justice of the peace to the criminal courts as well. Thomas Jarvis, a J.P. in Suffolk County, was also a tavern-keeper, and he usually held court at his inn. During one civil suit, he allowed one of the parties to purchase "strong Liquors" for the jury and thereby swayed their verdict. As a result he soon found himself on trial in the Supreme Court.[29] There were many similar cases, but in a colony with an expanding population and a shortage of men with adequate legal training, it should not be surprising to find that some justices of the peace were less than scrupulous about the performance of their duty. And, of course, such performance of duty could be most difficult regardless of the abilities of individual justices.

Life in the colony of New York, as in most new societies, could be precarious. One reason was precisely because the nature of public authority could be so ephemeral and open to question—and sometimes such questioning could be less than polite. I shall have a great deal more to say about this subject in a later chapter. For

[27] Mayor and Aldermen (April 11, 1738).

[28] *Doc. Hist. N.Y.*, III, 950 (no date given).

[29] King *vs.* Thomas Jarvis, S.C.M. (April 24, 1767).

the moment, however, one example should suffice to demonstrate just how contemptuous New Yorkers could be of authority they deemed to be illegitimate.

In September of 1696, thirteen men marched on the courthouse of Kings County with "swords guns and Pistoles" in hand. They attacked the courthouse, attempting to "disfigure and deface" it. The sheriff of the county apprehended them; they were tried; and they received a very light fine of ten shillings per man.[30] That such a severe attack on the most visible manifestation of public authority could be carried out with relative impunity is extraordinary and points once again to the peculiar position of law-enforcement officials, especially in the counties. An excessive punishment in this particular case might have done more harm than good. The colony was still reeling from the Leisler troubles, and Kings County had been a center of Leislerian sentiment. Surely, discretion was the better part of justice in this situation, and the local justices levied light fines in the hope of forestalling even more disruptive and dangerous behavior.

The variety of criminal behavior in colonial New York was considerable, then, and occasionally even bizarre by twentieth-century standards. But the courts of New York tried the usual group of "killers and thieves" as well as drunken justices and rebellious citizens. Theft was an especially persistent problem. New York underwent enormous economic expansion in the middle decades of the eighteenth century, and the pickings could be extremely fruitful for the enterprising thief, particularly in the busy port of New York City. Edward Lee, for example, made off with an especially good haul when he robbed the home of Thomas Perry in 1752. When he was arrested, a list was made of what he had stolen. In addition to some clothing, he had taken "sixty-nine dollars, one double doubloon, a two pistole piece, one English guinea, one-half gold Johannes, one quarter Johannes, one eighth Johannes, some Spanish Pistoles, one-hundred and forty-two shilling pieces, one English

[30] King *vs.* [?], K.C.S. (Sept., 1696).

piece of silver, two pounds Sterling, one penny, fifty-two shillings in English copper half-pence, and several pair of pinch back buttons."[31] Lee was caught and indicted for his crime; but James Mills, the sheriff of New York, negligently allowed him to escape.[32] The plunder was recovered, but the criminal himself eluded prosecution.

Not all thieves were lucky enough to escape, and some were acquitted only to find themselves under indictment in another colony. David Smith, for example, who was acquitted with his wife Elizabeth on two counts of burglary in New York in April of 1767, was immediately remanded to the custody of the Sheriff of Philadelphia where he had allegedly committed "divers Fellonies."[33] There were no formal extradition procedures in the colonies, since there was no precedent in English legal experience.[34] In a case like Smith's, extradition was entirely dependent upon informal communication between local officials. There are many examples of such communication—especially when an individual proved persistently troublesome in several localities. The case of David Smith and that of Owen Sullivan discussed earlier in this chapter are examples of how effective such communication could be despite the lack of any formal procedural mechanisms.[35]

But most thieves found the pickings in New York to be more than adequate to their needs, as one Mary Daily proved repeatedly between 1767 and 1771. She first appeared in court in October of 1767 on trial for burglary and grand larceny. She was acquitted of the burglary indictment but convicted of grand larceny. Although this was a capital offense, she received benefit of clergy and was

[31] King *vs.* Edward Lee, S.C.M. (Aug. 1, 1752).

[32] King *vs.* James Mills, S.C.M. (Aug. 2, 1752).

[33] King *vs.* David and Elizabeth Smith, *et al.,* S.C.M. (April 28, 1767).

[34] See Julius Goebel, Jr., and T. Raymond Naughton, *Law Enforcement in Colonial New York,* 288–293.

[35] For one example of such cooperation between local officials, see the following: Kempe Papers, Lawsuits A-B, a warrant for the return of "two Indians" in Rhode Island to Albany to stand trial for murder (May 1, 1762).

accordingly branded on the thumb. The following summer she was on trial again—this time for petit larceny and with two accomplices—but the Attorney-General dropped the case. She was on good behavior for the next year or so when, in October of 1769, she was indicted for petit larceny. But in January of 1770 the Attorney-General once again entered a *nolle prosequi,* and the case was dropped. Four months later Mary Daily was on trial once more. She was found guilty of grand larceny and received a moderate whipping of twenty-one lashes. This was most fortunate, since grand larceny was a capital offense; and having already received benefit of clergy, Daily might have been sentenced to hang.

By now, one would think, Mary Daily might have been more prudent, for the hangman's noose was uncomfortably close, but she chose to tempt fate once more and, in October of 1770, she was convicted of petit larceny for the second time. The patience of the court was running low, and this time she was punished with a whipping of thirty-nine lashes. Thus, Mary Daily had appeared five times on theft charges of one kind or another when, in April of 1771, she was arrested for burglary. She pleaded not guilty, but her luck had run out, and on April 27, 1771, she was sentenced to hang.[36]

Mary Daily's story is not a happy one, and we can only speculate about the forces which brought her to the gallows. Surely the fact that she was unmarried, unskilled, and unemployed drove her to thievery; but as to specific circumstances, the records are silent. Fortunately, there is somewhat more information available in the case of another woman, Anna Maria Cockin, who was accused of murdering her own newly born infant. She confessed that "great poverty [had] forced her to commit fornication with Joe the Negro Man," and then while she was in labor with his child, she had

[36] King *vs.* Mary Daily, S.C.M. (Oct. 24, 26, 31, 1767); King *vs.* Mary Daily, *ibid.* (July 29, 1768); King *vs.* Mary Daily, *ibid.* (Oct. 24, 1769, and Jan. 20, 1770); King *vs.* Mary Daily, *ibid.* (April 27–28, 1770); King *vs.* Mary Daily, *ibid.* (Aug. 4, 1770, and Oct. 22, 26, 1770); and King *vs.* Mary Daily, *ibid.* (April 22, 24, 27, 1771).

gotten out of bed and the baby "fell from her upon the ground." Cockin further stated that she did not know whether the baby had been stillborn or whether it "had fallen to death." In another deposition, she embellished her story further, explaining that Joe had gotten her "half Drunk" and had promised her a pair of shoes which she desperately needed. As for the story of the baby falling to the ground while she was standing up, she explained that "she had never had so easy a Labour before not having any pain."[37]

Whether the court believed Anna Maria Cockin's story, or whether it was merely showing mercy to a poor widowed woman is not clear; but she was not convicted of murder. Rather, she was convicted of having with her "two black Bastard Children—the Eldest being a boy about three years old which children she doth own and nourish to the Evil Example of others." She confessed to this charge and was punished with a whipping of thirty-one lashes and banishment from Albany County.[38]

Murder was, of course, the most serious of all crimes in colonial New York. But the manner in which the courts dealt with a killing very much depended upon circumstances. When eleven-year-old Bartholomew Noxon accidentally shot a playmate in a children's game, he was found guilty of homicide by "misadventure" and released.[39] When Frederick London was tried for manslaughter in 1764, he was found guilty of "homicide in his own defense" and discharged from custody.[40] Even insanity could be an appropriate defense, as in the case of Elizabeth Horton of Suffolk County, who was tried for murder in 1733. Horton refused to speak at her own trial, and the jury found that "she does not stand mute through malice or obstinacy and also [found] that before and at the time of committing the fact she was mad and is so at the present time."[41]

[37] A.C.S. (June, 1719); N.Y.S.L. Mss., LXI, 146 (June 18, 1719). See *Cal. Hist. Mss.*, 442.

[38] King *vs.* Anna Maria Cockin, A.C.S. (June, 1719).

[39] U.C.S. (Aug., Sept., and Nov., 1714).

[40] King *vs.* Frederick London, S.C.M. (Aug. 2–3, 1764).

[41] Circuit (Sept. 11, 1733).

On the other hand, the penalties for murder could be swift and merciless, especially if slaves were involved. In 1708, for example, Lord Cornbury reported to the Lords of Trade that "a most barbarous murder had been committed upon the Family of one Hallet by an Indian Man Slave and a Negro Woman." A mother and father of their five children had been murdered, and Cornbury "immediately issued a special commission for the Tryal of them, which was done, and the man sentenced to be hanged and the Woman burnt."[42] Thus, even in cases of murder the courts were seldom bound by hard and fast rules. They handed down judgments and sentences that reflected the specific circumstances of the particular case.

III

The range of criminal activity and court proceedings was, then, very wide indeed. In every case for which some detail has survived, one can find a peculiar twist that sheds light on the texture of provincial life. A more difficult task, however, is to tender generalizations regarding the socioeconomic status of criminal defendants. The court records provide only occasional and fragmentary information—an occupation perhaps, or a statement that the defendant owned "no goods, Chattells, Lands and Tenements."[43]

[42] *N.Y. Col. Docs.,* V, 39. See also Kenneth Scott, "The Slave Insurrection in New York in 1712," 45.

[43] Although I have not done so, it may be possible to compare tax lists, assessment records, and the like to court records and thus precisely outline the socioeconomic structure of the population of criminal defendants. The problems of such an analysis are manifest, however. To be accurate, such a comparison would probably have to be done with computer assistance. Therefore, the preparation of the data for analysis would, by itself, be very time consuming. Second, the investment of time and effort might prove fruitless, since many criminal defendants seem to have owned little or no property and, therefore, would probably not appear in records containing data on economic position, though, of course, even their failure to appear would be useful since it might indicate the frequency with which propertied individuals were prosecuted as compared to those without property. At a

But this information does permit some cautious and very tentative conclusions. First, and perhaps most obviously, certain crimes were specific to members of particular social groups, while others were not. Neglect of duty and theft were, for obvious reasons, specific to persons of higher and lower status respectively. But murder and assault prosecutions were undertaken against members of all groups.[44] Defendants accused of keeping disorderly houses tended to be either male tavernkeepers and their wives or single women. Rioters might be either men of substance or poorer people.

In short, socioeconomic status does not seem to have been the prime determinant of criminal activity. Inconsistent though the records may be, they clearly indicate that members of almost every occupational group—from vagrants to artisans and tradesmen to wealthy merchants and government officials—were tried for all sorts of crimes. There is no question, of course, that persons with a greater stake in society were probably less likely to commit serious crimes than those who were deprived of the basic necessities of life. But those necessities might have been psychological as well as physical, and, given the present state of our knowledge, it would be a mistake to attach too great a causal significance to socioeconomic position. What can be done, however, is to offer interpretations that emphasize the effect of specific conditions at given moments in time upon particular groups as they relate to the commission of particular categories of crime. I will attempt to do so in a later chapter.

This said, it must still be acknowledged that there was one occupational group that posed persistent and difficult problems. Indeed, if the members of any particular group of New Yorkers

future date, I intend to undertake such a project, but, for the moment, readers will have to be satisfied with the impressionistic comments which follow.

[44] See, for example, King *vs.* Roper Dawson, S.C.M. (Jan. 22–24, 1766). Dawson was a substantial merchant who was tried and convicted of manslaughter. For evidence of his economic status, see *M.C.C.*, VI, 125.

can be said to have been a plague on New York society, it was certainly the men of the British armed forces. Aside from the very considerable problem of desertion, authorities found that the presence of so many soldiers and sailors in the province could have a most disruptive effect.[45] And the range of crimes committed by military men was extraordinary.

For example, soldiers might get drunk and cause trouble for upstanding townspeople, as the Albany City Council complained one group had done in June of 1716.[46] They might steal from military stores as another group did in December of 1711.[47] Or they might even rob churches as did one sailor named Hamilton in 1769.[48] But soldiers and sailors were most often responsible for acts of violence, and it is to these that I would like to devote some brief attention.

[45] The subject of desertion from the British armed forces in America is large and beyond the scope of the present discussion. Suffice it to say that evidence from many sources indicates that it was a constant and difficult problem. A complete listing of citations would be pointless, but see the following examples. Laws to prevent desertion and prescribing the death penalty in *Col. Laws N.Y.,* I, 417–418 (1699), 434 (1700); *ibid.,* II, 135 (1723), 348 (1726), 501 (1729), 748 (1732), and 858 (1734), as well as later in the century. A multiplicity of warrants and proclamations for the arrest of deserters are also extant. See, for example, N.Y.S.L. Mss., LXXXI, 49 (Sept., 1755), and *Cal. Hist. Mss.,* 644; N.Y.S.L. Mss., LIV, 79 (Oct. 11, 1710), and *Cal. Hist. Mss.,* 356; N.Y.S.L. Mss., LI, 113 (April 27, 1706), and *Cal. Hist. Mss.,* 347; N.Y.S.L. Mss., XLIV, 77 (April 1, 1701), and *Cal. Hist. Mss.,* 282; and others. In addition, deserters sometimes sold their "cloathing, accutrements and provisions" for a profit. See Joel Munsell, ed., *Annals of Albany,* VII, 41–42. For an example of how deserters were punished see "Minutes of the Court Martial of the Schenectady Deserters" in *N.Y. Col. Docs.,* IV, 162–164 (April 21, 1696).

[46] Munsell, ed., *Annals of Albany,* VII, 56. For a similar complaint see *ibid.,* V, 202 (Dec., 1709).

[47] N.Y.S.L. Mss., LVII, 36 (Dec. 26, 1711). See *Cal. Hist. Mss.,* 401.

[48] "On Tuesday evening was examined and committed to gaol a Man who has called himself Hamilton and says he is a Sailor, who confessed that he had in his Possession and sold to Different Persons the three Damask covers off the Cushions, and three Prayer Books, lately stolen out of St. Paul's Church in the city." *New York Journal* or *General Advertiser,* July 20, 1769.

The crimes of violence committed by soldiers and sailors stationed in New York ranged from riots and assaults to rapes and murders. John Tabor Kempe received a letter from Mayor Peter Silvester of Albany in March of 1764 which told a typical story:

> The night before last a Couple of Officers with a large number of Soldiers armed kicked up a most Terrible riot here and for what no one can tell. But as the officers were Intoxicated Somewhat in Liquor it is to be presumed that they did not know all the harm they were doing—several Doors were broken open—many windows broke—goods to considerable value for poor people burnt and destroyed—several people and some of the magistrates wounded in the affray.[49]

Such incidents were not uncommon, and they proved a more-than-bothersome problem for civilian and military officials alike, since they were bound to engender deep antipathy for British authority among civilians. Yet the harsh feelings aroused by an occasional riot of drunken soldiers could not have compared to those generated by the violent personal attacks that New Yorkers sometimes suffered at the hands of members of the military.

One such assault occurred in 1701 when Luykus Gerritse entered a complaint on behalf of his daughter, Maria. It seems Maria had been gathering huckleberries in the woods with some friends when she was "grievously mishandled" by three soldiers. The Albany Mayor's Court called a jury of six women to "search the Body of said Doghter and to see if they could finde any syn of her being ravished." Their verdict was that although they found her "hard handled," they could find no evidence of her being "carnally known in body." They concluded, therefore, that she was "not bereaved of her virginity." The Mayor's Court referred the case to the military authorities who "promised to see [the soldiers] severely punished."[50] We can only speculate about just how severe that

[49] Peter Silvester to John Tabor Kempe (March 13, 1764), Kempe Papers, Box BSW 1. See also William Goodwin to Kempe (March 15, 1764), Kempe Papers, Box I, John Tabor Kempe Letters, "Fisher-Guest," wherein Goodwin assured Kempe that the soldiers involved would be made to pay for the damages and asked how he ought to proceed.

[50] Munsell, ed., *Annals of Albany,* IV, 128–129.

punishment was, but we can be certain that the incident could hardly have endeared the British Army to Luykus Gerritse and his family, or to the citizens of Albany.

Not all crimes committed by soldiers and sailors were as purposeful at the attempted rape of Maria Gerritse. Sometimes members of the military could be capricious in their violence, and often to disastrous effect. In the early summer of 1750, His Majesty's Ship *Greyhound* was in the port of New York. On Thursday, June 7, two members of the crew were on deck when they apparently decided to scare some of the local residents. At two or three in the afternoon, John How, commanding officer of the ship, and James Parks, a gunner's mate, gave the city a sample of thc power of His Majesty's Navy by firing one of the ships' swivel guns at a small boat owned by William Ricketts of Elizabeth Town. The bullet struck one Abigail Stubbins "above the orbit of the Right Eye" and killed her. How and Parks were committed to jail, but escaped New York on board the H.M.S. *Hector* on June 8. There is no evidence to indicate that either man was ever recaptured or punished for the crime.[51]

Crimes like these could hardly have been greeted favorably. Aside from traditional English fears about the dangers of standing armies, this particular standing army gave New Yorkers more than their share of trouble. As the American Revolution approached, such acts surely proved to be more than a mere bother. Indeed, they became grounds for the most serious sorts of grievances. New York society in the eighteenth century was already fragmented, pluralistic, and under intermittent threat of war. The addition of large numbers of British soldiers and sailors to an already volatile social situation generated tensions both in the barracks and outside them, and the result was not only assaults by soldiers on citizens, but violent confrontations between soldiers and sailors as well as attacks by native New Yorkers on His Majesty's troops in the colony of New York.

[51] C.M. (June 7, 1750).

Such incidents were quite common, and one example may be illustrative. James Sprowl, a sailor, was murdered in early May, 1757. It seems that "a Certain Serjeant and three Grenadiers . . . belonging to Some or one of the Marching Regiments posted at [that time] in the Province of New York" attacked Sprowl with bayonets. The resulting wounds killed Sprowl, and he died on May 4. The names of the four soldiers who committed the crime were unknown at the time of the coroner's inquest and, insofar as the court records indicate, were never discovered.[52]

Of course, such crimes were not everyday occurrences, and it would be a mistake to see New York as a society in constant chaos and panic as a result of the presence of the British military. On the other hand, the importance of such incidents ought not to be minimized either. Occasional though they may have been, they were a significant ingredient in the social mix of eighteenth-century New York. New Yorkers shared contemporary anxieties about standing armies, and the behavior of the soldiers and sailors stationed in the colony tended to confirm and strengthen their darkest suspicions. It is, therefore, no surprise that the Quartering Act was so thoroughly resisted in the American colonies. It was bad enough that the colonists had to depend upon British troops for their defense and must welcome them into their cities and towns. Accepting them into their homes was unthinkable.

IV

The variety of crimes and criminals was, then, considerably greater than the figures in previous chapters might at first suggest. Such aggregation is useful, since it allows the historian to take a wider view and permits the perception of general patterns and trends that would otherwise be obscured. Moreover, this is also true of the treatment prisoners received while they were awaiting trial and after they had been convicted. It is to this topic that we now turn, and it should become clear that although conditions in

[52] *Ibid.* (May 5, 1757).

New York's jails were anything but idyllic, the administration of justice could be as personal and specific as crime itself.

Jails had a different function than they do today. They were devoted, almost exclusively, to holding prisoners awaiting trial. It was very rare for an individual to receive a prison term as punishment for the commission of a crime.[53] This was the result both of economic imperatives—it was very expensive to hold a prisoner in jail—and of the fact that few men of the eighteenth century believed that a term in jail would have a deterrent effect. The prison, therefore, had no corrective function, and conditions within its walls could be very harsh indeed—even by the standards of the eighteenth century, which were none too high.[54]

The jail of the city of New York was in the City Hall, at the head of Broad Street. It was here that court sessions were held. In front of the building there was a whipping post, a pillory, and stocks, and it was here, as well, that unfortunate prisoners were confined.[55] Physical conditions were horrendous. One prisoner complained that he had "nothing but the bare floor to lay on—no covering—almost devour'd with all kinds of Vermine and no refreshment of Apparel."[56] Another wrote that he was "almost Deprived of the use of [his] Limbs" and was "Inclining to a Consumptive Disorder."[57] A third said that he "suffered Daily for want of the Common Necessities of Life" and feared that he would "perish for want of food and Raiment."[58] Other prisoners com-

[53] I have found only nineteen such cases for the entire century. See, for example, case of King *vs.* Richard Cooley who was sentenced to three months in prison for assaulting a jailer, S.C.M. (Oct. 25, 29, 1773).

[54] See Leon Radzinowicz, *A History of English Criminal Law* (New York, 1948), I, 32, and the accompanying citations of W. L. Clay, *The Prison Chaplain: A Memoir of the Reverend John Clay* (1861) and John Howard's famous *The State of the Prisons* (1771).

[55] John F. Watson, comp., *Annals of New York . . .* (Philadelphia, 1846), 179.

[56] Patrick Mulvany to John Tabor Kempe (May 19, 1766), Kempe Papers, Lawsuits M–O.

[57] Anthony O'Neal to John Tabor Kempe (Oct. 8, 1762), *ibid.*

[58] John Young to John Tabor Kempe (Jan. 29, 1770), Kempe Papers, Lawsuits V–Z.

plained that they were starving and would die without relief.[59] Still others were removed from jail when illness seemed to threaten their lives or the cold of winter threatened to freeze them to death.[60] In short, prisoners suffered terribly. In fact, in March of 1751, they made a public appeal in the *New-York Gazette* because they had not "one Stick to burn in freezing weather."[61]

If the physical conditions were not bad enough, jail-keepers could make them even worse. In April of 1694, for example, the Sheriff of New York was presented for stabbing one of his charges.[62] One prisoner wrote to complain that the Sheriff had locked him up in a "lone Gail" where he almost died. He escaped and "sent to the Sheriff and told him that I would com to him and mak [?] if he would not put me not in gail." The Sheriff agreed and then proceeded to lock the man in irons for fourteen days.[63] Another prisoner wrote that he was "grossly used" by the jail-keeper "in being Close Confined and locked up alone."[64]

Abominable physical conditions and brutal jail-keepers were not the only things that prisoners had to fear. Their fellow prisoners might prove dangerous as well. On a July evening in 1756, for example, Edward Pendegrass was attacked by John Carr, a fellow inmate. Carr struck Pendegrass with "his Right fist in the pitt of his

59 See, for example, the petition of John Thorpe in N.Y.S.L. Mss., LXX, 114 (Aug., 1734). See *Cal. Hist. Mss.,* 522.

60 See King *vs.* Mary Yates, S.C.M. (Jan. 29, 1764); and the petition of the sheriff relative to John Roads in S.C.M. (Oct. 21, 1729).

61 Quoted by Carl Bridenbaugh, *Cities in Revolt,* 118. Other references to the conditions in New York's jails abound. The following notice appeared in the *New York Journal* or *General Advertiser* in February of 1772: "As the Distresses of the prisoners confined in the gaol of this City, appear to be very great, they being in want not only of firing but even the common Necessaries of Life, Charity Sermons for the Relief will be preached next Sunday Morning." Quoted in *Collections of the New-York Historical Society for the Year 1870* (New York, 1870), 220.

62 S.C. (1912), 55 (Aug. 1694).

63 John Bell to William Kempe (April 1, 1756), Kempe Papers, Box IV, William Kempe Letters, "Armstrong-Correy."

64 John Clarke to William Kempe (April 20, 1754), *ibid.*

Stomach" and Pendegrass "then and there immediately died."[65] No wonder, then, that prisoners were sometimes driven to suicide by their incarceration, as was Stephen Porter, an occupant of New York City's jail who hanged himself in his cell in June of 1769.[66] Still others became so desperate that they attempted to burn the building down. This was true in the case of Martha Cash who, when she was tried for arson in May of 1733, explained to the court that "her only Design was to Gett out of Gaol."[67] The court no doubt appreciated her honesty, but ordered that she receive eleven lashes just the same for being an arsonist.

Life was, therefore, anything but pleasant for prisoners awaiting trial. But accused criminals enjoyed one advantage denied to internees in our own jails. Public officials in colonial New York were far more accessible to men and women in trouble with the law; they were besieged with letters and petitions from prisoners or their friends and relatives requesting relief from the burdens of life in prison or applying for pardon on one basis or another. Such letters and petitions often went on for pages, arguing the facts of a particular case and requesting the intercession of the public official in question.

A common defense for criminal behavior was that the alleged act was committed under the influence of alcohol. Joseph Burras of Newtown petitioned in 1693 for the remission of a fine "imposed on him for words spoken whilst in drink."[68] Conversely, a defendant might argue that the crime was committed as a result of extreme provocation from another individual who was intoxicated. It was on such grounds that John Degvaty [?] protested his innocence in an assault case in October of 1754. He claimed that the victim of the assault had been drunk and that he was only attempting to remove her from his tavern.[69]

65 C.M. (July 26, 1750).

66 *M.C.C.*, VII, 169 (June 15, 1769).

67 N.Y.G.S. (May 2, 1733).

68 N.Y.S.L. Mss., XXXIX, 53 (May 19, 1693). See *Cal. Hist. Mss.*, 233.

69 John [Degvaty?] to William Kempe (Oct. 27, 1754), Kempe Papers, Box IV, William Kempe Letters, "Davenport-Flood."

Other grounds upon which defendants requested pardon were that the defendant was too young to understand the consequences of his act, that he was ignorant of the law, that he was "mentally deranged," that the crime was committed accidentally, that the crime was the result of being "seduced by Ill women," and that the prosecution was the result of an anti-Catholic bias.[70] One individual, Richard Tinker, tendered an entirely unique defense. Tinker, a blind man, was being prosecuted in the Supreme Court for harboring runaway servants. In his petition, he asked for a pardon and "declared that he never saw any such persons in his house."[71]

In short, the variety of prisoners' pleas for mercy was enormous, and no public official involved with the enforcement of the law could avoid receiving such requests. Nor were prisoners alone in their supplications to government officials. Friends and relatives often joined in as well. When Abraham DeWitt was locked up in Orange County for passing counterfeit money, a group of twenty-six of his neighbors got together and petitioned John Tabor Kempe to drop the charges. DeWitt, in their words, had "Bin a Dweller for Several years in our parts Ever since he was a young lad and never to oure knowledge or By any Report from any person, We never heard anything Against him as to his Dishonesty or misconduct but we do look upon him To Be a Very Honest Person."[72]

Two special categories of petition also deserve some brief atten-

[70] Evidence of such requests may be found in the following locations. *Youth:* King *vs.* Joseph Prosser, S.C. (1946), 98 (April 19, 1702). *Ignorance:* Elijah Dean to William Kempe (Feb. 22, 1754), Kempe Papers, Box IV, William Kempe Letters, "Davenport-Flood." *Mental Derangement:* Petition and Letter regarding John Snyder in *Cal. Hist. Mss.*, 829, 830. *Accident:* Letter from John Thorpe to John Tabor Kempe claiming he killed his wife accidentally, Kempe Papers, Lawsuits P–V. For additional material on the same case, see also N.Y.S.L. Mss., XCIX, 63, 64, 66 (Jan. 25, 1773, Feb. 2, 1773, and June 30, 1773). See *Cal. Hist. Mss.*, 813. *Seduction by* "ill women": N.Y.S.L. Mss., LXII, 75, 78 (March 19, 1720 and April 4, 1720). See *Cal. Hist. Mss.*, 450. *Anti-Catholicism:* James Lyons to John Tabor Kempe (June 20, 1764), Kempe Papers, Box I, John Tabor Kempe Letters, "La Grange-Lyons."

[71] N.Y.S.L. Mss., XLIV, 70 (March [?], 1701). See *Cal. Hist. Mss.*, 281.

[72] Kempe Papers, Box BSW 1 (March 31, 1762).

tion. Occasionally, a prisoner might admit his guilt, but ask that he be allowed to "enlist out of jail." That is to say, he would offer to make a deal with the prosecutor—a military enlistment in exchange for immunity from prosecution. Thus in 1711 William Baker, a convicted horse thief, wrote in a petition that he "hath constantly Demeaned himself in all things towards all her Majesties liege people . . . [and] never before hath offended." He had a wife and children and was "nearly related to Severall persons of good Creditt." He vowed to "Spend the remainder of His Days in her Majesty's Service either by Sea or Land," if only he could be released from prison.[73] There is no record of the disposition of Baker's case; but there can be no question that such pardons were not only occasionally requested, but granted as well.[74]

A second category of petition was that of masters asking that their slaves be pardoned. Slaves occupied an anomalous position: they were "persons" and could be tried in the courts; but they were also "property," and therefore the state had a responsibility for their protection. Masters understood this only too well and were compensated with twenty-five pounds when a slave was executed.[75] Moreover, masters sometimes attempted to obtain full pardons for convicted slaves by arguing that their livelihood depended on the work of the particular slave involved. Thus did the cooper Richard Elliott plead for mercy on behalf of two of his slaves in 1693. Emphasizing his own character and loyalty, Elliott went on to explain that he was old and sick and entirely dependent on the two slaves. Unless they were pardoned, he asserted, he and his children would starve.[76]

[73] N.Y.S.L. Mss., LII, 55 (May 11, 1711). See *Cal. Hist. Mss.*, 379.

[74] See, for example, two letters from Nathaniel Robinson and three other prisoners in Albany to William Kempe in Kempe Papers, Box IV, William Kempe Letters, "Gale-Hyatt" (April 23, and Nov. 4, 1750) in which Kempe is beseeched to allow the prisoners to "Inlist out of Gaol."

[75] For an example of this law at work, see the petition of Isaac Governour and ten others requesting compensation for their slaves executed in the conspiracy prosecutions of 1712 in N.Y.S.L. Mss., LVIII, 22 (Sept. 30, 1712). See *Cal. Hist. Mss.*, 409.

[76] N.Y.S.L. Mss., XXXIX, 110 ([?], 1693). See *Cal. Hist. Mss.*, 237.

Discussions of the "moral personality" of the slave aside, it is clear that slaves who committed crimes created very special problems for the courts since their punishment invariably affected their masters. That individuals should be punished for violation of the law, no New Yorker would have denied. At the same time, however, they would have argued that the government had a responsibility to protect private property, and these two notions came into serious conflict every time a slave was convicted of a crime. This conflict could never be entirely resolved since monetary compensation was not always adequate compensation for an executed slave. A slave trained as a cooper or as a blacksmith was not so easily replaced as a horse might be. Implicitly, then, albeit for entirely selfish reasons, masters had to recognize that slaves were people with special talents, abilities, and personal qualities; and although twenty-five pounds might repay the slave's value as a piece of property, it never could restore his value as a person. The irony was that it was the slave's legal status as a chattel which, in cases of criminality at least, forced the master to recognize his real status as a person.

Public officials in colonial New York were assaulted, therefore, with a veritable barrage of petitions and letters requesting pardons or reprieves for defendants. Of course, these letters and petitions would never have been drafted if the writers did not believe that there was some chance of obtaining the desired results. In fact, there is ample evidence to suggest that public officials read the many requests for pardon and often acted upon them and, in addition, that the courts themselves often acted to assure fairness and equity in the prosecution of crime.

Pardons were frequently granted to capitally convicted defendants. Of all those sentenced to death, 51.7% were pardoned after their trial by one or another agency of government. Occasionally, such pardons were conditional upon the fulfillment of certain other requirements. Convicted felon Dennis Hall was pardoned in 1765 on condition that he "quit the province."[77] Pardons for slaves

[77] N.Y.S.L. Mss., XLIII, 30 (Feb. 4, 1765). See *Cal. Hist. Mss.*, 752.

might sometimes be granted if the master would provide security for their good behavior or if he would agree to have the slave sold and transported out of the colony.[78] Other conditions which might be invoked included enlistment in the army or navy or leaving the colony permanently.[79] The reasons for or conditions of a pardon were not always explicitly stated in the records, but there is abundant evidence that the requests of capitally convicted defendants were taken seriously before they were refused.

Capital cases were not the only crimes in which the courts and other governmental bodies showed their willingness to consider the personal situation of defendants. Poverty, for example, was often a powerful argument for leniency in the passing of sentence. There are numerous cases of the courts intentionally reducing a fine "in consideration of the poverty of the defendant."[80] The youth of the accused might also help to mitigate a penalty as in the case of Mansfield Hunt, convicted in a riot case in 1721, but "being a Youth . . . [was] remitted to the correction of his Father."[81] Moreover, if a defendant had been in prison for some months

[78] See, for example, the pardon of bricklayer Dyrck Vandenburgh's slave, Jack, convicted of "burglary at the house Mr. Ives." The pardon was granted in consideration of a three hundred pound surety for Jack's good behavior provided by Vandenburgh. The original petition and the pardon itself may be found in N.Y.S.L. Mss., XLII, 72, 118 (Oct. 10, 1698). See *Cal. Hist. Mss.*, 263, 265. For a case where pardon was granted on condition of transportation, see pardon of William Pontine's slave, Tom, in N.Y.S.L. Mss., XCIII, 85, 87–88, and 92 (missing). See *Cal. Hist. Mss.*, 756 (Aug. 9, 14, and Sept. 5, 1765).

[79] For example, see the pardon of Abraham Van Ornem, John Likens, Peter Donnelly, George Sears, William Thomas, John Dislow, and David Miller on condition of enlistment in N.Y.S.L. Mss., XC, 130 (May 22, 1762). See *Cal. Hist. Mss.*, 731. Also see the case of King *vs.* Mary Clarke, who was pardoned and banished, in S.C.M. (Jan. 22–25, and April 27, 1752).

[80] Penalties were reduced for this reason in the following cases, among others: King *vs.* Rynier Quackenboss in S.C.M. (Jan. 16, 1765) for riot; and King *vs.* John Martine in S.C.M. (April 29, 1763) for refusing to give evidence.

[81] Circuit (Aug. 11–12, 1721).

awaiting trial and then was convicted, the penalty might be reduced in consideration of the duress of a lengthy stay in jail.[82] In addition, servants or slaves who were convicted of crimes after having already been punished by their masters might also find that the courts could show them considerable leniency. This was true in the case of James McKensey who was convicted of petty theft and sentenced to receive a whipping of twenty-one lashes. The punishment was remitted, however, "in Consideration of his Ingenious Confession and his having been severely punished for the Crime by his Master."[83]

A final consideration which almost always resulted in at least a reprieve for a defendant was pregnancy. Pregnant women were occasionally brought before the courts on a variety of charges. In such a situation a standard procedure was followed. The defendant would "plead her Belly" and would then be examined either by a midwife or a "jury of Matrons." If they agreed that the woman was, in fact, pregnant, a variety of courses might be taken. The court might put off sentencing until the following term, it might recommend that the defendant be removed from jail until the baby was born, or, in the case of capital offenses, the defendant might receive a stay of execution.[84] In short, the response of the courts in cases involving pregnant women was as individual and personalized as in other cases. Each case was decided on its merits, and decisions were made not only with reference to the law but reflected, as well, the court's understanding of the particular circumstances of a specific criminal act and its perpetrator.

[82] The case of King *vs.* Anne Wright is an example. Wright was a servant who stole a teakettle in August of 1742. She was arrested and remained in jail until November of that year. She was convicted and her sentence of six lashes was remitted, since she had already been in jail for three months. N.Y.G.S. (Aug. 14, 1742, and Nov. 2, 1742).

[83] S.C.M. (Aug. 4–5, 1742).

[84] Examples of each of these alternatives may be found in the following cases respectively: King *vs.* Frances Malone, S.C.M. (July 29, and Aug. 11, 1767); King *vs.* Mary Jeffrys, S.C.M. (Aug. 1–2, and Oct. 22, 1765); and King *vs.* Margaret Grass, S.C.M. (April 21, 23, 26, and 27, 1736).

Having observed the behavior of a number of individual defendants and having seen the system of criminal justice at work, what can be said about the social context of the aggregate data examined in earlier chapters? The overwhelming conclusion must be, I think, that criminal behavior was infinitely varied and touched many aspects of life. Social mobility, servitude, family life, public authority, and the British military presence—to name only five—all impinged upon and, in turn, were themselves affected by criminal behavior. It bears repeating that the crimes were as individual as the people who committed them, and although conditions in the jails of the colony were uniformly unbearable, the courts and the other agencies of government showed considerable flexibility in their handling of criminal cases. Penalties were harsh, but they were not uniformly applied, and there is reason to believe that a real, if not entirely articulated, effort was made to personalize the system of criminal justice by making public officials accessible to prisoners and by providing pardons and respites of judgment when circumstances seemed to warrant them.

Aggregation, therefore, can be an effective, but occasionally dangerous tool since it imparts a deceptively smooth texture to historical phenomena. History—if I may be permitted a somewhat crude analogy—is like a relief map which indicates not only the borders of political units, but also the elevations and depressions of the land itself. By grouping implicitly discrete pieces of historical information into general categories, we may tend to level the historical landscape and thus suggest the general outlines of the map without providing any sense of specific contours. The purpose of this chapter has been to restore the rough edges by demonstrating the wide diversity of private and public behavior which must play a part in any study of crimes, criminals, and courts in eighteenth-century New York. In the next chapter, I shall attempt to restore some of the topography itself by adding a chronological perspective to our view of crime in the colony of New York.

CHAPTER 5

The Chronological Dimensions of Crime

The dimension of change over time is central to all historical study: the broad generalization is probed and tested in the crucible of time; a pattern or trend is broken down into its component parts; and analysis takes on a specificity which at once deepens and clarifies an interpretive framework. This is especially true when the data of history can be expressed quantitatively. Thus far, for example, I have tried to elucidate several interpretive themes regarding crime in eighteenth-century New York. For the most part, however, I have relied upon figures computed for a period of almost one hundred years. The various patterns I have described are important, but they do not account for such variations from century-long averages as may be attributed to forces which were chronologically specific. The purpose of this chapter, therefore, is to examine several aspects of crime from a more explicitly chronological perspective by relating changes in the business of the criminal courts to developments in the society at large.

Discussion centers first upon the question of crime rates and the problems inherent in computing them and then moves on to an evaluation and analysis of long-term patterns of prosecution. Insofar as it has been possible to do so, I have tried to make this section as comprehensive as possible by examining specific categories of crime on both a colony-wide and geographically specific basis. But I have also exercised the historian's prerogative of selectivity, choosing for analysis only those computations which seem most informative and useful, since an encyclopedic compilation of calculations would serve to confuse more than it would to clarify.

I

The calculation of crime rates is a tricky business. Population figures for New York are excellent—probably the best for any of the British colonies in North America.[1] But the quality and completeness of the court records themselves create problems that cannot be entirely surmounted. The only complete set of records is that for the Court of General Sessions of the Peace for the city and county of New York. The minute books of all the other county courts, and the Supreme Court as well, have chronological gaps that complicate what would be, under other circumstances, a relatively straightforward series of calculations. For example, there is no year for which we have a census *and* complete records for each of New York's colonial courts. In addition, the Supreme Court records for the decade of the 1740's are missing. Thus, although we have two censuses taken during those years, in 1746 and 1749, it is impossible to compute crime rates which could be legitimately compared to those for years that do include Supreme Court records.

The central problem is the degree of confidence one can place in the comparability of rates generated from different record sets and computed for different population groups. Although complete rates can be computed for New York City throughout the century (with the exception of the 1740's), no equivalent rates may be calculated for the other counties. Moreover, although rates may be calculated for the counties where records are extant, any comparison of such rates would be very tenuous indeed.

Still, having acknowledged these problems, some calculations are possible for the years during which we possess both census data and complete court records. Such calculations indicate that the serious crime rate in New York was substantially higher than in

[1] For a convenient summary, see Evarts B. Greene and Virginia D. Harrington, *American Population,* 88–105.

Massachusetts.[2] The lowest crime rate in New York during the eighteenth century was 150 prosecutions per 100,000 of population and 80 convictions in 1723. The highest rate was 300 prosecutions per 100,000 of population and 170 convictions in 1703. Moreover, in the city of New York rates were even higher, reaching a zenith of 450 prosecutions per 100,000 and 210 convictions. By any standard of comparison, this would seem to be an extraordinary variation from the Massachusetts pattern, where in 1725 the crime rate was only 12.5 prosecutions per 100,000 and 4.7 convictions. Colonial New York, as innumerable contemporaries and not a few historians have observed, was a "factious" society. And these crime rates would appear to support that generalization —at least in comparison to Massachusetts. But beyond the comparative dimension, there are other questions we should ask. How widely did these rates vary over the course of the century? Did they rise or fall as time wore on? No dramatic increase in crime rates took place over the course of the century; if anything, a slight decline may be noted both in New York City and in the colony as a whole. The relative stability of these rates may be deceptive, however. There were two very sharp increases in criminal activity— the first in the 1730's and the second in the 1760's. Moreover, these sharp increases in the crime rate parallel similarly acute fluctuations in population and severe economic dislocation. In the thirties crime was increasing at a rate even faster than that of population, and there was a very clear rise in crime rates during that decade. In the sixties, the volume of convictions rose more sharply

[2] The accompanying calculations for eighteenth-century Massachusetts have been generously provided by David H. Flaherty who is at work on a book concerned with crime and law enforcement in the Bay Colony. It should be noted, however, that Flaherty's rates are not *strictly* comparable to my own calculations since the population of New York did not reach 100,000 until the middle of the 1750's, while the population of Massachusetts had reached that level during the 1720's. Nonetheless, while there is a dearth of comparative data, the differences between Massachusetts and New York noted below are striking enough to be suggestive if not entirely conclusive.

than at any point in the century, though not quite so rapidly as population. As a result, there was a very slightly increased rate for that decade in the colony as a whole and a slightly depressed one for the city alone. But it is nonetheless clear that the population growth of the 1730's and 1760's was accompanied by a rise in the number of both criminal prosecutions and convictions.

Therefore, at two points in New York's history—the periods from 1731 to 1737 and 1756 to 1771—crime was rising faster than population, but it should also be recognized that the actual rates were less than those for the very earliest census years of 1698 and 1703. Moreover, in New York City proper this pattern was also evident, with crime rising faster than population only between 1723 and 1737. It would be a mistake, however, to conclude that the gross volume of crime was not on the rise; indeed, the actual volume of convictions multiplied more than sixfold both in the city and in the colony as a whole over the course of the century. And the volume of prosecutions rose in even greater magnitude. In the colony as a whole, the overall case volume increased more than eight times between 1691 and 1774. Volume increased almost as dramatically in New York City, and similar increases may be noted both in the rural counties taken as a group and in each of the individual regions of New York.

Again, I am not suggesting that this increase was steady and uninterrupted. There were periods when prosecution slackened, and the volume of criminal business handled by the courts declined, but the general trend seems to have been one of increasing volume over the course of the century. How ought this increase to be interpreted? Remembering that, for the most part, crime was not rising as fast as population, there is still reason to believe that crime was a social problem of increasingly serious proportions. The legal institutions of New York, which had first been systematized by the Judiciary Act of 1691, were ill-equipped to handle a rapidly accelerating volume of criminal cases. That the growth of criminal prosecutions was usually slower than the rate of population increase is certainly true. That a society changing as rapidly as colonial New York could easily absorb and deal with the problems its growth created is much less certain and is the subject of a later chapter.

Like everything else in the colonies, then, the prosecution of crime was changing, increasing, and expanding. What was the nature of this growth? To what extent did certain crimes begin to consume a greater share of the courts' attention while others declined? Did patterns of prosecution change over the century among the different ethnic groups? How extensively were colony-wide trends reflected in the different regions of the colony? All of these questions are related in significant ways, and perhaps the best way to begin to answer them is to divide the century (quite arbitrarily) into two periods in an attempt to delineate the broad outlines of change underway.

The first period stretches from 1691 to 1749 and the second from 1750 to 1776. Striking differences may be noted between the two periods, and it is possible to provide a precise description of the changing character of the criminal cases appearing before the courts. Case volume was increasing over the course of the century, but it is also vital to describe the nature and direction of that increase.

Generally speaking, serious, and especially violent crimes assumed a more important role from 1750 to 1776 than they had in the period 1691–1749. Thefts and cases involving disorderly houses were both up slightly, and acts of personal violence and violations of public order rose sharply in the last twenty-five years of New York's colonial history. Crimes by slaves against their masters declined sharply, on the other hand, from 9.6% of all prosecutions in the period 1691–1749 to only 0.2% of all cases in the later period. This sharp decline is, of course, related to the fact that both of New York's major slave conspiracies took place in the earlier part of the century—the first in 1712 and the second in 1741. One of the results of these massive prosecutions is to inflate the percentage of cases involving crimes by slaves against their masters.[3]

Although violent crime seems to have been on the rise in the colony, contempt of authority cases dropped from 7.9% of all prosecutions to 4.3%, and crimes by officials increased slightly. In other words, although serious crimes do seem to have been on the rise, it also appears that they were more arbitrary and less specifically directed in the later period. Crimes against masters and contempt of authority cases are clearly focused offenses. The individual attacked is, in both cases, the object of institutional as well as personal antagonisms. But offenses like theft, assault, and rioting are less definite in purpose. To be sure, they may reflect grievances of a social, economic, or political nature, and they are committed with clear objectives in view, but they are more often the result of more generalized social dislocations than would be at work, for example, in a case involving an insult to a justice of the peace or an assault on a cruel slavemaster.

It is, in my opinion, fair to argue that patterns of criminal prosecution seem to have reflected the impact of the enormous demographic and economic expansion of New York during 1700's. But before tendering a more detailed interpretation, an examination of the nature of regional variation is in order. As we have seen, New York was not a socially homogeneous colony, and the diversity of its social history is very much in evidence in calculations that are geographically and ethnically specific. The two major geographic divisions of the colony, New York City and the outlying counties,

[3] For details of these prosecutions, see the following representative works: Kenneth Scott, "The Slave Insurrection in New York in 1712," 43–74; Edgar J. McManus, *A History of Negro Slavery in New York* (Syracuse, 1966), ch. 7; Ferenc M. Szasz, "The New York Slave Revolt of 1741: A Re-Examination," *New York History,* 55 (1967), 215–230; Daniel Horsmanden, *The New York Conspiracy;* and T. Wood Clarke, "The Negro Plot of 1741," *New York History,* 25 (April, 1944), 167–181. Both prosecutions had an unsettling effect on New York society. The first resulted in 39 indictments against slaves and, in the second, 154 bondsmen and free blacks were accused.

evinced markedly different changes in patterns of prosecution, changes which add precision to the general colony-wide trends noted above.

In the city, theft increased from 16.9% of all prosecutions between 1691 and 1749 to 24.1% between 1750 and 1776. Acts of personal violence swelled to an even greater extent, growing from 12.5% to 27.6% of all cases. Violations of public order, on the other hand, rose by a relatively meager amount from 5.9% to 8.8%. Moreover, in the counties, a contrary configuration of prosecutions appears to have developed. Thefts *declined* in the counties, and acts of personal violence rose only slightly. Violations of public order, however, picked up markedly, increasing from 27.0% to 33.7% of all cases. The figures suggest clearly different directions of change in urban and rural New York.

Such an interpretation is supported by other evidence as well. The increase in cases of theft in the city was apparently accompanied by a corresponding rise in the percentage of prosecutions for keeping disorderly houses. The disorderly house was, as noted earlier, a characteristically urban phenomenon popularly associated with theft. Such prosecutions were of only marginal significance in the countryside, while an increase in their number in the city confirmed and reflected the contemporary view, since it paralleled a similar rise in cases of theft.

The only offenses which seem to have undergone similar change in patterns of prosecution between rural and urban New York are violations of public order and contempt of authority. In the former case, however, there appears to have been a striking dissimilarity between city and country in terms of the significance such cases took in the larger scheme of things. In both periods, riots and the like were the single most frequent source of prosecution in the countryside, while they accounted for a relatively small percentage of cases in the city. Insofar as the decline in contempt cases is concerned, there do appear to have been parallel changes occurring within and without the city of New York. That is to say, in both areas such cases comprised a smaller percentage of the courts' total caseload in the period 1691–1749 than in the period 1750–1776. Cases of crime by officials, on the other hand, maintained a stable 2.2% of all prosecutions in the city during each of the two periods, while rising slightly from 4.0% to 6.5% in the counties.

There is as much danger, of course, in presenting the counties as a single unit as there is in treating the entire colony without regard to rural and urban distinctions. Yet the various regions did share certain common characteristics. Without exception, in every area of the colony except New York City, thefts constituted a smaller percentage of all prosecutions later in the century than they did earlier. Similarly, violations of public order increased markedly between 1750 and 1776, with the lowest percentage of all cases accounted for by these crimes being 20.5% in Albany and Charlotte counties—more than double the volume in New York City in the same period. For the two crimes of theft and violation of public order, therefore, the patterns of prosecution in individual regions confirm the observed differences between the urban and rural sections of New York.

For other offenses, patterns of prosecution were somewhat less consistent with general trends. Acts of personal violence declined slightly in Suffolk, Albany-Charlotte, and the borough counties of Kings, Queens, Richmond, and Westchester, while rising sharply in the river counties of Ulster, Dutchess, and Orange. Contempt of authority, on the other hand, dropped off in the borough and river counties, while increasing ever so slightly in Suffolk and Albany-Charlotte. In addition, crimes by public officials rose everywhere but in Albany, where they declined by a meager 0.5%.

But these variations from the more general trends are, in my view, relatively insignificant. The actual differences are very slight for the most part, and I am disinclined to attach too much importance to the discrepancy between an increase of two percent and a decline of two percent—especially considering the uneven quality of the court records. This is especially true in calculations for the particular regions, since the numerical base on which the percentages are computed is smaller, and, therefore, the percentage itself is more subject to fluctuation. The only dramatic variation is a jump in cases of personal violence in the river counties from 23.4% to 35.2%.

At the very least, then, the direction of changing patterns of prosecution for the major categories of crime differed between urban and rural New York. Trends in the prosecution of ethnic groups, on the other hand, were remarkably consistent. In the colony as a whole, in New York City, in the rural counties taken as a group, and in each of the regions individually, the English accounted for a greater and greater share of all criminal cases, while the number of Dutchmen appearing before the courts declined. In addition, in every part of New York, slaves constituted a far smaller percentage of prosecutions between 1750 and 1776 than between 1691 and 1749.

Patterns of criminal prosecution underwent striking and clear changes over the course of the eighteenth century. Throughout the colony, levels of violence rose dramatically, taking the form of assaults and similar personal attacks or riots and other more general violations of public order. Proceedings involving contempt of authority seem to have been on the decline, while cases involving official abuse or neglect of duty were on the rise. In the city, cases of theft drew an increasing share of the courts' attention while declining in relative importance in the countryside. Disorderly houses, which never occupied a very important position in the rural counties, jumped sharply in the city, while crimes by slaves against their masters dropped off to a small fraction of all prosecutions. Finally, persons of English descent, who had always accounted for the greatest percentage of criminal cases, took an even more preponderant proportion of the total caseload in the third quarter of the century. This rise in the number of Englishmen prosecuted was accompanied, moreover, by a corresponding decline in the percentage of cases involving persons of Dutch descent and black slaves.

What are we to make of these facts? To what extent do they offer any insight into the social history of the colony? In short, what relation do changes in patterns of prosecution have to developments in the society at large? The most central facts in the social history of the colony were economic and demographic growth of unanticipated and unprecedented proportions. The population grew from 18,067 in 1698 to 168,007 in 1771.[4] The economy of the province expanded and diversified as ships from all over the empire docked in the port of New York, unloaded their cargo, and then sailed off again to do New York's business in Virginia, the Carolinas, the Caribbean, and England. Settlement—which in 1691 had centered in New York City, Albany, and Long Island—had, by 1776, not only covered the Hudson River Valley, but had begun to move west along the Mohawk. The city of New York itself, little more than a small town in 1691, was a major metropolitan center in the 1770's, with shops of every description, a college, a coffeehouse society not unlike that of London, and an active and vociferous press. In sum, the texture of life in New York changed to an extraordinary degree between 1691 and 1776, and it is in these broad social transformations that I believe we can find the sources of altered patterns of criminal prosecutions.

Theft, which rose so dramatically in New York City and declined so precipitously in the countryside, is essentially an offense that depends upon intensive settlement. In other words, a high rate of theft might be expected in a society where population density is high. In such a situation, the temptations for thievery are greater, since highly concentrated population necessarily implies an equally high concentration of the goods and services which most attract thieves. Of course, the colony of New York between 1691 and 1749 was anything but densely settled. Population was, for the most part, thinly spread all over the colony. Even in 1773, only one-fifth of the whole province was occupied.[5]

But the wide distribution of New York's people conceals some of

[4] Greene and Harrington, *American Population,* 92, 103.

[5] Stella H. Sutherland, *Population Distribution in Colonial America* (New York, 1936), 72.

the more subtle aspects of settlement. Early in the century, when thefts were at their highest in the counties, it was more likely that people would live in towns and villages than on isolated farms. Under intermittent threat of war with the French and the Indians, people found it necessary to live in widely scattered but intensively settled clusters. After 1750, and especially after 1763, as the threat of war diminished and immigration rose sharply, people spread over the entire landscape, and settlement became more extensive than intensive. Moreover, if the Puritan towns of Long Island followed the example of their New England cousins, the tightly organized family and community structures of the early years may well have broken down in the latter half of the century as younger sons began seeking their own land.[6] As a result of these developments, the temptations for thievery may have declined in the countryside. More remote from each other as well as from law-enforcement officers than they had been earlier in the century, people living outside the city were both less likely to steal and less likely to be caught if they did.

In New York, on the other hand, the original high concentration of population did not decline, but rather was augmented as the city grew from village to metropolis. All of the factors that make cities an attractive home for thieves were on the rise in New York, and, in fact, a close examination of the statistics suggests the prudence of emphasizing density of population as a determining factor in the prosecution of theft. In the period 1691–1749, for example, thefts accounted for 16.9% of all prosecutions in New York City—which was certainly the most densely settled area in the colony at the time. But in neither the countryside as a whole nor in any individual region did the percentage of thefts approach that for the city in the early period. This is precisely the result that might be expected on the basis of distribution of population. Further, if we turn to the later era, 1750–1776, it is clear that as New York City grew and expanded, so too did the volume of cases

[6] For the playing out of these themes in one New England town, see Philip J. Greven, *Four Generations.*

of theft. At the same time, however, theft declined in each of the rural areas as a source of prosecution—and, it should be added, this was also a period when New York's population began, for the first time, to enjoy a degree of physical security that had not been possible earlier in the century. The declining percentage of thefts in the counties may fairly be attributed to the fact that between 1750 and 1776 the population of New York, for the first time, began to move beyond the protective boundaries of the first villages and towns. This diffusion of rural population discouraged thievery to a considerable degree by removing the thief from the sources of wealth.

These developments were reflected in the changing patterns of prosecution for other crimes as well. The expansion of the colony's trade brought increasingly large numbers of soldiers and sailors into the port of New York. In the previous chapter, we examined some of the more concrete manifestations of the British military presence, but there were indirect effects as well. In the period 1750–1776, the percentage of prosecutions for keeping disorderly houses rose to twice what it had been between 1691 and 1749, and there can be no question but that these prosecutions were related to an increased demand for the services of prostitutes in a bustling port city. In addition, the presence of the British military in the colony contributed to the heightened levels of violence. Violations of public order as well as personal attacks were encouraged by the behavior of soldiers and sailors who could be less than courteous in their treatment of New York's citizens.

It would be unfair, however, to be too eager to blame the British army and navy for New York's rising volume of violent crimes. Certainly, the mere physical fact of New York City's growth contributed to the increased percentage of acts of personal violence. With a larger population living at closer quarters than ever before, the possibilities for personal antagonism increased, and social tensions sharpened. Serious crime focused less and less on the most visible manifestations of authority—contempt proceedings dwindled from 6.9% to 3.9% of all prosecutions in the city—and became more and more arbitrary. Violations of public order, on the other hand, rose only slightly and were never the major source of prosecution in the city that they were in the outlying counties. Indeed, the slight rise in these offenses which the city did experience was probably more the result of the essentially political disturbances of the prerevolutionary decade than of any dramatic change in social conditions in the city.

Crimes of violence in the rural areas underwent a slightly different sort of change in the later years of the colonial period. In each of the regions and in the counties as a group, the single largest increase in case volume was among offenses that violated public order. In fact, of all the changes that can be identified this is probably the most striking. Cases involving riots rose by more than twenty percentage points in the borough counties and Albany-Charlotte, more than fifteen points in the river counties, and more than ten in Suffolk County. These increases may be attributed, in large part, to the so-called antirent riots of the 1750's.[7] But these disturbances did not occur throughout the colony—they centered in the river counties. Yet, an increase in riot prosecutions may be noted in every rural section of the colony in the period 1750–1776, and, in fact, the greatest increase was in the borough counties.

It seems clear, therefore, that the increased volume of riot cases was a general phenomenon for which the land disturbances of the middle of the century do not entirely account. This most pro-

[7] These conflicts resulted from the peculiarities of New York's land system and have been variously interpreted by historians. Generally, however, they centered around conflicts between New York's great landlords and tenants on their lands in the Hudson River valley. In the pages which follow discussions of "antirent riots," "land disturbances," "land riots" and "tenant rebellions" all refer to this ongoing series of violent outbreaks in rural New York at mid-century. For details see, Irving Mark, *Agrarian Conflicts in Colonial New York;* Patricia Bonomi, *A Factious People;* Sung Bok Kim, "A New Look at the Great Landlords of Eighteenth-Century New York," *William and Mary Quarterly,* Ser. 3, 28 (Oct., 1970), 581–614; and Kim, "The Manor of Cortlandt and Its Tenants, 1697–1783" (Ph.D. diss., Michigan State University, 1966).

nounced of all changes in patterns of rural prosecution has perhaps a more fundamental significance as an indication that many of the traditional channels for the adjudication of public issues were beginning to break down. With the size and distribution of New York's rural population commencing to outstrip institutions of government, with disputes over land titles occurring throughout the colony, with political tensions constantly on the rise, and with the economy of the colony heading away from mere subsistence and toward aggressive profit making, it was becoming even more important that government generally and local officials in particular devise effective means for the adjudication of disputes. Since, in a frontier society where effective police powers were virtually nonexistent and where people no longer lived exclusively in the more manageable pattern of clustered settlement, this was practically impossible, the result was often a violent public disturbance of one kind or another which did not focus on specific grievances as the anti-rent riots did, but rather reflected a decline in social and political authority structures in the countryside.

There is additional evidence which suggests an erosion of the ability of governmental and social institutions to maintain order. Contempt cases (as a cause for prosecution) either declined or rose very slightly. At first, this might appear to indicate a bolstering of the foundations of public authority. But contempt cases, unlike violations of public order, usually involved single individuals rather than groups of people, and there can be no question that many violations of public order carried with them an implicit, but nonetheless clear, contempt for authority. Therefore, the relatively small changes in the volume of contempt cases do not necessarily indicate strengthened public institutions. Rather, it merely suggests that antagonisms, which in the early part of the century had been expressed on an individual and *ad hoc* basis, took a more organized and therefore more disruptive form in the later years of the century.

Richard M. Brown has recently argued that one of the legacies of the colonial period to the Revolutionary generation was the use of organized violence as a form of social and political protest.[8] If this is true, the citizens of New York surely made their contribution. I do not mean to suggest that each and every riot or breach of the peace was laden with dire threats to the entire sociopolitical order of the colony. However, I would emphasize that riots in rural areas required far more planning and organization than those in cities. There were no ready and available crowds in New York's outlying counties, neither transportation nor communication was very good, and there were few occasions which brought many people together in one place. Since careful planning was required, cold calculation almost certainly played a more important role than spontaneous response to an inherently emotional situation. This sophistication of crime, which touched on matters of public authority, represented a marked departure from, or rather a modification of, trends already apparent earlier in the century. The point is simply that the experience of organized and controlled public violence was almost certainly a fact of life in mid-century, and if the nature of that violence was not always overtly political in the 1750's and early 1760's, there was no difficulty involved in channeling those techniques in more explicitly political directions when circumstances so required during the late sixties and early seventies.

If the colony of New York experienced palpable alterations in the prosecution of certain kinds of crimes, and if those changes reflected other, more fundamental, trends in the society, it is no less true that the patterns of ethnic prosecution also bore a clear relationship to the changing composition of New York's population. The undeniable conclusion is that persons with Anglo-Saxon names, always constituting a majority of criminal defendants, became even more frequently the subject of prosecution in the latter half of the century than they had been earlier. This phenomenon

[8] Richard Maxwell Brown, "Violence and the American Revolution," in Stephen G. Kurtz and James H. Hutson, eds., *Essays on the American Revolution* (Chapel Hill, 1973), 81–120.

reflects two fundamental characteristics of the demographic history of colonial New York. The first is the increasing anglicization of the Dutch population. Of course, Dutch immigration to New York had virtually ceased well before 1700, and the Dutch therefore constituted a decreasing percentage of the population; but it is also true that many Dutch New Yorkers anglicized their names and intermarried with the English. The precipitous decline in Dutch names among those appearing in the criminal courts thus reflects both the assimilation of the Dutch population and the floodtide of immigrants from the British Isles which swept over the colony of New York in the eighteenth century.

Similarly, the diminution of crimes against masters in the period 1750–1776 and the parallel drop in the percentage of slaves among the population of criminal defendants indicates changes in the population as a whole. First, the percentage of slaves in the population of the colony dropped between the censuses of 1756 and 1771 from 21.1% to 11.8%.[9] Moreover, the proportion of slaves in the population of the city of New York, where most slave crimes were committed, declined even more drastically from high points of 21.6% and 21.1% in 1749 and 1756 to 14.3% in 1771. To some extent, then, the dwindling percentage of slaves among criminal defendants may be explained by the simple fact that they no longer constituted as high a percentage of the population.

But the decreasing proportion of slaves in the population of New York is not an adequate explanation of the declining percentage of slave defendants. The slave population dropped, to be sure, but even in 1771 slaves constituted 14.3% of the population of the city and 11.8% of the population of the colony as a whole—not an inconsiderable proportion, especially since the same group accounted for only 2% of the criminal defendants between 1750 and 1776.

There are two possible explanations for the discrepancy between the position of slaves in the population as a whole and in the popu-

[9] Computed from Greene and Harrington, *American Population,* 96–103.

lation of criminal defendants. The first is that antislavery sentiment was rising during the 1760's, not only in New York, but also in the colonies generally. Newspapers attacked the institution of slavery and reprinted the polemics of British critics as well.[10] This altered public attitude may have had some effect on the institution itself, softening the treatment of slaves and easing conditions somewhat. We also know, for example, that voluntary manumissions rose significantly in the sixties and seventies, and the possibility of obtaining freedom may have encouraged slaves to be more careful about their behavior than they might otherwise have been.[11]

A second and even more speculative interpretation depends upon the nature of the slave trade itself. Philip D. Curtin has established that the British slave trade from Africa declined significantly between 1751 and 1770.[12] In other words, fewer "unseasoned" slaves reached the colonies in this period than at any other time in the eighteenth century. Although there are no figures for the colony of New York *per se,* and despite the fact that Curtin also argues that the majority of slaves reaching the northern colonies had been seasoned in the Caribbean or the southern mainland colonies, it is still reasonable to argue that a smaller number of new slaves reached New York in the 1750's and 1760's than in earlier years. The slave population of New York in the last two decades of the colonial period was, therefore, one which was probably more experienced with the New York variant of chattel slavery than at any time during the entire history of the colony.

But what has all this to do with a declining volume of slave crime? The seasoned slave dealt with his plight in ways which were fundamentally different from those of his more recently arrived fellow bondsmen. Acquainted with the language and culture of the white man, and familiar with their physical environment,

[10] See McManus, *A History of Negro Slavery in New York,* 151–152, for a brief discussion and some representative citations.

[11] *Ibid.,* 153.

[12] Philip D. Curtin, *The Atlantic Slave Trade: A Census* (Madison, 1969), 142, Table 41.

seasoned slaves were wise enough to realize that the master would harshly punish the slave who directly threatened his life. But as Kenneth Stampp and Gary Nash have so persuasively argued, there were many ways to threaten the institution of slavery without engaging in outright rebellion.[13] Although crimes against masters constituted 67.6% of slave crime between 1691 and 1749, they accounted for only 11.4% of such offenses between 1750 and 1776. Theft, on the other hand, comprised a mere 12.9% of slave crime in the earlier period, while in the later era it accounted for fully 56.8% of all the cases involving slaves. Thus, not only did the volume of slave crime decrease, but the nature of the offenses committed by slaves was altered as well. Crimes against masters would be more likely among slaves recently arrived in New York, while thefts would be more characteristic of the seasoned slave who had learned to subvert his master's influence without needlessly endangering his own safety. Furthermore, it should also be recognized that the slave who directly attacked his master was far more likely to be caught and prosecuted than the slave who stole. Therefore, the decline in the volume of slave crime may be misleading, since the crimes which the unseasoned slaves of the earlier period were most likely to commit were also the crimes for which they were most likely to be caught and successfully tried, while the crimes which the experienced slaves of the later period were most likely to commit were the very offenses for which prosecution was least likely.[14]

[13] Kenneth Stampp, *The Peculiar Institution: Slavery in the Ante-Bellum South* (New York, 1956); and Gary B. Nash, *Red, White and Black: The Peoples of Early America* (Englewood Cliffs, N.J., 1974).

[14] This interpretation runs counter to the argument recently advanced by Gerald Mullin that the more seasoned a slave was, the more likely he was to engage in elaborate plans to overthrow his master. This may have been true in eighteenth-century Virginia, the subject of Mullin's study, but the New York evidence does seem to indicate a contrary trend. New York's two major slave conspiracies took place in 1712 and 1741, while in the later periods to which Mullin attaches considerable importance no such prosecutions were undertaken. Mullin argues persuasively that the Gabiel Prosser plot

In sum, then, how ought the dwindling volume of slave crime in colonial New York to be interpreted? Clearly, none of the foregoing explanations is entirely adequate. They all suffer from serious gaps in our knowledge of the demographic dimensions of slavery. If the sources are adequate to the task, these gaps may soon be filled. But for the moment, only the most tentative generalizations may be offered. The marked decrease in the proportion of case involving slaves between the periods 1691–1749 and 1750–1776 may be ascribed to four developments whose relative importance is, at the present time, impossible to assess with any confidence. The first is that slaves composed a smaller percentage of the population of New York in the latter part of the century than they had earlier. The second is that the emergence of appreciable antislavery sentiment may have sensitized masters to the brutality inherent to the institution of chattel slavery, and encouraged them to treat their slaves more humanely with the result that slaves reacted less sharply to their bondage through the commission of criminal acts. A third possible explanation is that a rising rate of manumission in the colony engendered an increasing reluctance by slaves to commit crimes lest they antagonize their masters. Finally, the declining volume of slave crime may be interpreted as a reflection of the quality of the slave population rather than its quantity—an indication of the changing nexus of the particular experience of New York's slaves rather than their declining numbers. None of these interpretations is entirely satisfying but seem

marked the culmination of a century of acculturation in Virginia. Of course, we do not know very much about the origins of the individual slaves tried in 1712 and 1741. If they were, in fact, slaves with some experience in the colonies—and Curtin's statistics suggest they may have been—Mullin's thesis would seem to be confirmed. Until such time as further research reveals the precise experience of those slaves, however, I do not believe that Mullin's very suggestive formulations may be fairly applied to other colonies—especially not to those in the North. See Gerald W. Mullin, *Flight and Rebellion.* See also Peter H. Wood, *Black Majority,* 284–307. Wood's reading of the South Carolina evidence is more in line with the interpretation advanced here.

at least to indicate some directions for future research and study which may perhaps render the declining volume of slave crime in New York more comprehensible than it is at present.

Patterns of criminal prosecution changed in a variety of ways in the colony of New York over the course of the century. But these changes ought not to conceal the fact that in the middle of the eighteenth century, New York was moving in directions which had been established at the end of the seventeenth. After all, the categories of crime that dominated the courts' business between 1691 and 1749 were the very same offenses that preoccupied them later in the century. New York was already a society that had suffered considerable violence, and the increased levels of the latter part of the century merely exacerbated a problem with which New Yorkers had lived for many years. Cases of theft were never *uncommon* in New York City, they merely became *more* common later in the century. Englishmen had always composed a majority of those appearing as criminal defendants. The rising percentage of Englishmen appearing in the courts between 1750 and 1776 only continued a trend already very much in evidence.

In short, if the Massachusetts figures, referred to above, provide a reliable standard of comparison, New York had never been free of serious crime. The direction of criminal prosecution in New York, like the direction of the society itself, was not so much toward a radical alteration of previously existing trends as it was toward a continuation, an expansion and, to some extent, a modification of social phenomena in progress as early as the 1690's. The remarkable thing is not that patterns of criminal prosecution changed as markedly as they did, so much as it is that they were not transformed to an even greater degree.

CHAPTER 6

The Effectiveness of Law Enforcement: The Institutional Setting

The business of the criminal courts of colonial New York was dominated by several major categories of crime—most notably thefts, acts of personal violence, and disruptions of public order. During the course of the eighteenth century, moreover, these offenses grew in relative importance, absorbing a greater share of the courts' attention between 1750 and 1776 than between 1691 and 1749. This is an important trend for the historian and one with wide implications, yet it should also be noted that such a perception does not provide an answer to what, in some ways, is one of the most fundamental questions to ask about the history of crime: How much did eighteenth-century New York suffer—"a lot" of crime or "a little"?

Clearly, this is not an either/or question, and an answer does not come easily. The problem, of course, is one of definition—how much is "a lot" of crime? One way to attempt a solution would be to compare the New York experience with that of the other British colonies. Crime, after all, was a fact of life, and a comparative approach would permit a more balanced assessment of the New York data. As we noted in the last chapter, New York's crime rate *does* seem to have been higher than the Massachusetts rate. Massachusetts is the only colony for which comparable data exist, but does an exclusively quantitative answer really resolve the issues which the question raises? Can we be satisfied to discover that crime rates in New York were generally higher than those for Massachusetts? I think not, for the phrase "how much" has clear qualitative implications in this case. A crime rate of fifty per 100,000 in Massachusetts would have been significantly different from a crime rate of fifty per 100,000 in New York. An extensively settled, politically factious, and ethnically heterogeneous colony like New York might have been much more able to tolerate high levels of crime than an intensively settled, politically stable, and ethnically homogeneous province like Massachusetts. Or the reverse might be true. The point is that even if comparisons were possible, they would have to be made over a broader range of issues than crime rates. The crucial question, then, is not whether New York had more or less crime than other colonies, but how well it coped with the crime it did have.

Thus, our original question—How much crime was there in eighteenth-century New York?—must be answered in terms of the legal system itself. How well did it do its job? Was criminal business processed quickly and efficiently or did the volume of cases stretch the system to the breaking point? The measure of "how much" crime occurs in a given society must be based on the tolerance of the society itself and its ability to deal with criminal behavior. Our own society is often termed "crime-ridden," but this is so at least partly because our techniques of enforcement, our courts, and our methods of rehabilitation are so inadequate to the task. Therefore, in this chapter and in the one that follows, I intend to examine the system of criminal justice from the perspective of its effectiveness in enforcing the law, for I am convinced that such a perspective is essential to an understanding of the wider significance of crime in the colony.

Just how effective law enforcement was in colonial New York depends upon the answers to a series of interrelated questions. Among them are whether the system of criminal justice and law enforcement was adequately staffed, whether the jails of the colony were sufficiently secure to hold prisoners for trial, whether there were obstacles of one kind or another that hindered attempts to enforce the law, whether most cases were seen all the way through the courts from indictment to judgment, how long this process took, and whether individuals, once punished for their offenses, reappeared to be tried again for similar crimes at a later date. Some of these questions require quantitative answers while others do not, but all of them bear directly upon the effectiveness of law enforcement in colonial New York.

I

The apprehension, detention, and trial of criminal suspects made many demands upon the limited human resources of the colony. Perhaps the greatest of these was finding adequate numbers of competent personnel. No system of criminal justice can be effective without a core of dedicated public servants charged with law enforcement, but throughout the century New York suffered from a severe shortage of able nightwatchmen, constables, sheriffs, jailkeepers, and justices of the peace. As a result, the authority of the law and the efficiency of the courts suffered greatly.

The police powers of the state were exercised in several ways. In New York, as in the other major cities of Europe and America, there was no professional police establishment, and peace-keeping functions were delegated in different ways at different times. The major instrument of police protection in New York City was the nightwatch charged with going "round the Citty Each Hour in the Night with a Bell and there to proclaime the season of the weather and the Hour of the Night and if they Meet in their Rounds Any people disturbing the peace or lurking about Any persons house or committing any theft they take the most prudent way they Can to Secure the said persons."[1]

The character of the nightwatch varied from time to time. Sometimes it was composed entirely of civilians forced to take their regular turn as watchmen or pay for a substitute to replace them. At other times, especially during the intercolonial wars, the militia

[1] *M.C.C.*, II, 62 (Oct. 17, 1698).

took over the watch.[2] At still other times, a paid constables' watch was used, or citizens themselves were paid to guard the city.[3] Unfortunately, none of these measures was adequate. The unpaid citizens' watch was unfair, since it forced the poor of the city either to lose precious time while doing their duty or to pay substitutes to perform their service. Indeed, in requesting funds from the assembly for a paid watch, the mayor and aldermen of the city argued that, in addition to making lives and property more secure, such a system would allow the poor of the city "in great measure [to] be Eased of the Burthen and hardship they now groan under."[4] In addition, since the unpaid watch was often staffed by substitutes of questionable reputation, the inhabitants of the city were sometimes less than sanguine about the safety of their society.[5] The paid citizens' watch was a better solution, but while it lacked the disadvantages of the unpaid watch, it did not possess "the authority or the resources to prevent crime and maintain order."[6] Moreover, a military watch was impractical, expensive, and unpopular. A paid constables' watch was the best solution to police problems in the city; but it was difficult to staff properly. In short, police protection in the city of New York was never regularized or systematized in any coherent fashion, and was never adequate to the

[2] During Queen Anne's War, for example, the watch was manned by militiamen. Arthur E. Peterson, *New York as an Eighteenth-Century Municipality Prior to 1731* (New York, 1917), 165.

[3] The first paid constables' watch was established in 1699 and ordered to prevent "any danger that may happen to the Inhabitants . . . by fire thieves or any other inconveniencyes." N.Y.G.S. (June 4, 1699). The first paid citizens' watch of six men was created in 1714 and paid £8 a man for a half year's service. *M.C.C.*, III, 61 (April 20, 1714).

[4] James F. Richardson, *The New York Police: Colonial Times to 1901* (New York, 1970), 10; undated petition, Kempe Papers, Box V.

[5] For example, *The Independent Reflector* termed them "a Parcel of idle, drinking, vigilant Snorers who never quell'd any nocturnal tumult in their lives . . . but would, perhaps, be as ready to join in a Burglary as any Thief in Christendom." William Livingston, *et al., The Independent Reflector* . . . , 73.

[6] Richardson, *New York Police,* 11.

needs of a growing port city.[7] Furthermore, in the later years of the colonial period, as other municipalities of the colony began to grow in size, they faced similar problems, and the Assembly passed several bills designed to aid them in keeping the peace by providing funds for a paid watch.[8]

The nightwatch was only a stopgap measure in any case. The ultimate burden for the arrest and confinement of suspected criminals fell upon the sheriffs and constables whose legal responsibility it was to ensure compliance with the law. Usually recruited from among the artisans and tradesmen of the colony, these men were saddled with a wide variety of duties for which they received little compensation. In addition, the performance of these duties could be anything but pleasant. The obstacles that peace officers faced when they attempted to enforce the law were considerable, not only for the inconvenience they caused, but also because they created very real dangers for the constable or sheriff who dared to do his job.

Perhaps the most obvious danger to constables was that they were often assaulted and resisted when they attempted to make an arrest. In fact, of the 312 cases of contempt of authority I have collected, more than 70% involved attacks by citizens on officers of the law.[9] Such assaults were probably even more frequent than the court records indicate, since there is considerable evidence that many such acts were committed but never brought to court. In

[7] Carl Bridenbaugh, *Cities in Revolt,* 376. Attempts to increase the effectiveness of the watch are scattered throughout the records of the Common Council and other governmental bodies. More comprehensive citations for this and the other phenomena described in this chapter may be found in Douglas Greenberg, " 'Persons of Evil Name and Fame.' "

[8] See, for example, the following acts to support a night watch in Albany: *Col. Laws N.Y.,* V, 145 (Jan. 12, 1771); 294 (Feb. 26, 1772); 459 (Feb. 6, 1773); 661 (Feb. 8, 1774); 722 (Jan. 31, 1775).

[9] The following cases are typical: King *vs.* William Osborn, N.Y.G.S. (Feb. 4, 1730); King *vs.* Solomon Fowler, S.C.M. (Jan. 21, 1752); King *vs.* John Ferguson, *et al., ibid.* (Oct. 28–30, 1760); King *vs.* Anthony and John O'Neal, *ibid.* (Oct. 24, 1763, April 17, 28, 1764).

January 1757, for example, William Kempe received a letter from Catharine Van Alstyne of Canajoharie in Albany County. She explained that her husband, John, had been deputized by the sheriff, and that when he attempted to arrest David Mariners during the course of his duty, Mariners had stabbed him to death. Mrs. Van Alstyne claimed that Mariners had been confined and then "released out of Gaol," and she asked that Kempe intercede on her behalf and secure a speedy trial, but there is no indication that he was able to do so.[10]

A similar case is revealed in a letter from Jacob Van Schaack, the Sheriff of Albany, to Cadwallader Colden on December 21, 1760. "This week I arrested Lieut. George Coventry. . . . After I had made an arrest, he seized a pistol, swore he would blow my Brains out, and so kept me off from further prosecuting the arrest, uttering all the time the most violent oaths and other abusive Language against me. It is impossible for me to execute my office . . . not only my life, but my fortune also is in the utmost danger by these insults."[11] There were many such cases which, for one reason or another, did not reach the courts.[12]

Granting that constables and sheriffs often had inadequate means at their disposal to secure defendants for trial, it is still difficult to explain the frequency of these attacks on law-enforce-

[10] Catharine Van Alstyne to William Kempe (Jan. 31, 1757), Kempe Papers, Box IV, William Kempe Letters, "V-Yeamans."

[11] Jacob Van Schaack to Cadwallader Colden (Dec. 31, 1760), "Cadwallader Colden Papers" in *Collections of the New-York Historical Society for the Year 1921,* 383. Colden's papers occupy the *Collections of the New-York Historical Society* for the years 1917 through 1923 with volumes numbered consecutively. Hereafter cited as "Colden Papers," followed by the appropriate volume number.

[12] For other such attacks which did not result in trial, see for example, *Cal. Hist. Mss.,* 655, for a deposition by Westchester Constable James Kniffen claiming that he was attacked at the house of William Hooper Smith by three men; and a deposition describing an attack on John McClean, deputy sheriff of Ulster, who was almost killed in attempting to serve a writ on Samuel Clarke, in N.Y.S.L. Mss., XCVIII, 137 (Sept. 3, 1772). See also *Cal. Hist. Mss.,* 809.

ment officials. It is true, of course, that this was an amateur constabulary and that respect for authority of government in New York seems often to have been lacking. But such attacks appear to have resulted also from popularly held notions about the rights of suspects. James Wilkes was convicted of murdering John Christie, the Sheriff of New York, in 1756. Soon after his trial, Wilkes was reprieved and eventually pardoned. In the text of the reprieve itself (presumably written by the governor of the colony, Sir Charles Hardy) may be found a clue to the frequency of attacks on peace officers. Hardy acknowledged that Wilkes was unquestionably guilty, but granted the reprieve because the accused "had imbibed and strongly believed a common Error generally prevailing among the Lower Class of Mankind in this part of the world that after warning the Officer to desist and bidding him stand off at his Peril, it was lawful to oppose him by any means to prevent the arrest."[13] In other words, Hardy's view was that there was a general conviction that there was no reason for any citizen to submit to an arrest unless the personal authority of the peace officer made such a course the most prudent one. Hardy was but one man, to be sure, and his opinion may have been mistaken. Still, such a view seems to jibe with the frequency with which constables and sheriffs were attacked in colonial New York and, at the very least, it confirms the impression that the dangers attendant upon law enforcement were considerable.

There were, in addition, other barriers in the way of law officers who wished to do their job properly. Most important among these is the fact that they lacked the force necessary to subdue suspects who did resist arrest. New Yorkers, as we have seen, could be most contemptuous of authority, and it was very difficult indeed to convince them that the law could or would be enforced. John Munro of Westchester related a story to John Tabor Kempe on the arrival of Governor Tryon in 1771 which, perhaps, sums up this attitude. "I payed a visit to my good Neighbours," he wrote, "when I acquainted them that they ought to consider the fate of

[13] N.Y.S.L. Mss., LXXXII, 163 (Feb. 5, 1756). See *Cal. Hist. Mss.*, 648.

the Regulators and that now the same Governor is sent here to punish you; they told me that they did not value all he could do."[14]

Munro's friends had grasped a crucial fact—there really was not much that government could do if citizens were intent upon resisting the law. Kempe discovered this himself in 1765 when mobs of up to 200 men ousted four families from their homes in Dutchess County. He found that it was simply too difficult to arrest 200 men—or even ten. Indeed, it was dangerous enough to apprehend just one offender.[15] New York society in the eighteenth century simply lacked the resources to resist such disorder. To be sure, the Assembly made an occasional gesture toward strengthening the law-enforcement capabilities of constables and sheriffs, but these were piecemeal measures without lasting effect.[16]

[14] John Munro to John Tabor Kempe (Nov. 10, 1771), Kempe Papers, Box I, John Tabor Kempe Letters, "McComb-Munro." William Tryon was the former governor of North Carolina and had been responsible for forcefully quelling the so-called "Regulator" movement in that colony at the Battle of Alamance in 1771. See Alonzo T. Dill, *Governor Tryon and His Palace* (Chapel Hill, 1955).

[15] Unmarked file (Nov. 23, 1765), Kempe Papers, Box BSW I, "Unsorted Legal Mss." Other evidence of such cases may be found in the court records themselves which contain a number of cases in which people were tried for refusing to assist an officer of the law. See, e.g., King *vs.* Johannes Tieboot, in S.C.M. (1946), 133, 154, 175 (April 9, Oct. 7, Oct. 12, 1703); and King *vs.* Jacob and William Dikeman in *ibid.* (Jan. 21, and April 25, 1763).

[16] See, for example, "An Act for preventing tumultuous and riotous Assemblies in the Places therein mentioned, and for the more speedy and effectual punishing of Rioters," in *Col. Laws N.Y.*, V, 647–655 (March 9, 1774) which, as the following excerpt demonstrates, detailed with great eloquence the nature of the problem: "Whereas the Spirit of Riot and Licentiousness has of Late prevailed in some Parts of the Counties of Charlotte and Albany, and many Acts of Outrage and Cruelty have been perpetrated by a Number of turbulent Men who assembling from Time to Time in Arms have seized insulted and menaced several Magistrates and other Civil Officers so that they dare not execute their respective Functions; rescued Prisoners for Debt; assumed, to themselves . . . Judicial Powers; burned and demolished the Houses and Property, and beat and abused Persons off many off his Majesty's Subjects; expelled others from their Possessions and finally have put a Period to the Administration of Justice." But these were hollow words, and the act failed to provide effective solutions.

The position of constables and sheriffs, therefore, was anomalous. Charged with enforcement of the law, they might be punished themselves if they failed to do their duty. But they were often deprived of the means necessary to function as effective keepers of the peace. One case epitomizes the ambiguous position of the sheriff and constable better than any other. This was the lengthy and complicated case of Sheriff Harmanus Schuyler and his repeated attempts to arrest John Henry and Baltus Lydius, an Albany fur trader and his son.

In May of 1762, Attorney-General John Tabor Kempe sent two writs to Sheriff Schuyler to be served on the Lydiuses for intrusion on Crown lands. Schuyler apparently failed to do his duty and arrest the two men; identical writs were sent to him on May 23, 1763, and August 3, 1764, but with similar results. In December 1764, Kempe wrote to Schuyler instructing him to arrest the Lydiuses even if he had to break into their house to do so. The following month Kempe received a letter from Schuyler saying that he had "not been able to get them." By the third week in January 1765, Kempe was beginning to lose patience and warned Schuyler to serve the writs and arrest the two men or suffer the consequences. In fact, Kempe had already begun proceedings against Schuyler, whose excuse for his neglect was that "he did not think it safe, the said Lydius and Son being very resolute Fellows." The court ordered Sheriff Schuyler to show cause in the April term why such an attachment should not be issued. At the following sitting of the court, Albany's Sheriff did appear and "the Court having heard what he had to offer and Judging it insufficient to excuse him; Therefore set a fine on Him of twenty pounds."

Schuyler paid his fine, but the case was not over yet. On the same day that Schuyler was fined, an information was filed against Baltus Lydius for assaulting and wounding the Sheriff of Albany, Harmanus Schuyler.[17] And who, of all people, was ordered to arrest

[17] This offense apparently took place when Schuyler attempted to collect from Baltus Lydius a fine imposed for an assault on Elisha Smalley. See

Lydius and put him in jail? None other than the Sheriff of Albany! Neither Lydius was tried, and John Henry later became a Loyalist, dying in Kingston, England, in 1791 at the ripe old age of ninety-eight. As for Schuyler, he was involved in several cases similar to this one and finally left office permanently in the early 1770's.[18]

The story of Sheriff Schuyler and the Lydius family is amusing, but not trifling, for it points up the difficulties that every constable and sheriff faced when he attempted to arrest a suspect. Caught between understandable fears for his own safety and Kempe's equally understandable desire to see justice done, Schuyler faced a difficult dilemma. His failure to secure the two suspects for trial does not indicate a failing on his part so much as it suggests a weakness in enforcement capabilities which he shared with constables and sheriffs throughout the colony.

Given the considerable hazards and meager rewards of office, many New Yorkers preferred to pay the requisite fines rather than serve as law officers. Throughout the century and in every part of the colony, there appears to have been great difficulty in keeping a sufficient number of constables in office. Many people preferred the payment of a fine to the dubious "honor" of holding office; and after virtually every election the Mayor and Aldermen of New York City collected fines from a less than public-spirited freeholder

---

King *vs.* Baltus Lydius, S.C.M. (Oct. 30, 1764; April 18, July 26, Oct. 27, 1765, and April 18, 1765).

[18] The preceding account was reconstructed from the following sources: "The King *vs* John Henry Lydius" (two files), Kempe Papers, Box BSW 3; King *vs.* John Henry Lydius, S.C.M. (Oct. 9, 29, 30, 1762; April 29, July 30, Oct. 27, 1763; Jan. 28, Aug. 3, 1764; April 18, Aug. 3, 1765); King *vs.* Harmanus Schuyler, *ibid.* (Jan. 19, April 18, April 27, 1765); King *vs.* Baltus Lydius, *ibid.* (April 18, April 27, 1765; May 2, 1767; Jan. 19, 1771); King *vs.* Harmanus Schuyler, *ibid.* (July 29, 1768); and *Doc. Hist. N.Y.*, III, 893. I have purposely eliminated some of the more complicated legal details of the case. See Julius N. Goebel, Jr., and T. Raymond Naughton, *Law Enforcement in Colonial New York,* 448–452, for these. In addition to filling in the legal minutiae, Goebel's and Naughton's account differs slightly from my own, but the differences are relatively minor and do not affect the substance of the incidents described.

or two who had decided that discretion was the better part of law enforcement and had refused to serve as constable.[19] In fact, there is some evidence to indicate that election as constable did not signify the community's respect for an individual at all. Rather, it seems to have been a device used occasionally to punish a freeholder who had antagonized his neighbors. In April of 1714, for example, Jacques Cortelyou petitioned "to be relieved of the obligation of acting as constable for the town of New Utrecht to which he has been maliciously chosen he being unacquainted with the English dialect."[20]

The office of constable was, then, hardly the most sought-after public office in colonial New York. As a result, persons who were neither qualified to vote nor to hold office were often elected and then excused from office.[21] In addition, those who did qualify and could not or would not pay the fine for refusing to serve tended to be negligent in the performance of their duty. The most obvious manifestation of this negligence was the failure of constables to appear at court sessions. Throughout the colony and over the entire century, this was a problem that plagued the courts, and one which was never satisfactorily resolved.[22]

[19] See the following representative examples: *M.C.C.*, II, 289 (Oct. 15, 1703); Adrian Man, Hugh Craw, Stephen Janau, fined five pounds each for refusing to serve as constables; and *ibid.*, VII, 451 (Oct. 14, 1773): William Mariner fined five pounds for refusing to serve as constable.

[20] N.Y.S.L. Mss., LIX, 45 (April 29, 1714). See *Cal. Hist. Mss.*, 419. For two similar cases, see Abraham Delamontagne's complaint about his election to the City Council of New York in September of 1713 in *M.C.C.*, III, 49, and the several prosecutions in Brooklyn against Hendrick Wyckoff for refusing to serve as constable. Wyckoff was elected in two successive elections, refused to serve both times and finally was released from being chosen again. K.C.S. (Nov., 1707, and May, 1708).

[21] Once again the examples are copious, and the variety of reasons offered for disqualification was wide, but the single most common ground for disqualification was that the individual was "neither a Freeman nor a Freeholder."

[22] The following case is only illustrative. On October 27, 1769, the entire "List of Constables was called and no one appearing," the Supreme Court fined them all forty shillings each. S.C.M. (Oct. 27, 1769). Similar nota-

The reluctance of reputable citizens to serve in peace-keeping offices had other effects as well. Persons chosen as constables sometimes met the formal requirements of office but were ill-suited in other ways to assume their duties. Men of questionable integrity and scruples were sometimes the only people willing to serve, and the result was to decrease the authority of law in the colony. Sheriffs and constables took bribes to release prisoners in their custody or to fix juries; they extorted money from prisoners in exchange for preferential treatment, assaulted innocent citizens without cause, charged excessive fees, committed a variety of other crimes, and used their office as a protective device to advance their private interests.[23] Furthermore, fines levied by the courts had a habit of ending up in the pockets of the men charged with collecting them. This problem became so serious that the Supreme Court had to issue an order in April, 1765, demanding that the "Several Sheriffs of the respective Cities and Counties within this province . . . account for the fines received by them."[24]

---

tions are to be found in the records of all the county sessions courts with as many as forty constables at a time fined for nonattendance.

[23] See the following examples of law enforcement officers abusing their positions. *Bribery:* A letter from T. Kay to John Tabor Kempe in August of 1769 complaining that a prisoner bribed Patrick Welsh and, as a result, was released from jail. Kempe Papers, Lawsuits G–L. *Extortion:* King *vs.* James Mills, sheriff of New York. S.C.M. (July 28, Oct. 28, 1769; Jan. 20, April 28, 1770). *Assaults on innocent citizens:* King *vs.* John Christie, sheriff of New York, for assault and battery. S.C.M. (Jan. 18, 1753). *Charging excessive fees:* Petition by an Orange County J.P. complaining about the conduct of Thomas Husk, the sheriff, and accusing him of assaults on His Majesty's subjects, extortion, *and* charging excessive fees. N.Y.S.L. Mss., LXII, 57 (Dec. 29, 1719). See *Cal. Hist. Mss.*, 449. *Commission of criminal acts:* King *vs.* Isaack Haselbury, a sheriff's deputy, for theft. K.C.S. (May and Nov., 1696). *Use of office to advance private interests:* Petition of Elizabeth Barker of Albany complaining that Thomas Clarke, undersheriff of New York, had impeded workmen from building on a lot which she owned in the city of New York. N.Y.S.L. Mss., XXXVII, 243 (Sept. 3, 1691). See *Cal. Hist. Mss.*, 215.

[24] S.C.M. (April 18, 1765). See also a similar order in Queens County Court of General Sessions, Q.C.S. (Sept., 1763). Until 1765, this sort of

We do not know how effective this Supreme Court order was, but the behavior of law officers certainly did not improve, for in March, 1773, the Assembly itself saw fit to take up the issue of the conduct of constables and passed an act to "oblige [them] to give Security for the faithful performance of their respective offices." The preamble of the act summed up New York's experience with officers of the law when it stated that "many Inhabitants of the said Counties [had] sustained Losses by the Misconduct and Insolvency of the Constables of said Counties."[25] In short, law enforcement in colonial New York suffered not only from the reluctance of honest citizens to serve, but also from the eagerness of unscrupulous men to exploit such power as did accrue to the position of constable or sheriff.

Cases involving public officials who had neglected or abused their offices were common in colonial New York, constituting 3.8% of all prosecutions (199 cases); and it should be noted that many more instances of official neglect never even appeared before the courts. In February of 1752, for example, Cadwallader Colden wrote to Governor George Clinton that the Sheriff of Ulster County had declined to continue in his office and attempted to convince Clinton to take vigorous action against the man, "especially if it be true as I am informed . . . that he is very negligent in his office. There were several persons in Jail for Felony, one of them for Murder of an Officer in the Execution of his Duty, they have all made their escape. The Sheriff by what I am told has justly laid himself under Suspicion of Negligence, if not connivance in suffering this Escape."[26] Insofar as the court records indicate,

---

thing had usually been done on an individual basis. See the 1734 bond of Charles Gerrets, sheriff of Richmond, to "pay over all moneys collected by him," in N.Y.S.L. Mss., LXX, 697 (March 25, 1734). See *Cal. Hist. Mss.*, 521.

[25] *Col. Laws N.Y.*, V, 529 (March 8, 1773). See also an act of similar intent passed the same day to "regulate the office of Under or Deputy Sheriff within this Colony" which bemoaned the corruption of the men filling these offices. *Ibid.*, 527.

[26] Cadwallader Colden to George Clinton (Feb. 15, 1752), "Colden Papers," IV, 309.

no action was taken against the Ulster sheriff—perhaps because he had decided to vacate his office in any case.

New York suffered greatly from an inability to fill important police positions with qualified men. Moreover, as the century wore on, and the population of the colony grew, this problem became even more pressing, since an even larger number of constables was required. As a result, the Assembly passed several bills to increase the number of constables in several of the counties.[27] In sum, there can be no doubt that the first link in the chain of criminal justice in colonial New York—the exercise of police powers by constables and sheriffs—was a very weak one indeed. Lacking the resources to attract qualified men to these positions, the colony suffered not only from the incompetence and corruption of those they were able to hire, but from the insufficiency of their numbers as well.

Other posts in the system of criminal justice were equally hard to fill. For example, two prisoners who had been sentenced to hang on January 18, 1762, were reprieved until February 19 because "the sheriff cannot find any person to act as hangman." On February 12, however, the sheriff of New York made it known that he had "taken all Possible Measures that the Time allow to procure a hangman for the two Persons that were to be executed . . . and that he [could] procure none." In this case, the reason for the difficulty seems to have been that the people of the city opposed the hanging of these two prisoners, for the sheriff was "apprehensive an Attempt would have been made to rescue them." The execution did take place, but only after a "party of his Majesty's Forces quartered in the City Barracks" was called out "to guard the Sheriff and Civil Officers against any Insult."[28]

[27] See "An act to . . . elect a greater Number of Constables (in Suffolk County)" in *Col. Laws N.Y.*, V, 21 (Dec. 20, 1769), and a similar bill for Ulster County passed on Feb. 8, 1774. *Ibid.*, 613. Dutchess County had faced this problem as early as 1735, when additional constables were appointed, since the problem was so pressing that it could not wait for the next election. D.C.S. (May, 1735).

[28] N.Y.S.L. Mss., XC, 66 (Jan. 18, 1762). See *Cal. Hist. Mss.*, 728; Benjamin Pratt to Cadwallader Colden (Feb. 12, 1762), "Colden Papers," VI, 120; Cadwallader Colden to Sir Jeffry Amherst (Feb. 17, 1762), *ibid.*, 122.

When men could be found to act as hangmen or as jailers, they were often of less than exemplary character. New York City had a long history of troubles with jail-keepers who either overcharged the city for their services or were accused of mistreating prisoners.[29] One man provided a vivid description of the cruel and sadistic behavior of one Thomas Shreeve who served as coroner and jail-keeper of the city in the early 1770's. Aside from describing Shreeve as—among other things—an idiot, a glutton, a drunk, a frog, a fool, and an ignoramus, the prisoner, Daniel Coe, charged that Shreeve had extorted an exorbitant amount of money from him and severely mistreated him. He concluded by saying that he prayed that Shreeve would "be confined in a lonesome goal, fed with nothing but bread and water and have none but dead carcasses for [his] companions."[30]

The citizens of the colony experienced great difficulty in finding jail-keepers who did their job decently and humanely. One reason may have been that the job of guarding prisoners in colonial New York must have been a harrowing and frustrating experience, owing to the inadequacy of the jails. The prisons of the colony were never sufficiently secure to effectively detain suspects awaiting trial. I have discovered in the various records of the colony almost 240 complaints against the sufficiency of the jails. Such complaints occurred in every county from the 1690's to the end of the colonial period. They were made by grand juries, sheriffs, jail-keepers, the Common Council of the city, justices of the peace, and the Assembly itself.[31]

[29] See George W. Edwards, *New York as an Eighteenth-Century Municipality, 1731–1776* (New York, 1917), 104–105.

[30] Daniel Coe, *An Address to Mr. Thomas Shreeve, coroner for the city of New York . . .* [*ridiculing him for his failings. Signed by his*] *dear, dear brother and afflicted prisoner Daniel Coe. New York Goal, 13th May 1772* (New York, 1772).

[31] The number of complaints against the jails was so large that citations would be superfluous. Suffice it to say that there is evidence of dissatisfaction with prisons in the records of each of the county courts, in the minutes of the Supreme Court, in the records of the New York City Common Council, and in the *Colonial Laws of New York.*

An act of the Assembly passed in October, 1730, indicates the general tenor of these complaints. The act was passed in order to fund a variety of important public projects in the city of New York, and among these were repairs to the jail. The preamble of the act merits lengthy quotation since it outlines in some detail why improvements to the jails were so vitally necessary.

> WHEREAS the Publick and Necessary Charge of Keeping the Peace, Maintaining of good Rule and Government . . . and putting the Laws in Execution daily Increases Occationed by great numbers of Idle and dissolute Persons Privately Conveying them Selves into the said City, many whereof are Suspected to be Convict Felons transported from England. Several of whome have Lately been Committed for Felonys by them Perpetrated . . . and tho Loaded with Irons and very Strong Goals have found means to escape from there with Impunity. AND WHEREAS . . . the Common Goals of the same are now very much out of Repair, and it appearing there is an Absolute Necessity not only to repair but to Enlarge the said Prisons and Gaols.[32]

Although this act was passed in 1730, there are strong indications that the conditions which prevailed then remained equally serious later in the century. Concern about the inadequacy of the jails increased considerably in later years. In fact, there were almost five times as many complaints between 1760 and 1769 as between 1700 and 1709. And despite a flurry of bills passed by the Assembly in the late 1760's and early 1770's to build new jails or repair old ones, the protests continued unabated, with a greater number filed in the seven years between 1770 and 1776 than in any single decade except the 1760's.

During his tenure as Attorney-General, John Tabor Kempe occasionally commented on the problems of law enforcement which attended the decayed conditions of the jails. He indicated in one letter (albeit in another context) the connection between the jails and the indifferent performance of the constabulary. Kempe was concerned about the arrest of a certain counterfeiter named Charles Hamilton and one of his accomplices, and he wrote Clear Everitt, the Sheriff of Dutchess County, that he understood Hamil-

[32] *Col. Laws N.Y.*, II, 645–648 (Oct. 17, 1730).

ton had been apprehended and that the other man would be taken into custody soon. "I know not what Conditions your Gaol is in," Kempe wrote, "but trust that you will keep them secure that they may make not their Escape from Justice. The Reason of my mentioning this to you, is because several Criminals have broke Gaol and made their Escape lately from some of the Counties . . . and I should be very sorry should you be liable to be punished . . . for the Escape of a Felon. You will excuse my mentioning this to you as I have no other Inducement but to take care Justice be done."[33]

Thus did Kempe warn Sheriff Everitt, although Everitt was himself in no position to build a more adequate jail. Therefore, the man who assumed the responsibilities of sheriff found himself in a most precarious situation, since he might often be helpless to detain a prisoner before trial, but would be criminally liable himself if the suspect escaped. This anomaly in the criminal justice system not only discouraged otherwise scrupulous and public-spirited men from assuming the duties of sheriff and constable, but, more importantly, provided a further inducement for those who did take office to disregard their duty and be negligent in serving writs and making arrests.

Given the deficiencies of the jails, therefore, it is not surprising that it was so difficult to hire sheriffs and jail-keepers to guard prisoners. Nor should it be astonishing to discover that prisoners often "broke gaol" and escaped prosecution altogether.[34] Occasionally an escapee might be recaptured and tried, as was Daniel Stewart in March 1705.[35] But constables and sheriffs were generally so lax in the performance of their duty that a jailbreak

[33] John Tabor Kempe to Clear Everitt (May 1, 1761), Kempe Papers, Box BSW 1.

[34] Once again, these are too numerous to list, but see the following example: a presentment against the sheriff of New York and his deputies for allowing a murderer to escape from jail on Jan. 20, 1769. Kempe Papers, Lawsuits P–V.

[35] King *vs.* Daniel Stewart, S.C.M. (March 9, 17, 1705).

could usually be carried off with impunity. And there were jurisdictional problems as well. An escapee could not be apprehended once he had crossed county lines, since arrest warrants were only valid in the county of issue. Apparently, this was a source of considerable frustration for scrupulous law-enforcement officials, and in 1771 the assembly provided a remedy by passing an act "for the apprehending of Persons in any County or Place upon Warrants Granted by Justices of the Peace of any other County or Place."[36]

The decrepit condition of New York's jails often combined with the inadequacy of her peace officers to entirely undermine the system of criminal justice and render even the most scrupulous justice of the peace and attorney-general impotent to protect the public interest. In 1770, for example, Henry Van Schaack, a Kinderhook J.P., wrote John Tabor Kempe about just such an incident. It seems that a prisoner had escaped from the local jail, and one of the constables had pursued him. On capturing the prisoner, the constable had purposely allowed him to escape (presumably as the result of a bribe). Another constable was enlisted in the cause, but he refused even to attempt an arrest. The prisoner, a "notorious Offender" who "eluded the Punishment which he Several Times deserved by keeping Off the Officers of Justice" had thereby eluded prosecution, and Van Schaack asked Kempe how to proceed "as the Administration of Justice seems in great measure to be Affected by Cases like that."[37]

II

However poorly they did their jobs, the constables, the sheriffs, the jailers, and even the jails themselves had a function that was only preliminary to the actual administration of justice. Once a

[36] *Col. Laws N.Y.*, V, 209 (Feb. 16, 1771).

[37] Henry Van Schaack to John Tabor Kempe (July 18, 1770), Kempe Papers, Box I, John Tabor Kempe Letters, "Van Benthuissen-Vrooman." For a similar incident, see N.Y.S.L. Mss., XLIV, 95 (April 12, 1701). See *Cal. Hist. Mss.*, 283.

defendant was secured for trial, the major nexus of responsibility for sound law enforcement shifted from the constabulary to the courts, to the judges, juries, and prosecutors who were the very heart of the English tradition of criminal law. But in these areas, as in others, the judicial system of colonial New York was sadly lacking.

The jury was the pivot upon which the wheels of justice turned. The smooth functioning of the system required grand juries to hand down indictments and presentments, and petit juries to determine innocence or guilt. But it was difficult to find people who were willing to serve on juries of any kind. In almost every session of every court, fines were levied on veniremen who failed to appear.[38] Sometimes a juryman might appear, but refuse to serve, as did Ekin Jones of Westchester, who told the Marshall who summoned him that "the Sheriff might Kiss His * *."[39] Occasionally, courts might even be forced to adjourn until a sufficient number of jurymen could be found. This happened on May 16, 1727, when the court minutes for the Queens County Court of General Sessions noted: "Court Opened but Adjourned till four of the Clock in the Afternoon for want of a Competent number of Grand Jurymen."[40] In addition, since juries were drawn from among the local freeholders who might sometimes have an interest in the outcome of a particular case, they sometimes performed their duties with less than total honesty. Thus, an entire jury was fined twenty shillings in January of 1772 for "Irregular behavior" in a trial involving Jeremiah Miller of Albany.[41]

Throughout the century, the inadequacy of juries was a cause for considerable concern on the part of the Assembly, and a num-

[38] Again, these are so numerous as to prohibit full citations, but see the following notation in O.C.S. (Oct., 1749) which indicates how difficult this problem could become: "Whereas a great number of the Grand Jurors [were] Absent and [did] not appear" the fine for nonappearance was increased.

[39] Fox, ed., W.C.S., 100 (June 4–5, 1695).

[40] Q.C.S. (May 16, 1727).

[41] King *vs.* Jeremiah Miller, A.C.S. (Jan., 1772).

ber of bills were proposed and passed in order to assure "the returning of able and sufficient jurors." One of these, enacted in November, 1741, spelled out the dimensions of the problem in some detail. It seems that the inadequacy of juries was related to the character of the sheriffs charged with calling them. The act was designed to correct several specific abuses, and one of them was that of "sheriffs and other Ministers who for Reward may be Tempted to Spare the most able, and Sufficient, and Return the Poorer and Simpler Freeholders and others less able to descern the Causes in Question." As a remedy, the Assembly ordered that "no Persons . . . Shall be Returned as Jurors to serve on Trials at any Courts . . . who have Served therein within the space of one year before." In addition, the bill noted that "many evil Practices have been used in the Corrupting of Jurors . . . and many people lawfully summoned to Serve on Jurys have neglected to appear" and ordered fines for nonappearance, ranging from thirteen shillings, four pence, to three pounds.[42]

This act appears to have been a thorough attempt to reform jury practices in the colony of New York, but the court records do not indicate that it was even temporarily successful. It seems to have fallen into disuse in the 1760's, moreover, and consequently the assembly passed several more acts of similar intent. The preamble of one, passed in 1765, pinpoints the nature of the continuing difficulty:

> Whereas thro' a defect of Sufficient Power in the several Courts of this Colony in levying Fines for the Defaults of Jurors, Constables, and other Persons, they are become very Remiss in their attendances, to the Prevention and Great Delay of Justice, more especially in the Causes of the Crown [Criminal Cases].[43]

The problem, then, was that the courts themselves had not "Sufficient Power" to make the system work. This bill was renewed in January, 1770, and revived in April, 1775.[44] There is no indica-

[42] *Col. Laws N.Y.*, III, 185–189 (Nov. 27, 1741).

[43] *Ibid.*, IV, 1000 (Feb. 6, 1768).

[44] *Ibid.*, V, 67 (June 27, 1770); *ibid.*, 875 (April 13, 1775). See also an

tion, however, that the fundamental problem—the authority of the courts themselves—was ever solved, and the minute books of the courts suggest that continuing efforts to secure "able and sufficient" juries were seldom successful.[45]

If, as the jury bill of 1768 suggested, the courts of colonial New York lacked sufficient authority to summon proper juries, from what sources did such a weakness derive? To some extent, justices of the peace themselves were almost certainly responsible. J.P.'s, like juries, constables, and sheriffs were not always anxious to perform their duty, and they sometimes even failed to appear at their own court sessions. The Dutchess sessions court, among others, was forced to fine its own justices several times between 1740 and 1760.[46] In fact, the bill of 1768 discussed above was also intended to assure the attendance of judges as well as juries at court sessions.[47] No wonder, then, that it was so difficult to obtain sufficient juries. If judges were reluctant to appear, why should jurors have been any more diligent in the performance of their duties?

Of course, limitations on the power of local courts derived from more fundamental causes than the occasional nonappearance of a justice of the peace. Indeed, there is much evidence to indicate that judges in colonial New York were, on the whole, an ignorant lot, ill-suited to hold office, and often anxious to abuse the power which such office afforded them. William Smith, Jr., the preeminent historian of colonial New York, wrote that "there are

---

order "to sheriffs to levy fines on jurors who make default" in *Cal. Hist. Mss.*, 823 (Dec. 27, 1773).

[45] Other references to this problem include a "report of a committee of the council" on an act similar to those described above in June of 1716. N.Y.S.L. Mss., LX, 113 (June 27, 1716). See *Cal. Hist. Mss.*, 430; and amendments of the council to a similar bill in June of 1734. N.Y.S.L. Mss., LXX, 121 (June 20, 1734). See *Cal. Hist. Mss.*, 522; and readings of such acts before the various county courts. See, for example, S.C.S. (Oct., 1744) and Q.C.S. (Sept., 1765).

[46] D.C.S. (May, 1740; Oct., 1740; Oct., 1741; Oct., 1753; and May, 1760).

[47] *Cal. Hist. Mss.*, 771 (Dec. 28, 1767).

some [J.P.'s] who can neither write nor read."[48] Indeed, the ignorance of the judges in the colony was appalling. In 1763 there were 328 justices of the peace in the province (excluding New York City), and of these 194 (59%) had no legal training or knowledge at all.[49] There were, to be sure, copies of legal guides like Michael Dalton's *The Countrey Justice,*[50] but these were of no use to a man who was illiterate and, in any case, much of a J.P.'s authority and ability to enforce the law depended upon his standing with the local populace. A justice who was widely known to be as ignorant of the law as those he tried was likely to find his position in legal matters frequently challenged; and, lacking any formal qualifications to legitimize his position, he may have found his ability to enforce the law severely compromised.

There is much reason to believe that the administration of justice in colonial New York was undermined by just such a situation. The provincial government was flooded with a continuous outpouring of petitions from local residents asking that one justice or another be removed from office for maladministration, malfeasance, neglect of duty or some related offense.[51] There is no question that some of these petitions were justified; however, some of them almost certainly resulted from petty grievances and were prompted by the ease with which the authority of an ignorant J.P. might be challenged. Cadwallader Colden commented to Governor Clinton on the dangers of granting such petitions in September of 1749. "I think it may be of consequence to the future administration of Government," he wrote, "not to incourage such kind of Petitions. . . . For if these kind of Petitions be incouraged the officer will not depend on the Governor but on the humours of the

[48] William Smith, Jr., *The History of the Province of New York,* Michael G. Kammen, ed. (Cambridge, Mass., 1972), I, 261.

[49] Goebel and Naughton, *Law Enforcement,* 91, note 159.

[50] (Reprinted: New York, 1972).

[51] The following example is typical: a petition from the inhabitants of Bedford "complaining of the oppressive conduct of Zachariah Miller, justice of the peace." N.Y.S.L. Mss., LXXI, 47 (Oct. 19, 1736). See *Cal. Hist. Mss.,* 527.

populace or on popular men among them . . . which may be of bad consequence in the execution of Justice. . . . It is likewise necessary that officers should think that they hold their offices not on precarious terms but on the Opinion the Governor has of their being faithful otherwise they cannot be depended on in any cases where they may have temptations to act against their duty."[52]

With his usual acuity, Colden seems to have understood quite clearly the dangers for central government inherent in responding too precipitately to complaints against officers appointed by the governor. What he failed to note, however, was that whether such petitions were granted or not, the authority of a justice of the peace still depended very much upon the acquiescence of the local populace. Thus, in practice, officials were governing by the consent of the governed before the full development of the democratic idea and its formal institutionalization. The authority of central government in colonial New York had but one vehicle of expression in the hinterlands of the province—the justice of the peace and other officers of the court. If the legitimacy of their power was questioned by the people, there could be no effective law enforcement, since provincial authorities lacked the ability to buttress the power of local officials in any but the most serious circumstances—as for example, in the land riots of the last three decades of the colonial period. This being the case, a form of *ad hoc* democracy functioned in the outlying communities. Colden's fears notwithstanding, local justices of the peace had no choice but to depend upon the willingness of local citizens to accede to their position as representatives of legitimate governmental authority. The consent of the community was vital, for without it they were impotent to do their jobs properly. The governor had the power to remove a J.P. from office, but once in office a justice could not do his job without the cooperation of the people.

As the numerous petitions for the removal of J.P.'s demonstrate,

[52] Cadwallader Colden to George Clinton (Sept. 15, 1749), "Colden Papers," VII, 348–349.

however, the cooperation of local citizens was not always forthcoming. Nor was it always deserved, for there is reason to believe that justices of the peace did often act arbitrarily and "not according to the dictates of law." The shortage of judges sometimes led to the appointment of men who were unsuited to public office or, as David Colden put it in a letter to his father in 1758, "men who are much fitter to break the law than to keep it."[53] I have already commented upon several such cases in earlier chapters, but perhaps an additional example may further serve to illustrate how the power of a justice might be abused.

Thomas Strickland entered a complaint against two Dutchess J.P.'s on April 29, 1763. It seems that one John Edwards and other "Divers persons . . . much Abused and Robbed" Strickland, and when he asked Justice Lawrence Van Kleeck to issue warrants for their arrest, the judge "declined taking any steps for apprehending the offenders." Strickland then sought the aid of Justice Henry Vanderbergh, who issued a precept against Edwards and the others. But when Edwards appeared before Vanderbergh, he was allowed to swear on oath "that he was Innocent of the Fact Charged against him" and was discharged. Finally, Vanderbergh charged the victim of the crime, Thomas Strickland, with court costs of one pound, six shillings, and refused to take any further action in the case.[54] On April 30, Attorney-General Kempe drafted a letter to Vanderbergh in which he made it clear that he felt the two judges had acted in a manner which was "very irregular and unjustifiable, and inconsistent with the duty of a Magistrate." Kempe warned the two men to take action to rectify their misconduct, or else he would vigorously pursue the criminal proceedings which he had initiated against them and see that they paid a stiff penalty for their abuse of office. Apparently, they did so, for a *nolle prosequi* was entered for their case in the next term of the Supreme Court.[55]

[53] David Colden to Cadwallader Colden (March 2, 1758), *ibid.*, V, 220.
[54] S.C.M. (April 29, 1763).
[55] Draft of a letter from John Tabor Kempe to Henry Vanderbergh

III

Common as cases like these were, merely to condemn local justices of the peace for their stupidity, laziness, and arrogance would be a mistake. There is no question that such traits were all too common among the judges of colonial New York and that the personal failings of justices often contributed to weakened law enforcement in the province. But it ought to be remembered, as well, that a variety of obstacles stood in the way of even the most diligent judge, and consequently in the way of effective implementation of the law. Climate and geography, the expense involved in keeping the peace, the character of New York's population, and the unsettled nature of its politics all impinged upon law enforcement and made the tasks of the courts and their officers more arduous and complicated than they might otherwise have been.

Communication and transportation were major problems in the colony of New York. The Hudson River constituted the major thoroughfare between New York City and the northern parts of the colony. Beyond the banks of the river, roads were poor where they existed at all, and travel was, at best, difficult. Distances easily traversed in our own time represented journeys of major proportions, and some parts of the colony were virtually inaccessible during the winter months. Thus, persons in need of good law enforcement were often remote from the institutions designed to provide it. In July, 1760, for example, William DeNoyelles was assaulted and forcibly ejected from his own land in Orange County. But in a letter to John Tabor Kempe, he commented that "by reason of the Distance from a Justice of the Peace [I] have no opportunity to make affidavit thereof so must transmit this to you that you may prosecute him at his majesties Suit for these actings."[56] Such a situation was hardly favorable to the administration of justice,

(April 30, 1763), Kempe Papers, Lawsuits C–F; S.C.M. (July 30, 1763). There were many similar cases. See the cases of justices Thomas Jarvis and Francis Pelham discussed in Chapter 4 above.

[56] William De Noyelles to John Tabor Kempe (July 9, 1760), Kempe Papers, Box I, John Tabor Kempe Letters, "Dalzell-Eustace."

which depends on the accessibility of those charged with trying and punishing those accused of criminal behavior. DeNoyelles made his complaint in mid-summer. How much more difficult things must have been during the winter! In Dutchess County, for example, the Court of General Sessions was forced to cancel the January term of 1765 owing to "the Excessive Great Snows" which made the roads "in Great Measure impassable."[57]

Nor were weather and geography the only problems. The control of epidemic disease was in its infancy in the eighteenth century, and when a measles epidemic swept New York City in the late winter and early spring of 1728, thc Supreme Court was forced to cancel its March term for fear that persons attending the court might spread the epidemic over the whole province.[58] In addition, law enforcement could be very expensive. Money had to be allocated for many vital purposes—the construction and repair of jails, stocks, and gallows, the care, housing, and feeding of prisoners, the salaries of jailers, constables, sheriffs, prosecutors, and judges, and so on.[59] In many cases, of course, government was throwing good money after bad, but even ineffective law enforcement could be expensive.[60] There is, in fact, some evidence to

[57] D.C.S. (Jan., 1765).

[58] S.C.M. (March 11, 1728).

[59] See the following examples: "John Tudor, Esq. High Sheriff . . . exhibited his account to the court amounting to 12 pounds and sixpence . . . itt being for . . . Carpenters Worke building a gibbet and hanging a Negro convicted of Murder." N.Y.G.S. (Feb. 3, 1697); a similar account presented by Ebenezer Willson "for the Maintenance of Several Criminals in Prison," *ibid.* (Aug. 2, 1698); a letter from Cadwallader Colden to Earl of Halifax on August 11, 1760 reading, in part: "It may perhaps be proper to inform your Lordship that the highest Sallary hitherto given by the assembly to the Chief Justice and the perquisites of the office are not sufficient to support a family in this country." "The Colden Letter Books, 1760–1775," in *Collections of the New-York Historical Society for the Year 1876,* 10. A second volume was published in 1877. Hereafter referred to as "Colden Letter Books," volumes I and II respectively.

[60] An excellent example of this sort of thing is the enormous amount of money expended to repair the colony's jails—usually to no effect. The following case also indicates how costly, but futile, such expenditures might

suggest that the financial burdens of administering justice were not always met with dispatch. Jarvis Marshall, the Under Sheriff of New York, petitioned for his pay in May, 1691, claiming that he had not been paid since the arrival of Governor Ingoldesby.[61] Similarly, in 1737 the attorney-general sued the Ulster County supervisors for failing to pay him for prosecuting three criminals in June of 1735.[62] This seems to have been a chronic problem for prosecutors until the 1760's when John Tabor Kempe, with the support of Cadwallader Colden, was able to secure more equitable compensation for his services as well as a guarantee of payment for his expenses in the execution of his office.[63]

A third factor which impeded the courts in the performance of their duty was the populace of the colony itself. It bears repeating that 5.3% of all the criminal cases under study involved cases of contempt of authority of one kind or another. The legitimate authority of government was often subject to question. Even surveyors were prevented from doing their job when residents feared encroachments on their land.[64] And, of course, officers of the law and the courts themselves often suffered direct challenges to their authority, which, as we have seen, could sometimes be expressed

---

be. In August of 1770, New York's constables were paid a considerable sum for "pursuing George Seymour the person suspected of having murdered Anthony Collins." But Seymour was never imprisoned or tried, and thus the money paid the constables, though possibly well deserved, did not contribute to the administration of justice or the enforcement of law. *M.C.C.*, VII, 224 (Aug. 11, 1770).

[61] N.Y.S.L. Mss., XXXVII, 97 (May 13, 1691). See *Cal. Hist. Mss.*, 207.

[62] S.C.M. (April 26, 1737).

[63] An undated "Draft of an Act to defray the Charges of the Public Prosecution in this Colony" authored by [John Tabor Kempe?], Kempe Papers, Box V; Cadwallader Colden to Earl of Halifax (Aug. 11, 1760), "Colden Letter Books," I, 10; Catharine Snell Crary, "The American Dream: John Tabor Kempe's Rise from Poverty to Riches," *William and Mary Quarterly*, Series 3, 14 (April, 1957), 176–195.

[64] See, for example, a warrant to the Suffolk County Sheriff for the arrest of Nathaniel Bishop for "molesting Thomas Cardale, deputy provincial surveyor in the discharge of his duty." N.Y.S.L. Mss., XLVII, 71–73 (March 25, 1703). See *Cal. Hist. Mss.*, 308.

violently. Even more frustrating perhaps were the cases of individuals who refused to acknowledge the authority of the courts at all. In March of 1692, for example, when the constable of Newtown attempted to arrest one Daniel Lawrence, a laborer, Lawrence held him off and said: "God dam their souls and blood, he would see them all damned in hell before he would undervalue himself fore to come afore them and further that he would not be taken alive."[65]

A host of similar incidents may be found in the records of the colony, and several of them were more complex than simple cases of resisting arrest. Rather, they seem to reflect real questions about the legitimacy of the authority of the public officials involved. When Canning, a slave belonging to a Kings County Leislerian named Myndert Courten, was sentenced to pay a fine of six shillings or receive thirteen lashes, Courten made it clear what he thought of the court, saying that "he did not value the Courts order a fart for their power will not stand long . . . and that he would obey none of their orders."[66] Similarly, when Simon Smith was fined for a misdemeanor in 1701, he told the court with "very Abusive language" that "he would pay none, that they had no authority to Compel him, that he would find a law for them and that he Cared not for their illegal proceedings."[67]

The frequency of cases like these was paralleled by occasional attacks on the physical symbols of criminal justice as well. A proclamation issued in March, 1702, for example, offered a reward of sixty pieces of eight for "detection of the person or persons who have cut down the gallows in New York."[68] This sort of

[65] N.Y.S.L. Mss., XXXVIII, 74 (March 2, 1692). See *Cal. Hist. Mss.*, 22. See, as well, an affidavit by Zachariah Mills, sheriff of Queens, relating to his attempt to arrest Thomas Willet. Willet threatened to cut his throat if he proceeded with the arrest. N.Y.S.L. Mss., XLV, 117 (May 13, 1702). See *Cal. Hist. Mss.*, 294.

[66] K.C.S. (Nov., 1696).

[67] King *vs.* Simon Smith, N.Y.G.S. (Feb. 5, 1701).

[68] "By the Honourable John Nanfan, Esq. . . . A Proclamation" [offering a reward of "sixty pieces of eight" for the detection of the persons who

thing was common during the twenty years following Leisler's Rebellion when the authority of government was especially precarious, but contempt cases continued to appear before the courts throughout the century and, as one J.P. complained to John Tabor Kempe, "if a stop is not put to Such behaviour . . . There soon must be an end to Government. When I am injured as a Magistrate, I have no other persons to Apply to but his Excellency and the Attorney-General for Redress."[69] Kempe was surely sympathetic but too often he found himself helpless to quell a deep strain of antiauthoritarianism in the people of New York.

As the population spread to even more remote parts of the colony, and the tensions which culminated in the American Revolution mounted, concern about the government's ability to enforce the law grew as well. After a serious riot in an isolated section of Charlotte County in 1774, Cadwallader Colden described his fear of

> the Danger of Suffering a number of People in such a Situation to Live in open Defiance of the Authority—pretending to appoint officers and to erect Courts among themselves—executing in the most illegal and cruel Manner, the high Power of trying, condemning and punishing their Fellow Subjects while their strength is daily increasing by the function of idle, desperate Vagabonds from all Parts of the Country.[70]

Colden was discussing a particular situation, but he had merely pinpointed, in a specific way, the "factious" character of the people of New York—a trait which plagued the courts and officers of the law from Leisler's Rebellion to the American Revolution.

Challenges to governmental authority were really the product of a symbiotic relationship between the character of the people of New York and the nature of the colony's politics. The antiauthori-

---

have cut down the gallows in New-York. Dated March 29, 1702] (New York, 1702). A copy of this Proclamation may be found in N.Y.S.L. Mss., XLV, 88 (March 29, 1702) and is calendared in *Cal. Hist. Mss.*, 291.

69 John Macombe to John Tabor Kempe (Feb. 16, 1769), Kempe Papers, Box I, John Tabor Kempe Letters, "Macombe-Munro."

70 Cadwallader Colden to General Gage (Sept. 7, 1774), "Colden Letter Books," II, 358. See also Colden to Lord Dartmouth (Oct. 4, 1774), *ibid.*, 364–366.

tarianism of New Yorkers, which grew primarily from social and ethnic heterogeneity, did little to bring stability to the chaotic political world of eighteenth-century New York. But it is also true that the instability of political life in New York engendered doubts about the legitimacy of government which, in turn, encouraged challenges to that legitimacy by a heterogeneous population. Thus, provincial politics might interfere with law enforcement in an indirect way by exacerbating tensions of which they were as much a cause as an effect.[71] But the relation between politics and law enforcement could be even more direct when the controversy touched issues of public justice.

During the tenure of the Earl of Bellomont as governor, a controversy raged in New York which directly touched the courts of law. Bellomont labored under very trying circumstances. He was concerned about piracy and the evasion of trade regulations and was anxious to put the administration of justice on a firmer footing in the colony. His commission and instructions, in fact, explicitly charged him with the suppression of piracy.[72] But he met with many obstacles. Among them were, in his words, "a divided people, an Empty Purse, a few miserable, naked, half-starved Soldiers . . . in a word the whole Government out of Frame."[73] But serious as these problems were, he wrote, "I should prefer an honest able judge and Attorney-General . . . before a Man of War, and Soldiers."[74]

The problem, as Bellomont viewed it, was that local politics hindered the "suppressing of Piracy and unlawfull Trade." He found himself caught between two rival factions warring for his favor while piracy continued. On the one hand, Paroclus Parmyter,

[71] The most thorough treatment of the political culture—and one which emphasizes its volatile characteristics is Patricia U. Bonomi, *A Factious People.*

[72] William Smith, *History of the Province of New York,* I, 103.

[73] *Ibid.,* 107.

[74] Earl of Bellomont to Lords of Trade (Oct. 20, 1699), *N.Y. Col. Docs.,* IV, 594.

a naval officer, trained in the law in England and "said to have read a good deal of the Law," ridiculed the Attorney-General, John Graham, for his ignorance of the law. On the other hand, Graham sought to enlist the Lieutenant-Governor against Parmyter to obtain his revenge. Bellomont, besieged with letters and complaints from both sides, begged the Lords of Trade to allocate money to bring a "good Judge from England" as well as "a good Attorney-General, if peace and good order in the Country are to be valued." Without two such men who were independent of local politics, Bellomont wrote, he was "like a man manacl'd and fetter'd."[75]

The essence of Bellomont's argument was that the administration of justice suffered because the politics of the colony interfered. Only men who were unconcerned with local contests for power could devote their full time and energy to the impartial execution of the law. Bellomont's advice was not followed, and in the 1760's a similar scenario was played out by Lieutenant-Governor Cadwallader Colden. In the midst of a controversy with the great landowners of the colony—especially the Livingston family—Colden wrote to the Earl of Halifax to request the removal of John Tabor Kempe as Attorney-General.[76] Two years earlier Colden had written that Kempe performed his duty "with great application Diligence and Fidelity in many cases under difficulties and hardships."[77] But he now said "as long as I can remember we have not had an Attorney-General fit for his office."[78]

Why the change of heart? Why was Colden now petitioning for the removal of a man whose diligence he had earlier praised? Colden had become convinced that there was a conspiracy afoot in

[75] *Ibid.* See also a representation by the Lords of Trade to the King on the administration of justice in New York (Dec. 14, 1699), *ibid.*, 598.

[76] Cadwallader Colden to Earl of Halifax (Jan. 23, 1765), *ibid.*, VII, 700–702.

[77] Cadwallader Colden to Lords Commissioners of Trades and Plantations (Nov. 25, 1763), "Colden Letter Books," I, 254.

[78] Cadwallader Colden to Earl of Halifax (Jan. 23, 1765), *N.Y. Col. Docs.*, VII, 702.

New York, led by men "of Sinister views and bad purpose"—a "desperate faction [opposed] to the legal administration of government and tending to sedition." Kempe, he believed, was the tool of this group which was led by Chief Justice Daniel Horsmanden and Justice Robert Livingston, whose removal he also requested. Colden insisted that Kempe had resolutely refused to assist him in the prosecution of the offenders, and Colden was convinced that "an able Attorney-General properly supported could have restrained them effectively."[79]

No action was taken by the English authorities; and on the basis of Kempe's earlier and later performance in office, it is difficult to believe that his behavior was as unscrupulous as Colden suggested it was.[80] But Colden continued to demand his removal and engaged Kempe in a lengthy conflict over a chancery controversy.[81] In any case, the battle with Colden almost certainly interfered with Kempe's ability to do his job properly—a job which was difficult enough without the additional hindrance of being the focus of a political dispute which was really extraneous to the day-to-day task of enforcing the law.[82]

The institutions of law enforcement in colonial New York were seriously attenuated in almost every particular. Poorly qualified

[79] *Ibid.*, 700–702.

[80] John Tabor Kempe to Lord Stirling (Oct. 6, 1770), Kempe Papers, Box 1, John Tabor Kempe Letters, "Schenck-Strong-Swan."

[81] See Cadwallader Colden to H. S. Conway (Nov. 9, 1765), "Colden Letter Books," II, 162 and *ibid.*, 280–316. See also Mary Beth Norton, *The British Americans: The Loyalist Exiles in England, 1774–1789* (Boston, 1972), 207–208, for evidence of continuing conflict with the Colden family even after Kempe had gone to England as an exiled Loyalist.

[82] For another example of the manner in which political controversies could undermine effective law enforcement, see *Doc. Hist. N.Y.*, III, 214–297, for the details of a long controversy over the churches and magistrates of Jamaica, Queens County. The details of this controversy are not nearly so important as the extent to which it demonstrates how the political position and interests of local justices could interfere with their ability to act as impartial arbiters of the law.

constables, reluctant to serve at all, presided over inadequate and insecure prisons. Legally ignorant justices of the peace, who exploited their power for personal ends, presided over courts which were indifferently attended by juries, sheriffs, constables, and defendants. Further, when law-enforcement officers did attempt to do their jobs, they faced the hazards of climate and geography as well as high costs, a populace which could be antagonistic to their efforts, and a political climate which could seriously hamper the administration of justice. Indeed, the only bright spot seems to have been an occasional official of real dedication—a man like John Tabor Kempe, who struggled to impose order on a system that was plagued by serious structural weaknesses.

This is a very bleak picture, and yet these problems were further aggravated by the fact that they were mutually supportive. That is to say, each specific point of weakness combined with others to engender a series of debilitating cycles from which escape was all but impossible. Police powers were enfeebled, thereby increasing the ease with which legitimate authority might be resisted and this, in turn, made the exercise of police powers more arduous. Jails were inadequate, and since sheriffs and jailers might themselves be punished for permitting an escape, the officers became reluctant to make arrests. Such a situation also discouraged qualified men from taking office and thus contributed to the continuing insecurity of the jails. The people of colonial New York have had a reputation among historians, as they did among their contemporaries, for their "factiousness," and the politics of the colony were certainly among the most turbulent in Anglo-America. These two factors fed upon one another and, in turn, both served to undermine effective law enforcement. But the failures of the law-enforcement agencies to do their jobs also affected the character of the people and the tenor of provincial political life, generating an even more restive population and an even more tempestuous political climate. In short, the weakness of law enforcement in colonial New York was but one of a complex matrix of interrelated factors which determined the texture of life in the colony. It was as much cause as effect, as much a reason for, as a result of, the other factors which made New York society and politics so extraordinarily volatile. But all of the factors which have been discussed in this chapter had concrete and measurable repercussions in the actual proceedings of the courts. Ineffective though arrest and detention procedures might have been, many cases did reach the trial stage, and the extent to which the courts dealt with them quickly and efficiently and discouraged offenders from repeating their crimes requires some attention.

CHAPTER 7

The Effectiveness of Law Enforcement: A Quantitative Analysis

The institutions of law enforcement in eighteenth-century New York were uniformly weak. Faced with a shortage of competent personnel, lacking sufficient inducements to secure faithful performance of duty from those who did serve in the constabulary or as justices of the peace, and blocked at every turn by a variety of other obstacles to effective law enforcement, the government of colonial New York oversaw a thoroughly debilitated judicial system. Because this was so, the effects of such emasculated law enforcement on the actual proceedings of the courts bear some examination. These effects may be measured in several ways. First, it is possible to compute the average length of time cases required in the judicial process before being either resolved through acquittal or conviction or dropped entirely because it was impossible to secure the suspect for trial.[1] A second measure of the efficiency of court proceedings is the percentage of cases which were left unresolved and which never reached the judgment stage at all.

[1] The average duration of cases is the arithmetic mean of the number of months each case spent in the court. The mean is the most appropriate measure of central tendency in this case because it reflects the effects of extreme values, i.e., very lengthy and very brief cases. Since I wished whatever summary statistic I chose to reflect the relative weight of both sorts of cases, the mean was more appropriate to my purposes than the median, for example. In this reasoning, I have followed the suggestions of Edward Shorter in *The Historian and the Computer* (Englewood Cliffs, N.J., 1971), 92–94.

These two measurements have value since they gauge, in a reasonably precise manner, the efficiency and effectiveness of the court system as an instrument of social control. The duration of cases indicates how much time the courts took to do their job, and may be considered to have a bearing upon the effectiveness of law enforcement, since the certain knowledge of speedy trial and punishment would almost certainly have served as a deterrent to criminal behavior. Similarly, if potential offenders knew that the courts would pursue them resolutely until a trial could take place, they would no doubt have been less inclined to engage in criminal activity. If, on the other hand, it was clear that the courts were often willing to let a criminal prosecution go unresolved because it was too difficult to capture the suspect, law enforcement would certainly suffer. Therefore, the average duration of cases and the percentage of cases which were unresolved are valuable tools in analyzing the effectiveness of law enforcement in colonial New York.

Aside from their precision, these quantitative indices make it possible to measure the effectiveness of law enforcement within the context of specific geographic and ethnic groups. In addition, they permit us to discover the extent to which certain crimes were more effectively prosecuted than others, and they may also be charted chronologically, thereby helping to define periods in which law enforcement was particularly difficult. In short, the average duration of criminal cases and the percentage of those cases which were unresolved allow us to move considerably beyond the structural weaknesses of law enforcement described in the last chapter by gauging precisely the ultimate effects of that weakness on the functioning of the courts themselves.

I

The average duration of criminal cases in the courts of New York between 1691 and 1776 was 3.7 months. In other words, the average case took that long to go through the courts from the day of its first appearance in the records to its ultimate resolution or to the first point at which it no longer appeared on the court docket. A slightly shorter period of 2.8 months was the average in New York City, whereas cases prosecuted in the countryside took somewhat longer—4.6 months. In Suffolk County, on Long Island, the average duration of cases was the briefest in the colony—only 2.3 months—while in the borough and river counties the averages were considerably higher—5.4 and 5.8 months respectively. In Albany and Charlotte counties, the average was 3.7 months—precisely the same as for the colony as a whole. The courts of New York City and Suffolk County, therefore, appear to have been the most efficient in speeding cases through the judicial process, while the courts of the borough and river counties seem to have been markedly slower in doing their job.

To understand these figures properly we must turn to resolution statistics for the same geographic areas. Thirty-six percent of all the criminal cases appearing in the court records were never resolved. Taken by itself, this percentage is certainly impressive evidence of inefficient law enforcement, since it demonstrates that an offender had better than one chance in three of never having his trial completed. But the potential criminal's odds were better in some parts of New York than others. In Albany-Charlotte, for example, 58.8% of all criminal prosecutions were never resolved, while in Suffolk County only 18.7% were never completed. The borough counties, the river counties, and New York City itself were closer to the colony-wide percentage, with New York slightly higher at 37.1% and the borough and river counties slightly lower at 29.0% and 32.6% respectively.

These figures suggest slightly different conclusions than those for the mean duration of cases. Once again, Suffolk County seems to have been most efficient in its handling of criminal prosecutions, but Albany-Charlotte, where cases moved through the courts with reasonable speed, was very ineffective in actually securing judgments. Similarly, a slightly greater percentage of cases was left unresolved in New York City than in the colony as a whole, while the average duration of cases was less than the colony-wide average. The evidence for the river counties would also appear to be contradictory, since in both areas the percentage of cases which were unresolved was lower than for the colony as a whole, while the average duration of cases was greater than that for the colony taken as a unit.

Given these apparent contradictions, how can we evaluate the relative efficiency of the courts in the different parts of the colony? The evidence from Suffolk is the clearest. The courts of Long Island were the most efficient in the colony. Cases were more rapidly processed there than in any other part of the colony; and a smaller, though still considerable, percentage of cases was left unresolved. Perhaps the consistency of the Suffolk evidence may be attributed to the character of life on Long Island. Suffolk County was settled by Puritans, who were far more likely to be zealous in their efforts to suppress social disorder. Suffolk was also the most homogeneous of the counties; and the characteristic unit of settlement there was, as it was nowhere else in colonial New York, the town. Each of these factors facilitated the job of the courts. As we saw in Chapter 2, although Suffolk County was anything but a "peaceable kingdom," the magistrates of Suffolk County were apparently more effective than those in other counties in coping with any lack of social harmony. An ideological fervor supported, in large measure, by a homogeneous population living in a manageable pattern of settlement greatly enhanced the enforcement capabilities of the Suffolk courts, making law enforcement more effective there than anywhere else in the colony. It should be emphasized, however, that such a judgment is relative; and the fact remains that almost one criminal case in five was never resolved in Suffolk County. In short, the courts of Long Island were more efficient than others in colonial New York, but they were far from being adequate to the needs of Suffolk County—especially when one considers the weakness of the other institutions of law enforcement.

Data from the other regions of New York are less consistent, but they are not beyond reasonable explanation. The figures for New York City, for example, may be indicative of the particular conditions in the city. On the one hand, the judges who ran New York City's courts were usually better trained than those in outlying areas, and the figures may reflect their inclination to be diligent in speeding cases through the judicial process. On the other hand, the courts of New York City were also the busiest in the colony, handling a greater volume of criminal cases than those in the outlying areas. Both the relatively brief average duration of cases and the relatively high percentage of unresolved cases stem from these two conditions. The great volume pressed the institutions of enforcement and confinement and thereby lessened the ability of the courts to see cases through from indictment to judgment. The relatively high quality of judges in New York, however, helped to ensure that the courts did their work in a briefer span of time. Moreover, the density of New York's population rendered unnecessary the hazards of travel which, as we have seen, interfered with the work of the courts in outlying counties.

It should also be noted that the courts of the city met more frequently than those in the counties—on a quarterly rather than a biennial basis—and, therefore, the average duration of cases in New York is not strictly comparable to the computed averages for the outlying areas. Thus, the relatively low average duration of cases in New York was in part made possible by the fact that the court met four times a year. The courts in Suffolk County enjoyed no such luxury, holding but two sessions per year. Therefore, the low average duration of cases there is all the more impressive, since the court met only at six-month intervals.

The borough and river counties experienced yet another pattern. In these areas, a smaller percentage of cases was left unresolved than in the colony as a whole, while the average duration of cases exceeded the colony-wide average. Again, despite the seemingly paradoxical nature of the data, a certain internal consistency can be discerned. The excessive length of time spent on cases in the borough and river counties may, in part, be ascribed to the extensive nature of settlement and the vagaries of geography and climate. It is significant, for example, that the average duration of cases in the smaller, more intensely settled borough counties was slightly lower than in the larger, more widely settled river counties which also suffered more severe winters. In addition, these figures reflect a dogged persistence in the pursuit of offenders, and it is this persistence which may help to explain the percentage of unresolved cases. The courts of the borough and river counties were unique in that they appear to have been reluctant to drop a case from the docket when it could not be resolved in a term or two. Instead, the case remained on the docket in hopes that the suspect would be apprehended. Of course, such efforts were often in vain, but they were occasionally successful, and the result was both to increase the average duration of cases and to decrease the percentage of cases that remained unresolved.

Finally, if we examine the figures for Albany-Charlotte, an even more anomalous pattern is apparent. Here the average duration of cases was briefer than for any of the rural counties except Suffolk, but the percentage of unresolved cases was phenomenally high at 58.8%. The mean duration of cases seems to indicate reasonably effective enforcement, while the percentage of unresolved cases suggests the reverse. The first thing to be said, of course, is that no court which left almost sixty percent of its criminal cases unresolved can be said to have been an effective instrument of law enforcement. Indeed, the low average duration of cases in these most northern areas of the colony merely indicates the many frustrations that officials had to endure. The mere physical size of the counties, coupled with the harshness of the climate, made for unparalleled difficulties in securing prisoners for trial; hence, the high percentage of unresolved cases. But the justices of Albany and Charlotte counties were certainly aware of these difficulties, and they undoubtedly knew that if a suspect's case was not tried quickly, it would probably not be tried at all. Therefore, those cases which were tried were usually resolved quickly, while those which were unresolved were soon dropped from the court docket.

In sum, then, how may the relative effectiveness of law enforcement in the several regions of New York be evaluated? Although there was no part of the colony where law enforcement was effective in an absolute sense, there can be no question that it was more potent in Suffolk County than elsewhere. Indeed, the calculated figures for other areas do not even approach those for Long Island. Only in New York City was the average duration of cases anywhere near that for Suffolk, but there a much higher percentage of cases was left unresolved. In the borough and river counties, the average duration of cases was high, but the percentage of unresolved cases was low, with the calculations indicating slightly better enforcement in the borough counties. Law enforcement was unquestionably weakest in Albany, where almost sixty percent of all prosecutions were never completed. If the regions of colonial New York were to be ranked, therefore, in order of decreasing effectiveness, they would appear in the following sequence: Suffolk County, New York City, the borough counties of Kings, Queens, Richmond and Westchester, the river counties of Ulster, Dutchess, and Orange, and finally Albany-Charlotte.

It is of some significance that, with the exception of Suffolk, effectiveness seems to have decreased in direct proportion to distance from the city and the authority of central government. Indeed, the central explanation for this pattern is the inability of local officials to depend upon support from central government in the enforcement of the law; and in an age of difficult transportation and communication, it stands to reason that the authority of central government was lessened as physical distance from its sources increased. Suffolk was exceptional because its magistrates derived legitimacy and authority from the cultural homogeneity of the population itself rather than from the support of provincial officials who were ill-equipped to provide it in any case. Even in New York City, where the authority of the Governor, Council, and Assembly was most visible and easily exercised, the effectiveness of law enforcement did not approach that of Suffolk County. These are noteworthy conclusions since they suggest the importance of provincial government in bolstering local authority as well as its weakness in doing so. Moreover, they indicate that even where central authority was strongest, law enforcement was not nearly as effective as in an area like Suffolk, where the power of the courts derived from the willingness of local residents to acknowledge the legitimacy of local institutions of law enforcement.

II

The effectiveness of law enforcement varied as much among the various categories of crime as among the geographic regions of the colony. Throughout the colony, certain crimes proved more troublesome than others. Actions against public officials, for example, were among the most complicated of court proceedings, and such cases invariably took a longer period of time than any other category of criminal offense. In the colony as a whole, the average duration of these cases was nine months, and only in Suffolk County was the average less than 5.9 months. In every county, actions against public officials for abuse or neglect of their duty were drawn-out affairs—more so than any other category of criminal offense. And it is also true that despite their length, these cases were, in most areas, more frequently resolved than those involving other crimes.

This evidence bears directly on issues of law enforcement and indicates a fundamental dilemma which faced the government of colonial New York. Cases of official neglect and abuse usually involved a complicated dispute between a justice of the peace, for example, and local residents. As a result of the complexity and character of the issues involved, such cases took longer to go through the judicial process; and because the fair adjudication of such disputes was necessary to good government, they were more frequently resolved than other cases.[2] Thus both the duration of such cases and the frequency of their resolution resulted from the

[2] Note, for example, that although 36.0% of cases involving public officials in Albany-Charlotte were unresolved, this was still a lower percentage than for any other crime in that area.

care taken in their prosecution. Unfortunately, this same diligence tended to undermine the very principles which actions against public officials were designed to uphold. The length of these trials, while perhaps necessary to their equitable resolution, left the institutions of law enforcement themselves in doubt while the prosecution continued. No sheriff or J.P. could carry out his official functions properly while under indictment for maladministration or neglect of duty. Therefore, even attempts to procure more effective law enforcement could backfire and do more to erode the authority of the law than to increase it.

Cases of contempt of authority followed a pattern strikingly similar to that for crimes by public officials. Contempt cases were generally of longer duration than other crimes. In no county, save Suffolk, was the average less than 4.5 months, and the colony-wide figure was 4.7 months. Insofar as the percentage of unresolved cases is concerned, 24.4% of all contempt proceedings were never completed, and in every county but Albany less than 30% of such prosecutions were left unresolved. There is, then, a sense in which contempt cases and crimes by officials shared a similar pattern. For both offenses, the average duration of trials was usually longer than the average of 3.7 months for the colony as a whole; and, similarly, the percentage of such cases left unresolved was, in every county but Albany, less than the 36.0% computed for the entire colony.

The parallel between these two offenses is of crucial importance, for it indicates that similar forces governed the prosecution of these two crimes. The clear sociopolitical significance of contempt cases and crimes by public officials militated against courts allowing cases to lapse without ever being resolved; and it also tended to lengthen these prosecutions considerably, since the matter at issue was never a simple case of antisocial behavior. Rather, such offenses reflected fundamental antagonisms of a social and political nature which had to be handled prudently. The irony was that in proceeding so slowly in such matters, the courts subverted their own authority. Despite the high rate of resolution for cases of contempt and official abuse, one may conclude that the courts were generally ineffective in dealing with such offenses and that, furthermore, a salutary effect of the lengthy duration of these prosecutions was to decrease the authority of the courts generally.

For no other crime is the evidence of the effectiveness of law enforcement as consistent as for contempt cases and crimes by public officials; but some patterns may be noted. Theft seems to have been more effectively prosecuted than any other crime. The average theft case was only 1.8 months in duration, and only 23.0% of such cases were left unresolved. Of course, these figures varied somewhat from one area to another, but only in the river counties did the average duration of larceny cases stretch beyond 2.8 months. Every county dealt more quickly with thefts than with crimes generally. The county courts do seem to have had considerably more trouble than those in the city in bringing theft prosecutions to completion—17.4% were unresolved in the city, while the rate for the outlying counties was 43.3%. Even in Suffolk, one theft case in five remained unresolved; and in the other counties, especially Albany, the percentages were substantially higher. In addition, the city courts were more scrupulous in resolving theft cases than they were in resolving criminal cases generally, but in the outlying areas, without exception, the reverse was the case, with the percentage of all cases left unresolved always smaller than the parallel computation for theft cases.

Several conclusions may be drawn from this evidence. First, it is clear that, whatever measure is used, New York City was more effective in trying larceny cases than even Puritan Suffolk County. Second, although theft cases were sped through the judicial process in the countryside more rapidly than other crimes, the percentage of theft cases left unresolved was higher than for all crimes. These facts derive primarily from the fact that larceny was a much more serious problem in the city than in the outlying areas; and, as a result, the courts prosecuted it with greater vigor. In the counties, on the other hand, theft was a relatively minor problem.[3] Because this was so, the county courts tended to be lax in the pursuit of larceny suspects, dealing with theft cases quickly—either by trying the case immediately or, if the offender had not been apprehended, recording the indictment and dropping the case from the court docket. The result was a high percentage of unresolved cases and a relatively brief average duration.

Like thievery, the disorderly house was primarily an urban phenomenon. But the city courts, like those in the countryside, were singularly ineffective in the prosecution of such cases. In the colony as a whole, 56% of all cases involving disorderly houses were never resolved. The figure was slightly higher in New York City at 56.3%, and slightly lower in the countryside at 53.8%. In the individual regions, the percentage of uncompleted prosecutions varied enormously—from none in Albany-Charlotte to 80% in the borough counties—but the number of individual cases in each region was so small that these percentages may not be reliable indices of effectiveness. In any case, because the disorderly house was so overwhelmingly urban in character and because it was a much greater cause for concern in the city, a brief discussion of why the city's courts were so much less successful in trying these cases than thefts, for example, is in order.

I argued in Chapter 3 that insufficient proof was the primary obstacle to securing convictions against persons accused of operating disorderly houses. The difficulties involved in obtaining sufficient evidence to convict made the acquittal rate higher, but they also affected the two indices of effectiveness. Cases remained on the docket for a longer period of time because prosecutors were unwilling to enter a *nolle prosequi* in a case where they knew, but could not prove, that a defendant was guilty. This reluctance to terminate prosecutions not only meant that many cases remained on the docket for a longer period of time, it also created conditions that impeded any final resolution of the case at all; and as a result,

[3] See Chapter 2 for the geographic distribution of theft cases.

judgments were not obtained in more than half of the 193 prosecutions against disorderly houses.

Crimes of personal violence not resulting in death were the most common criminal offense, but the courts of the rural counties were much more scrupulous in bringing such cases to a satisfactory conclusion. Sixty-one and six-tenths percent of these cases were never resolved in New York City. In the countryside, by contrast, a much smaller proportion—38.4%—of assaults and similar crimes were never fully tried. Moreover, in every area but Albany, less than 30% of these prosecutions were unresolved. Insofar as the average duration of such prosecutions is concerned, in all of the counties but Suffolk the mean duration was greater than three months—the average for New York City. In other words, cases of assault and the like tended to be more rapidly disposed of in New York City, but a smaller proportion of them were satisfactorily resolved.

This pattern may be at least partially explained by the fact that the city courts met quarterly while the county courts met biennially, a factor which tended to shorten the duration of all criminal cases in the city. But this is not an entirely satisfactory explanation, since the mean duration of cases of personal violence in the city was not only less than that for the same crimes in the countryside, but also less than for several other categories of crime in the city itself. Instead, perhaps we should examine the relative importance of crimes of personal violence in urban and rural areas. It will be remembered that assaults were slightly more common in the outlying counties than in the city, but that, along with thefts, such crimes constituted the single most numerous category of prosecution in the city.[4] But larceny was, in the city, a far greater cause for concern than assaults and, as I have indicated, the prosecution of theft in New York City was more effective than for most other offenses. I believe that it was for precisely this reason that assaults were so infrequently resolved in New York City.

[4] See Chapter 2.

Although there is no literary evidence on the subject, it is plausible to speculate that the heavy volume of cases in New York City made it necessary for the courts to trade off effectiveness in the prosecution of one crime for effectiveness in the prosecution of another—in this case, crimes of personal violence for theft. Rather than waste time attempting to secure assault suspects, the courts concentrated on thefts, which were more serious in any case. Thus, assault cases were foreshortened, and the percentage of unresolved cases increased, for when a suspect could not be secured for trial, the case was soon dropped from the docket. In the countryside, on the other hand, thefts posed a much less serious problem. While infrequent meetings of the courts may have tended to lengthen the time a case lingered in the judicial process itself, it was likely that persons accused of crimes of personal violence would be more vigorously prosecuted, since the courts in the countryside were not distracted by the thievery which so plagued New York City.

The pattern of judicial effectiveness was slightly different for violations of public order. More than half of these cases (51.7%) were unresolved in New York City. In the counties, on the other hand, resolution was considerably more frequent—only 29.5% of such cases were unresolved. Moreover, only in Albany-Charlotte and the river counties did the percentage of unresolved cases rise above 30%. The average duration of riot cases was 4.4 months in the colony as a whole. There was some geographic variation, but the only extraordinary deviation was in the river counties where the average case lasted 7.6 months.

Clearly, the river counties of Ulster, Dutchess, and Orange were less effective in handling cases involving violations of public order than any other area of the colony, with the possible exception of New York City. No doubt this is directly attributable to the tenant rebellions of the 1750's and 1760's. As Patricia Bonomi has persuasively argued, these riots had far-reaching implications, and their root causes are to be found in the demographic history of the counties and the nature of New York's land system.[5] These were

[5] See Patricia U. Bonomi, *A Factious People,* 200–228.

not isolated incidents. Rather, they grew from fundamental antagonisms which touched virtually every resident of the upriver counties. The weakness of institutions of law enforcement and the numbers of people involved in these riots help to explain why so many cases were never resolved and why the duration of prosecutions involving violations of public order was so great. Further, all the available evidence seems to suggest that most of the rioters escaped prosecution altogether. Bonomi cities contemporary estimates of the various mobs that gathered in 1766, ranging from 50 to two thousand men; yet the court records for that year, which are relatively complete, record only 48 cases involving violations of public order in the river counties.

III

On balance, there can be no question but that certain categories of crime were more effectively prosecuted than others. There was, in addition, considerable regional variation; and special conditions in different parts of the colony do seem to have influenced the speed and efficiency of the judical process. Patterns of effectiveness were far more consistent among the major ethnic groups. The average duration of actions against slaves, for example, was a very brief 1.3 months in the colony as a whole, and in neither the city nor any of the other regions was the average greater than 1.5 months. Similarly, the percentage of unresolved criminal cases involving slaves was uniformly low in every part of the colony except Albany-Charlotte, where, of the 14 cases tried, 7 were never resolved. These figures are especially striking when compared to those for the English and the Dutch. However ineffective law enforcement may have been in eighteenth-century New York, it was more effective against slaves than against any other group.

There are many reasons for the extraordinary consistency of this pattern. First among these is that the behavior and movements of the slaves were narrowly circumscribed by the law and by the imperatives of the institution itself.[6] This circumstance, in com-

[6] For the legal restrictions on slave behavior, see Chapter 2.

bination with the fact that the color of a slave's skin marked him for easy recognition, made the apprehension of suspects less difficult when the accused was a slave. In addition, slaves were frequently tried for thefts which, as we have seen, were a special cause for concern in the city of New York. Most important of all was the fact that slave crime was of a fundamentally different character than that committed by whites. Every time a slave broke the law he directly challenged the discipline his master had sought to impose. More than that, he threatened to undermine the authority of all slavemasters by setting an example which others might follow. Therefore, slave crimes had to be dealt with quickly and effectively. If they were not, if trials of slaves stretched on for months and if such cases were left unresolved, masters feared (perhaps rightly) that their slaves would rise in mass rebellion.

The effectiveness of prosecutions against slaves derived both from material and ideological conditions. The institutional setting in which slave crime occurred was designed to afford the master substantial social control and to limit the slave's physical and psychological freedom. The institution of slavery was itself designed to prevent slave crime. In the nature of things, it was impossible to oversee the slave's every movement and eliminate such offenses, but when a bondsman did violate the law his chances of escaping judgment were very low. Not only did the slave's appearance and condition make it more difficult for him to elude apprehension, but once he was secured for trial that complex of fear and hatred which was the ideological foundation of the slave system came into play and helped to ensure that the offender would be swiftly and efficiently tried.

Prosecutions involving persons of Dutch descent were handled far less effectively than those involving slaves, yet, for the most part, more effectively than those involving Englishmen. In the colony as a whole, 34.8% of actions against the Dutch were unresolved, while for the English, the percentage was somewhat higher. The real nature of this difference is indicated, however, when the figures are broken down geographically. In all of the outlying counties, prosecutions against the Dutch were more frequently resolved than those against the English, while in New York City the reverse was true. Insofar as the duration of these cases is concerned, the pattern is less consistent; but in the rural counties, trials involving Dutch men and women were usually lengthier than those involving their English counterparts.[7] In the city, on the other hand, the average duration of cases involving Englishmen was 2.8 months, while actions against Dutch defendants averaged 4.0 months.

It is apparent, therefore, that Englishmen were more effectively prosecuted in the city of New York, whereas in the countryside it was the Dutch defendant who was more vigorously pursued and tried. There can be no simple explanation for this difference between the urban and rural areas of New York, but some speculations are possible. In New York City, for example, where thefts were tried with relative speed and efficiency, 24.4% of all actions against Englishmen were for larceny of one kind or another. Such crimes accounted for only 4.0% of actions against persons of Dutch lineage. Thus, a large number of Englishmen stood accused in precisely that category of crime which was most frequently tried in the city. The important fact here, however, is the marked difference between the English and Dutch groups. The somewhat longer duration of cases and the higher percentage of unresolved prosecutions among the Dutch in New York City may be fairly ascribed to the fact that Dutchmen were so infrequently tried for theft—the very crime for which, in New York City, the average duration and percentage of unresolved cases was lowest.

Differences between the English and Dutch in the rural counties of New York are much more difficult to understand. Why should

[7] The two exceptions to this pattern were Suffolk and Albany-Charlotte. In Suffolk, there was only one case involving a Dutch defendant and thus the average duration of 6.0 months is of relatively little value. With respect to Albany-Charlotte, there seems to be no explanation other than that the behavior of the courts in that area was so erratic that it is often impossible to account for wide divergences from patterns which, in other parts of the colony, were very consistent.

Dutch defendants in the countryside have been more effectively prosecuted than English suspects? I have not been able to discover a satisfactory explanation.[8] For the moment, it can only be said that Dutch defendants appear to have been more effectively prosecuted in rural New York than their English counterparts. This pattern may have been the result of the attitude of the two groups toward each other, or it may have arisen from local political or social arrangements. We might posit, for example, that rural courts prosecuted Dutchmen more actively because they were considered to be a threat to the prevailing social and political order. But such an interpretation would be very tenuous indeed and entirely unsupported by evidence. The data described above must, therefore, stand without further comment in hopes that future research in New York's colonial history will uncover additional material upon which a satisfactory interpretive framework may be built.

IV

The effectiveness of the courts changed, not only according to variations within the population of criminal defendants, but also over time. The general pattern for the century was remarkably similar in the city and the outlying counties. In both areas, for example, the percentage of unresolved cases was generally lower before 1750 than afterwards. There were some exceptions to be sure. The period from 1711 to 1715 seems to have been particularly difficult in the countryside, and in the years between 1726 and 1735 the percentage of unresolved cases rose sharply in the city. In the first case, the trouble seems to have centered in the borough counties where 74.3% of all cases were unresolved. In the second case, the city was undergoing a period of economic

[8] I compared several sets of computations in an attempt to isolate the crime or crimes which were skewing the results. For example, I compared the average duration of cases involving violations of public order—the most common crime in the countryside—to the average duration of cases involving English and Dutch defendants, but the results were inconsistent and contradictory. Several similar comparisons proved equally futile.

distress, and the ability of the courts to resolve cases may have been affected.

Despite these exceptions, however, the general pattern in rural and urban areas alike appears to have been that a smaller percentage of cases were left unresolved before 1750 than after. Indeed the five years between 1750 and 1754 were marked by a sharp increase in unresolved cases throughout the colony. Even in Suffolk County where, during the course of the century, 18.7% of all cases were unresolved, the figure for 1750–1754 was 62.7%. In the next five years, moreover, the percentage of unresolved cases dropped off in most parts of New York, although the relatively low levels of the early years of the century were never again achieved. In addition, of course, the percentage of unresolved cases jumped markedly in 1775–1776, owing to the outbreak of the American Revolution, which commonly forced the suspension of court business.

A strikingly similar trend can be noted in the average duration of cases over the course of the century. Without exception, in every part of the colony, the average duration of cases rose considerably between 1750 and 1754. Only between 1706 and 1710, during the chaotic administration of Lord Cornbury, can a comparable increase be noted.[9] Of course, changes in the early 1750's were more extraordinary in some parts of the colony than others—notably the borough and river counties—but they occurred everywhere. During the next twenty-five years, moreover, there does seem to have been a downward trend, although it came later in some areas than in others. In New York City, the first sharp drop came in 1765–1769 when the average duration of cases fell from 4.2 months to 3.1. The situation in the counties was somewhat different, with a sharp decline occurring almost immediately in 1755–1759 and continuing until the beginning of the Revolutionary War. But this pattern varied slightly among different localities. In

[9] For a contemporary view of Cornbury, see William Smith, Jr., *History of the Province of New York,* I, 117–131.

the borough counties, for example, the average duration of cases dropped enormously in the period 1755–1759, only to rise again during the 1760's. In Albany-Charlotte, an area for which the records of the early 1750's have not survived, the average duration of criminal cases rose dramatically in the period 1760–1764 and then dropped off steadily in the prerevolutionary decade.

On balance, then, and with some exceptions, law enforcement was generally more effective before 1750 than after. Moreover, the five years between 1750 and 1754 appear to have been a moment of difficulty in the history of law enforcement in colonial New York. The percentage of unresolved cases as well as the mean duration of criminal prosecutions rose dramatically in those years. While there was considerable success in reducing the length of time for prosecution of cases in the 1760's and 1770's, the percentage of uncompleted prosecutions was higher in the third quarter of the century than at any previous time. From what sources did these developments grow? The problems of the early 1750's were certainly related to a number of circumstances which we have already discussed. One explanation might be that the land disturbances in the Hudson River Valley created unique enforcement problems to which the courts were not prepared to respond. (Indeed, the data do indicate that this crisis of enforcement was most serious in the areas beset by tenant rebellions. Yet similar developments were apparent elsewhere as well. In New York City and in Suffolk County, the percentage of unresolved prosecutions and the average duration of cases also rose sharply, and any explanation of the decline in effectiveness of law enforcement which the colony experienced in the first half of the 1750's must be valid for the entire province, for the crisis was colony-wide in scope.)

While the increase in all categories of serious crimes in the third quarter of the century was to be expected from tendencies apparent earlier, a similar analysis applies to the enforcement troubles of the 1750's. As we have seen, at other moments of political and economic confusion earlier in the century the percentage of unresolved cases and the average duration of prosecutions tended to increase, and thus another cause of the problems of the 1750's might be that the system of criminal justice in New York was extraordinarily sensitive to developments in the society at large. An incompetent and corrupt governor, an economic crisis, a local political dispute, could all have an inordinate effect upon the system of criminal justice because, as we saw in the last chapter, its fundamental structure was inherently weak from top to bottom.

In the early 1750's, the accumulated pressures of a growing volume of crime and the resultant increase in criminal prosecutions took their toll on the court system. The volume of cases handled by the courts between 1750 and 1754, for example, was more than five times what it had been between 1691 and 1695, but the features of the system itself were essentially the same. In addition, suspects were more difficult to apprehend in a more densely populated city and in a more widely settled countryside. In short, the institutions of justice had failed to keep pace with a growing society. In the 1750's the court system of New York was an institutional anachronism with neither the authority, the personnel, nor the strength to deal effectively with crime in a society which was in the process of fundamental transformation.

The legal system could not continue to function, of course, if sixty percent of all cases went unresolved and the mean duration of a case was eight months. During the tenure of William and John Tabor Kempe as Attorneys-General, efforts were made to increase the efficiency of the courts. It is impossible to read through the papers of either man and not be impressed with the care taken in the preparation of cases for trial, the issuance of warrants, the supervision of local officials, and the maintenance of an unimpeachable integrity and unswerving devotion to the law.[10]

[10] Julius N. Goebel and T. Raymond Naughton concur in this opinion: "There can be no doubt that about the time when William Kempe took over the duties of Attorney General, the judicial machinery was operating more effectively than earlier and it is not to be denied that Kempe and later his son, brought a greater degree of skill to the office than had their predecessors." *Law Enforcement in Colonial New York,* 194. For a prime

In addition, the overall volume of cases declined slightly in the late 1750's before rising sharply in the last fifteen years of the colonial period. This brief respite eased the pressures on the courts somewhat, and there are indications that during the sixties the courts did strive to increase their efficiency by being more scrupulous in the speedy completion of criminal cases.[11] But, by and large, the same problems which had plagued the system earlier in the century continued in the 1760's and 1770's. Never again did the situation deteriorate as seriously as it had early in the 1750's. The average duration of cases dropped dramatically, though the percentage of unresolved cases remained relatively high. With the overall volume of cases increasing so greatly, it was important that cases be moved through the courts more rapidly, but the problem of actually bringing a suspect to the bar for judgment remained, because the enforcement capabilities of the constabulary were as weak in the fifties and sixties as they had been earlier in the century. The case of John Henry and Baltus Lydius discussed in the last chapter is evidence of this continuing problem, and there are other examples as well.[12]

The Lydius case and others like it demonstrate that the limited effectiveness of institutions of law enforcement remained a subject of serious concern in the fifteen years preceding the American Revo-

example of this skill, see John Tabor Kempe's continuing correspondence with Peter Silvester in Albany between 1764 and 1771 on a variety of topics related to law enforcement. Kempe Papers, Box I, John Tabor Kempe Letters, "Schenck-Strong-Swan."

[11] See an order in the Dutchess County Court of Sessions in October 1761 that "all Indictments remaining Undetermined be also returned Next Court and that the Several Defendants have such Notice and also that Process go against them that have not appeared." D.C.S. (Oct., 1761). See also a similar order in O.C.S. (Nov., 1771) and the Supreme Court minutes of May 2, 1767, when the court apparently attempted to clear up all outstanding cases by declaring them judged for want of plea.

[12] See, for example, the case of the King *vs.* Rodman. John Tabor Kempe to Isaac Willet (May 12, and Feb. 16, 1767), Kempe Papers, Box I, John Tabor Kempe Letters, "Watts-Yates"; and S.C.M. (Jan. 28, 1764; Oct. 27, 1764; May 2, 1767; Aug. 1, 1767; Aug. 4, 1770; and Jan. 19, 1771).

lution, not, perhaps, as serious a problem as it had been in the early 1750's, but more troublesome than it had been earlier in the century. At no time, nevertheless, did the system of criminal justice function very effectively. In most places and at most times, the structural weaknesses of the system tended to lengthen prosecutions and enlarge the percentage of unresolved cases and, as John Tabor Kempe so clearly understood, the long-range effects of such circumstances could be disastrous, since a major deterrent to criminal behavior was the sure knowledge of the prospective offender that he would quickly be tried and punished if he dared to violate the law. Thus, one of the corollaries of weakened law enforcement in colonial New York was a high rate of recidivism, and it is to this topic that we now turn.

The statistical evidence in this study is based upon 5,297 cases gathered from the criminal court records of colonial New York; but not all of these cases involved different individuals since many people appeared before the courts more than once. At the very most, these 5,297 cases involved some 4,241 different individuals.[13]

[13] I obtained this figure by using the standard IBM "Sort" program to generate an alphabetized list of all the names in the file of 5,297 cases, each followed by a previously assigned identification number (which would allow me to locate that case in my notes) as well as all the other information which had been encoded on punchcards for each case. I then worked my way through the list checking all the names which appeared more than once against my notes on the corresponding cases. By comparing the county of prosecution, the year, and a variety of other variables, I was able to ascertain that certain prosecutions clearly involved two different individuals with the same name. Of course, this was not always clear, and I decided that unless I was virtually positive of an identity, I would assume that two different individuals were involved. To cite the most obvious sort of example, there were eleven cases involving "John Smith," but although I had some reason to believe that at least three of those prosecutions were against an innkeeper in New York City by that name, I decided to count each of them as separate individuals. This was the most conservative tactic, and I believe the most prudent one. Thus, the calculations for recidivism which appear below probably underestimate the extent of the phenomenon involved, but I am confident that I have not exaggerated it. The number of individuals was obtained by a series of calculations reproduced below:

Of these, 694 appeared more than once on criminal charges—a recidivism rate of 16.36%. In other words, about one person in six appearing in the criminal courts was a repeater. Moreover, the mean number of appearances for each recidivist was 2.52. That is to say, repeaters appeared not only more than once, but often more than twice.

Since we have, as yet, no reliable basis for comparison, these figures are somewhat difficult to interpret, but this would seem to be a relatively high incidence of recidivism in a society which tended to punish second-time offenders far more harshly than those making their initial appearance at the bar.[14] Indeed, for certain crimes such severities were established procedures. Grand larceny, for example, was punishable by death, but first offenders were permitted to "plead their clergy" and be branded rather than hanged for this capital crime, while repeaters were almost always executed.[15] Moreover, a chronological breakdown supports the conclusion that the effectiveness of law enforcement declined some-

---

5,297	Total number of cases
−1,750	Cases involving individuals whose names appeared in more than one case
3,547	Names which were not repeated
+ 694	Individual repeaters
4,241	Individuals

[14] In his study of crime in Massachusetts, David Flaherty of the University of Western Ontario has found very little evidence of recidivism and is inclined to ascribe the absence of repeaters from the court records to the severity of punishment in the Bay Colony, although penal procedures were, insofar as I have been able to determine, no more lenient in New York than in Massachusetts.

[15] For example, Catharine Bronson and Elizabeth Clarke were convicted of grand larceny in October, 1767. They asked for benefit of clergy, "but it appearing by the Judgement Rolls which were read that the prisoner Catharine Bronson in the Term of July and August last and the prisoner Elizabeth Clarke in the Term of April last were respectively convicted of grand larceny and were thereupon allowed their Clergy, the Court therefore pronounced Sentence," and the defendants were ordered hanged. King *vs.* Catharine Bronson alias Ranson alias Hannah Harding and Elizabeth Clarke, S.C.M. (Oct. 26, 1767, and Oct. 31, 1767).

what after 1750. Of the 694 repeaters, 285 appeared in the courts before 1750 and 409 after 1750. Because I have recorded more criminal cases after 1750 than before, we would expect a greater number of repeaters in the later period. But that number is greater than the chronological distribution of all criminal cases would lead us to predict. Among all cases, 44% occurred in the earlier period, and 56% occurred after mid-century. Among repeaters, however, 41% appeared before 1750, and 59% appeared after that date—a difference of 3%. In addition, the recidivism rate, which was 16.36% for the century taken as a single unit, was higher in the period 1750–1776 than between 1691 and 1749. In the earlier era, 15.16% of all individuals appearing in the courts were repeaters, while in the later period 17.31% reappeared.[16] The significance of these differences is difficult to gauge, of course, but they do seem to support the conclusion that the courts were less effective in preventing those convicted of crime from reappearing before the bar after 1750 than earlier in the century.

It should be apparent that although the ineffectiveness of law enforcement in colonial New York was a colony-wide and century-long phenomenon, the intensity of the problem varied consider-

[16] The relevant computations are as follows:

1691–1749	
2,332	Total cases
− 738	Cases involving individuals whose names appeared in more than one case
1,594	Names which were not repeated
+ 285	Individual repeaters
1,879	Individuals
1750–1776	
2,965	Total cases
−1,012	Cases involving individuals whose names appeared in more than one case
1,953	Names which were not repeated
+ 409	Individual repeaters
2,362	Individuals

ably. In Suffolk County, the courts met with considerably greater success than elsewhere in the colony, where the effectiveness of law enforcement seems to have declined as distance from the city increased; and among all areas of New York, patterns of prosecution were most erratic and ineffectual in the northernmost area of Albany and Charlotte Counties. Similarly, certain crimes were dealt with more satisfactorily than others. Theft, it would appear, was handled relatively well when compared to other categories of serious crime. In addition, the three major ethnic groups were tried with differing degrees of skill and vigor. Slaves, more than any other single group in the colony, were the subject of especially vigorous prosecution. The pattern for the English and the Dutch is confused, on the other hand, with the Dutch more effectively tried in the countryside and the English more steadfastly pursued in the city. Moreover, law enforcement generally seems to have been less effective during the first five years of the 1750's, with both the percentage of unresolved prosecutions and the average duration of cases rising dramatically. During the tenure of the Kempes as Attorneys-General, some small success was achieved in ameliorating these problems, but the level of effectiveness was lower during the 1760's and 1770's than in any other fifteen-year period in the century. Finally, recidivism was relatively frequent, occurring at a rate of 16.36% over the period from 1691 to 1776 and increasing slightly in the third quarter of the century.

Conclusions such as these are useful, since they provide new information about the social history of New York. Despite the wide variations which have been noted, however, we should observe that these were differences of degree and not of kind. The courts of Suffolk County were more effective than those in other parts of the colony; but it remains true that even on Long Island, almost one out of every five offenders escaped trial. Similarly, although law enforcement was less effective in the latter part of the colonial period than it had been in an earlier era, at no time did the courts of colonial New York function with the vitality and strength which the situation required.

Therefore, if we return to the question posed early in the last chapter—how much crime was there in eighteenth-century New York?—there would seem to be but one appropriate answer: too much. The volume of serious crime was, especially after 1750, clearly greater than the ability of the colony's agencies of law enforcement to cope with it. Thus, at least insofar as crime and law enforcement are concerned, the hallmark of New York's early history was the failure of institutional arrangements to keep pace with social change.

CHAPTER 8

Crime and Law Enforcement in Eighteenth-Century New York: An Interpretation

Discussing the people of New York in 1760, Andrew Burnaby observed that it was "almost impossible to give them any precise or determinate character."[1] So it has been with later historians of the colony as well. The people of colonial New York are not simply or easily described. We speak of the New England way of the Puritans, and of the plantation society of the Chesapeake. Even Quaker Pennsylvania, for all its ethnic diversity, has a more fixed image in the historical literature than its neighboring province of New York. Such uniform perceptions are perhaps illusory anyway, but it is also true that Puritan theology, the plantation system, and Quaker ethics deeply affected the texture of life in the colonies whose institutions they dominated. New York had no colony-wide staple crop or monolithic religious cast of mind to color its colonial history; indeed, it might even be said that the characteristic trait of New York's colonial history was a complexity that lacked any unifying theme or structure.

This complexity is nowhere more apparent than in the history of crime and law enforcement in New York. A bewildering array of factors touched and were, in turn, touched by the system of criminal justice. Moreover, the system itself was not administered with rigid consistency, and many patterns of criminal and judicial be-

[1] Andrew Burnaby, *Travels through the Middle Settlements,* 80.

havior may be noted as a result. Although it may be impossible to give the people of New York "any precise or determinate character," much can be said about specific groups of people living in the colony and their relationship to the criminal courts and the administration of justice. Because New York society was so multifaceted, and because the history of crime and law enforcement within its boundaries was so intricate, there may be considerable value in recapitulating some of the major conclusions of this study before considering their wider significance.

I

The vast majority of criminal defendants in colonial New York were white men of English descent. Women, blacks, and Dutch residents of the colony comprised a far smaller percentage of the population of criminal defendants than they did of the population at large. Similarly, certain categories of crime dominated the business of the criminal courts. Most important among these were acts of personal violence, violations of public order, thefts, instances of contempt of authority, crimes by public officials, and the keeping of disorderly houses. In addition, each of the ethnic groups was more frequently prosecuted for certain crimes than others. And women, for example, were frequently tried for theft and the keeping of disorderly houses, but rarely appeared for violations of public order or acts of personal violence. Similarly, certain crimes were characteristically urban, while others occurred more frequently in the countryside. Larceny cases were quite common in the city of New York, whereas violations of public order seem to have been primarily a rural phenomenon; and even in predominantly Puritan Suffolk County such crimes were the single most common source of prosecution. Generally speaking, patterns of criminal prosecution mirrored the antagonisms and divisions of the larger society, and reflected, as well the extraordinary heterogeneity of the colony's population.

Patterns of judgment were equally varied. Only about one-half of all defendants were convicted, but members of particular groups and persons accused of specific crimes were more likely to be convicted than others. Slaves were more commonly found guilty than members of other ethnic groups, while women were acquitted more often than their male counterparts. Similarly, convictions were most frequent among persons accused of theft, contempt of authority, and violations of public order. There were also significant geographic variations. Acquittals were more abundant in New York City than elsewhere in the province, but in Suffolk County guilty verdicts were more frequently the norm. Patterns of judgment were, then, extraordinarily responsive to particular circumstances and conditions, reproducing in microcosm many of the fundamental structural features of the society at large.

Yet it is deceptive to rely too heavily upon such generalizations. The personal experience of individual New Yorkers with crime and law enforcement cannot be subjected to simple characterization or description. The variations were simply too great. Young and old, rich and poor, immigrant and native-born New Yorkers all appeared in the criminal courts, and the ways in which they were treated were as different as the people themselves. The courts were flexible and could show great leniency or harsh severity as circumstances warranted. Moreover, although conditions in the colony's jails were deplorable, public officials were surprisingly accessible and responsive to petitioners, often pardoning convicted defendants when the interests of justice seemed to be served.

Despite these many variations, however, several clear patterns of change may be discerned in the history of crime and law enforcement in colonial New York. Although crime rates remained relatively constant over the course of the century, the volume of serious crime—and especially violent crime—became a more difficult problem in New York after 1750 than it had been before. Moreover, while collective violence in rural areas rose to new heights, New York City experienced a sharp increase in the percentage of cases involving disorderly houses and theft. The declining slave population and the increasing assimilation of Dutch New Yorkers were also reflected in New York's court records during the third quarter of the eighteenth century, but the most significant development appears to have been an intensification and expansion of trends which had been apparent earlier.

These developments were aggravated by a system of criminal justice that lacked the institutional resilience to handle an increasing volume of cases. In almost every particular—from the quality of the constabulary to the weakness of the jails, to the ignorance of the judges, to the indifference of juries—New York's judicial system was locked into a cycle of increasingly enfeebled law enforcement. Of course, the situation was more problematic in some areas and among some groups than others. The courts of Suffolk County were by far the most effective in dealing with crime; and slaves were more efficiently prosecuted than any other group. The overall picture, however, was anything but bright. In the years after 1750, the percentage of unresolved cases rose sharply, as did the average duration of prosecutions, and recidivism increased as well. Thus, during just the same period that violent and serious crime increased so dramatically, the effectiveness of law enforcement declined. Undoubtedly, there was a relationship between these two developments. Which was the cause and which the effect is difficult to tell, but there can be no question that each reinforced the other—with significant consequences for the larger society.

The multiplicity of groups living in the province shaped patterns of crime and law enforcement in a wide variety of ways, thereby imparting to our story—both collectively and as individuals—a variety which may obscure more general insights. Certainly several century-long and colony-wide trends seem to stand out, and we ought not lose sight of the forest simply because there are so many different kinds of trees.

The business of New York's criminal courts was dominated by serious crimes against persons and property, and this was inceasingly the case in the later years of the colonial period. For the most part, New York's institutions of law enforcement were inadequate to solve the dilemmas thereby created and failed to perform their key role as mechanisms of social control. Further, New York's ethnic diversity was everywhere apparent in its criminal court records, which reveal that African slaves were, in this area as in so many others, a group apart—living in society without being of it. Their behavior, as well as the response of the courts to them, make it clear that the institution of slavery had a profoundly unsettling influence on society in colonial New York.

Similarly, Suffolk County, settled by New Englanders and always the most homogeneous region in the colony, appears to have remained uniquely distinct from the rest of the province, evincing patterns of crime and law enforcement which, though hardly qualifying it for the status of pastoral utopia, were nonetheless fundamentally different from those apparent elsewhere. Indeed, regional variations in patterns of crime and law enforcement were very wide, and it may even be a mistake to regard eighteenth-century New York as one society. John Tabor Kempe and other provincial officials certainly thought it was, but their jobs virtually required such a perception. Yet crime and law enforcement were problems more local than provincial in origin, and they had to be dealt with on a daily basis by people in the localities who, as we have seen, labored under very difficult conditions. Therefore, discussions of "New York society in the eighteenth century" may be somewhat misleading. Perhaps the province may be more properly understood as a congeries of societies under the aegis of a single political system, with each society functioning with relative autonomy. Certainly, the variety of patterns suggested by the evidence would indicate that there were several societies in New York, each responding in its own way to the phenomena of growth and change.

Despite these differences, however, there were patterns of crime and law enforcement which the several societies of New York shared. In all of them, the volume of criminal cases appearing before the courts increased over the century, while the ability of the legal system to deal effectively with those cases declined. The principles of hierarchy and deference which had been—and remained—so central to Western social and political thought were severely and genuinely challenged in such socictics where the mechanisms of social control expressed in the criminal justice system found it increasingly difficult to keep pace with an increasing volume of criminal business. And yet the societies of New York were not *sui generis;* nor were their difficulties unique. All over Europe, and in America as well, the physical and cultural landscape was being transformed. There is good reason, therefore, to attempt to place New York's experience in the broader context of the eighteenth-century world.

II

In England, crime had been a cause for considerable concern for many years. At least since the later middle ages, the English court system had suffered from its inability to enforce the law.[2] The eighteenth century brought a renewed interest in these problems and a widespread belief that crime was increasing with alarming speed.[3] As a result, the system of justice in England was the subject of considerable public controversy, with parliamentary committees created to study the subject in 1750, 1770, and again in 1787. Moreover, a number of public figures—including Daniel Defoe, Henry Fielding, Patrick Colquhoun, Samuel Johnson, Edmund Burke and William Pitt—expressed their concern about the problem of rising crime; and an extensive pamphlet debate was devoted to the subject.[4]

Of all the English commentators Defoe and Fielding were perhaps the most astute. In *An Effectual Scheme for the Immediate Preventing of Street Robberies,* Defoe complained that the "Bold-

[2] See John Bellamy, *Crime and Public Order in England in the Later Middle Ages* (Toronto, 1973), esp. ch. 7.

[3] John Beattie has argued that such a belief was, in fact, justified and that crimes against property, especially, increased during the first half of the century. "Trends in Crime against Property and Its Punishment in England, 1660–1800," paper delivered at the meeting of the American Historical Association, New Orleans, Dec. 29, 1972. See Beattie, "The Pattern of Crime in England, 1660–1800," *Past and Present,* 62 (Feb., 1974), 47–95.

[4] Leon Radzinowicz, *A History of English Criminal Law,* I, chs. 8, 10 and 12, esp. 336–350, 399–415.

ness and Multitude of leud and disorderly Persons of both Sexes, which throng the Streets as soon as the Evening may be said to begin, are such that renders it not only unpleasant, but indeed unsafe to honest and modest People to be abroad."[5] Defoe argued that the problem was general and not merely confined to London; and, moreover, it had been heightened by the "Ill Conduct of Watch-men, Constables and other Officers."[6] In short, "the growth and Progress of Crime . . . has been owing chiefly . . . to a slack-handed Administration; the Reins of Justice being for sometime (as it were) let go."[7] Twenty years later, Henry Fielding voiced similar sentiments, suggesting that "the Introduction of Trade" had profoundly disturbed existing social arrangements and had "totally changed the Manners, Customs and Habits of the People." The result was an increased volume of crime which, owing to the "Lethargic State" of government, threatened to overwhelm the entire social order.[8]

Both Defoe and Fielding emphasized the institutional weakness of England's system of criminal justice and adduced what we would today call "sociological" analyses of the crime problem. Indeed, there is little question that enervated enforcement procedures were at the very heart of the issue. The English constable, like his counterpart in New York, had neither the authority nor the inclination to act as anything more than an "inferior helper of justice."[9] Clearly, some reforms were required. Unanticipated problems accompanied the unanticipated expansion of English economic life in the first fifty years of the eighteenth century; and since those problems seemed to threaten the prevailing social order in such basic ways, solutions had to be found if society were to continue on a steady course.

5 Daniel Defoe, *An Effectual Scheme,* 11.

6 *Ibid.,* 14.

7 *Ibid.,* 16.

8 Henry Fielding, *An Enquiry into the Late Increase in Robbers,* xxii, xxx, 1.

9 James Heath, ed., *Eighteenth Century Penal Theory* (Glasgow, 1963), 26–27.

Several measures were taken to quell the rising tide of crime in England. One was that the transportation of felons to the American colonies, which had been an informal and disorganized process in the seventeenth century, was regularized by a parliamentary act in 1717. This act, which "became the cornerstone of policy for the disposal of convicts throughout the century," had far-reaching consequences in the colonies and in England.[10] First, it allowed England to rid herself of her convicted felons—according to one estimate "at least seventy percent of those convicted at Old Bailey were sent to America."[11] Second, the transport of criminals provided a basic source of labor for the colonies of the Chesapeake, where three-quarters of these people were sent.[12]

Transportation of felons was central to changes in English penal policy, but other measures were taken as well. In the 1770's especially, imprisonment became an increasingly common punishment for convicted thieves. There were several reasons for this retreat from the corporal forms of punishment which had for so long dominated the sentences of English courts. A number of Enlightenment thinkers had undertaken re-evaluations of current penal theory. And Cesare Beccaria's *Essay on Crimes and Punishments,* first published in England in 1767, had a significant impact on changing attitudes and policies. In addition, the war in America ended transportation of criminals to the American colonies and forced a reconsideration of sentencing procedures.[13] John Howard's

[10] Abbot Emerson Smith, *Colonists in Bondage,* 111. See also Radzinowicz, *A History of English Criminal Law,* I, 110; and Marcus W. Jernegan, *Laboring and Dependent Classes in Colonial America, 1607–1783* (Chicago, 1931), 48–49.

[11] Smith, *Colonists in Bondage,* 117. John Beattie has found that "by the 1750's over half of those punished for crimes against property in Surrey were transported to America." Beattie, "Trends in Crime and Punishment."

[12] Smith, *Colonists in Bondage,* 117. It might be added that the impact of these people on society in Virginia and Maryland is an entirely unexamined phenomenon well worth more careful investigation.

[13] Of course, imprisonment did not entirely replace transportation, and soon after the war began the British began to discuss sending convicts to

State of the Prisons focused attention on conditions in English jails, and "it was," according to Professor John Beattie, "this intersection of theory and necessity that made hard labour so attractive a punishment: circumstances filled the gaols with convicts; the reformers provided Parliament with something to do with them."[14] Thus, in the last half of the 1700's, a movement for wide-ranging penal reform gained momentum in England, and by 1800 it had met with considerable success in making criminal justice more compassionate.[15]

In New York, as in the mother country, crime had become a problem of increasingly serious proportions; and, generally speaking, this change does seem to have resulted from similar economic and social circumstances—rising population, expanding ports, intensified urbanization, and a burgeoning economy. In New York, however, the volume of crime underwent dramatic increase some fifty years later than in England. After 1750 English concern about rising crime persisted, but was modified by a reform impulse which concentrated more upon humane solutions than upon increased severity.[16] In New York the first hint that crime might

---

Australia; the first group sailed in 1787. George Rusche and Otto Kirchheimer, *Punishment and Social Structure* (New York, 1939), 114. See also A. G. L. Shaw, *Convicts and the Colonies: A Study of Penal Transportation from Great Britain and Ireland to Australia and Other Parts of the British Empire* (London, 1966); and Eris O'Brien, *The Foundation of Australia: A Study in English Criminal Practice and Penal Colonization in the Eighteenth Century* (New York, 1952).

[14] Beattie, "Trends in Crime and Punishment."

[15] For example, by the early 1800's only one-tenth of all capitally convicted felons were actually executed—a considerable decline from a ratio of one in two in the middle years of the previous century. "The first sharp decline came in 1801, from which date, the ratio never again rose to its former high level." Radzinowicz, *A History of English Criminal Law,* I, 159.

[16] Note, for example, the difference between Fielding's view and that of the Parliamentary committee of 1751: "Fielding was primarily preoccupied with the repressive aspects of penal policy. The Committee's outlook was much more enlightened. It not only recommended reform of prisons and houses of correction, but emphasized the need to revise capital laws. Field-

pose a genuine threat did not come until the early 1750's at a time when law enforcement had virtually collapsed. Therefore, it would seem that at just the time that penal reform was beginning to gather momentum in England, crime was first becoming a subject of serious concern in New York.

Widespread crime was a new experience for New Yorkers in the 1750's and 1760's, and their response was relatively unsophisticated. Punishment became considerably more severe—especially for theft. Before 1750, whippings had been the most common punishment for convicted thieves, accounting for 70.9% of all sentences, while the death penalty was relatively uncommon and was used in only 9.5% of all larceny cases. After 1750, however, whippings dropped to 25.5% of all sentences, while executions rose to 22.2%, and branding, used most commonly when defendants were granted benefit of clergy, rose from 0.5% of all punishments for thieves before 1750 to 28.4% after that date. Thus, one way in which New Yorkers hoped to stem the rising tide of crime was by increasing the brutality of punishment.[17]

There are, in addition, other indications of change in New York during the third quarter of the century. In January, 1764, the Supreme Court of Judicature of the Colony of New York issued the following Proclamation:

The Court Considering that it has been the usage of most of the Civilized Nations in Europe to distinguish the different Orders of Men

---

ing's omission of this crucial matter made his schemes both unreal and retrogressive." *Ibid.,* 420.

[17] Moreover, this increased severity may well have affected the amount of crime reported to the courts. In England, many people believed that the increased severities of the criminal law encouraged victims to be reluctant in reporting crimes. Such a situation may also have been at work in New York. Thus, the crime rates presented in Chapter 5 may be less accurate for the later years of the century than earlier. Unfortunately, however, it is impossible to fully account for the "dark figure" of unreported crime, nor is it possible to gauge with accuracy changing patterns in reporting. For a discussion of these themes in the English context, see Beattie, "The Pattern of Crime in England," esp. 54–55.

in the learned Professions by their Dress and the Judges in our Mother Country having from the most Early Days been accustomed to appear at Westminister in Term Time, in Robes and Bands, and the Council in Bar in Gowns and Bands; and that Example being already imitated in several British Colonies. And the Court conceiving that the Practice at Home stands upon Good Reasons, and that the Introduction of the like usage in this Province would advance in Dignity Authority Solemnity and Decorum of the Court and have many useful consequences —And the Judges of this Court now Signifying their Intention to appear upon the Bench in October Term next ensuing in Robes and Bands—it is hereby Ordained that no person practising as Council at the Bar shall in the said Term appear in this Court or in any of the Courts of the Circuit unless he be habited in the Bar Gown and Band commonly used by the Barristers at Westminster under penalty of a Contempt.[18]

This extraordinary Proclamation indicates a genuine desire by the court to reassert an authority which it apparently felt was under attack. In addition, it indicates a peculiar self-consciousness, a sense that New York could now count itself as one of "the Civilized Nations," and that, as such, certain amenities ought to be observed in its administration of justice.

The true significance of the Proclamation goes deeper still but is also more difficult to demonstrate. There was a sense in which New York society had, over the course of the century, grown similar to that of England. The social dislocations caused by accelerated economic and demographic growth came later to New York than to Britain, but they did come. Moreover, the colony tried to apply what were perceived to be English solutions by making its system of justice more harsh. Certainly, the punishment statistics discussed above suggest as much. And the "Robes and Bands" Proclamation, when viewed in this light, would seem to be an explicit attempt to impose an English solution upon problems conceived to be similar to those of England.

John Murrin has aptly termed this process of imitation "anglicization," and Michael Kammen has described the tension be-

[18] S.C.M. (Jan. 24, 1764).

tween cultural anglophilia and political anglophobia that existed throughout British North America in the sixties and seventies.[19] But historians have not fully appreciated the extent to which these developments reflected a quite accurate perception of reality. New Yorkers understood—as perhaps imperial officials often did not—that theirs was a growing society whose problems had, to a remarkable degree, come to resemble those of England herself. What could be more natural, therefore, than to consciously imitate English courts in an attempt to augment the "Dignity Authority Solemnity and Decorum" of their own system of criminal justice. The anglicization of colonial law and the anglophilia of colonial culture were thus intimately related, in ways heretofore unrecognized, to underlying social processes. Anglicization was as much a social phenomenon as a cultural one; and, indeed, it might even be argued that cultural and legal anglicization grew directly from the social anglicization which preceded it.[20] At the center of the provincial self-consciousness of the prerevolutionary era was a recognition that the colonies had changed dramatically in the years since the Glorious Revolution (1688–1689); and that, for all the debates about American savagery so much in vogue in Europe, theirs was no pale copy of civilized society, but mature in the fullest sense, both enjoying the benefits and suffering the problems which such maturity brings.[21]

[19] John M. Murrin, "Anglicizing an American Colony: The Transformation of Provincial Massachusetts" (Ph.D. diss., Yale University, 1966); and Michael G. Kammen, *People of Paradox: An Inquiry Concerning the Origins of American Civilization* (New York, 1972), 184–185, 222.

[20] In using the term "social anglicization" here, I am describing social processes similar to, though not identical with, those which Kenneth Lockridge has termed "Europeanization." See Lockridge, *A New England Town*.

[21] For some extraordinarily perceptive observations on the question of the maturity of provincial society at mid-century and an analysis of the pervasiveness of the "parent-child metaphor," see Jack P. Greene, "An Uneasy Connection: An Analysis of the Preconditions of the American Revolution" in Stephen G. Kurtz and James H. Hutson, eds., *Essays on the American Revolution* (Chapel Hill, 1973), 32–80; and Edwin G. Burrows and Michael Wallace, "The American Revolution and the Psychology of National Liberation," *Perspectives in American History* (1972), 167–306.

For example, New York faced—as England had—a perplexing dilemma of law enforcement; that is, a desire to enforce the law efficiently, which sometimes conflicted with a long-standing commitment to the protection of civil liberties. This juxtaposition of individual freedom and community discipline was unique to the Anglo-American world. In eighteenth-century France, the police powers of the state were fully developed and efficiently administered, but at the expense of personal liberty.[22] Fielding himself was conscious of the problem, but argued that "wild Notions of Liberty . . . are inconsistent with all Government."[23] In New York, the quandary in which provincial law-enforcement officials found themselves appeared in sharp relief during the late 1760's.

For many years, New York had a law which provided for the "speedy punishing and releasing of persons from imprisonment as Shall Commit Offenses under the Degree of Grand Larceny."[24] The law granted wide discretion to local justices in punishing petty offenders and was designed to increase the effectiveness of law enforcement. Over the years, objections had been occasionally raised to the act on the grounds that it granted excessive power to ignorant and arbitrary J.P.'s.[25] In 1769, John Tabor Kempe wrote to several justices in Suffolk County about their "undue proceedings" against a servant named Wheeler who, according to Kempe, had done nothing more than defend the property of his master from attack. Observing that he did not want to "throw any difficulty in the way of [the Justices'] Duty," Kempe suggested very strongly that they had violated the "Bounds beyond which they ought not to pass" in their enforcement of the law.[26]

On May 20, the justices wrote to Kempe to ask for further clarification of his position and requested that he instruct them

22 Heath, *Eighteenth Century Penal Theory,* 27–28.

23 Fielding, *An Enquiry into the Late Increase in Robbers,* xxx.

24 See *Col. Laws N.Y.*, II, 745–747 and 766–768 (Oct. 14, 1732).

25 See, for example, *Journ. Leg. Council,* II, 1323.

26 John Tabor Kempe to Benjamin Strong, Selah Strong, and Richard Woodhull (March 3, 1769), Kempe Papers, Box I, John Tabor Kempe Letters, "Schenck-Strong-Swan."

how to proceed without violating the law. He wrote back that, in his opinion, the act itself was "destructive of that Grand Bulwark of our Freedom and Safety, the Tryal by Jury," since it provided for summary proceedings against petty offenders. Thereby, he argued, the law "[threw] down that Barrier against the Arbitrary Power of the Crown which it is the peculiar Happiness of our Constitution to have established." Therefore, Kempe continued, "too great Tenderness and Caution . . . cannot be used in Proceedings under this act." Kempe ended by once again repeating the provisions of the act and warning the justices that he expected them to use more caution in the future.[27]

This exchange between Kempe and the Suffolk J.P.'s points to a problem that law-enforcement officers faced on both sides of the Atlantic, one which plagues us still—how to secure the rights of the accused without abandoning the government's essential function of preserving order. It is significant, moreover, that this dispute occurred when it did, for it resulted from John Tabor Kempe's very complete knowledge of the English common-law tradition and his desire not to stray from it. This was the same Kempe who had struggled to increase the effectiveness of law enforcement throughout the 1760's, but he believed that New York's adherence to English criminal practice should be complete—including the protection of liberty as well as the control of crime. The Suffolk J.P.'s, on the other hand, faced with the day-to-day problems of law enforcement, were not nearly so concerned with guaranteeing fundamental liberty as with maintaining order. The dispute arose, therefore, not merely out of Kempe's superior legal knowledge, but also grew from the differing perspectives of local and provincial officials.

Social change in the colony of New York brought with it a pleth-

[27] Benjamin Strong, Selah Strong, and Richard Woodhull to John Tabor Kempe (May 20, 1769), *ibid.*, and Kempe to Strong, Strong, and Woodhull (June 9, 1769), *ibid.* Perhaps it should be added that Kempe maintained this position, despite the fact that he had himself been a victim of theft in 1760. See *New-York Mercury,* Jan. 7, 1760.

ora of difficult problems for which the province was institutionally unprepared. Dramatic increases in serious crime accompanied by an equally sharp decline in the effectiveness of law enforcement gave the colony "the look" of English society, and concerns about civil liberties took on a new significance when they seemed to conflict with effective peace-keeping. For New York, in the 1760's, shared with the mother country not only a common political culture, but common social experience as well—and it is to the intersection of the two that we now turn.

III

Much of our colonial history has been written with an eye on the American Revolution, and too often this perspective has colored and distorted our view of the prerevolutionary era. In these concluding paragraphs, however, I should like to examine some of the connections between the history of crime and law enforcement in colonial New York and the ideas and institutions that emerged in America during and after the Revolution. It is not my intention to read the Revolution back into an earlier era, but I am convinced that to properly understand the achievements of the colonists once their war was won, we must also understand the social experience they brought to the nation-building process.[28]

[28] The social origins of the American Revolution remain very perplexing. For the most recent reassessment, see Jack P. Greene, "The Social Origins of the American Revolution: An Evaluation and an Interpretation," *Political Science Quarterly,* LXXXVIII (March 1973), 1–22. In footnote 46 of that essay, Greene suggests that increasing crime may be one of several indices of "social strain" which he believes were related to the coming of the Revolution. My own feeling is that such a connection would be difficult to make conclusively and, at best, it would be "uneasy." For example, New York seems to have experienced far more "social strain" than Massachusetts. According to David Flaherty, not only was crime relatively infrequent in Massachusetts, but law enforcement was strikingly efficient. Yet when the Revolution began, the citizens of Massachusetts rallied to the cause in far greater numbers than did their neighbors in New York. In short, too many other factors touched on the coming of the Revolution in the various colonies, and the causal importance of "social strain" may have differed greatly from one to the other.

In the eighteenth century, the physical and cultural environments of England and Europe underwent a series of transformations which marked the emergence of "modern" Western society. Changes in the physical landscape—growing empires, urbanization, the beginnings of industrial development and the like—were vitally related to the changing cultural terrain of the Enlightenment. Societal developments prompted thoroughgoing re-examination of basic assumptions regarding economics, politics, and society. By the same token, the altered cultural climate itself prompted changes in self-consciousness, changes that had profound implications for the shape of futurc events and institutions. Indeed, the movement for penal reform in England and its eventual success evolved in just this way.[29] Although separated from the mother country by an expanse of perilous ocean, American colonists partook of the intellectual transformations of Europe at a time when their societies were only beginning to experience parallel growth and complexity.[30] As a result, when the Americans achieved independence from Britain, they enjoyed the unique opportunity of applying Enlightenment ideas to societies that had only recently reached the threshold of modernity and that had not yet experienced many of the problems which had originally prompted those ideas.

But the ideas were there for the using, ready to be applied to a socioeconomic and political order that was extraordinarily fluid and flexible. Thus, the American Revolution provided an opportunity for the colonies—soon to be states—to make a quantum

[29] J. H. Plumb is one of the few historians to appreciate the full importance of these developments. He writes: "Too often the eighteenth century enlightenment is dismissed as superficial, yet it marks the decisive turning point in the growth of European civility—that age that saw the spread of humane feeling—to women, to children, to criminals and to the insane." *In the Light of History* (American Edition: New York, 1973), 36.

[30] To understand the transatlantic dimensions of Enlightenment ideas one has only to examine the correspondence of such men as Benjamin Franklin and Cadwallader Colden. See also Michael Kraus, *The Atlantic Civilization: Eighteenth-Century Origins* (Ithaca, 1966).

leap, to overtake and surpass the European culture which had spawned them by fundamentally reordering attitudes, institutions, and social organization without having to overcome the inertia of history—that force, that heavy weight of the past which at once had allowed and encouraged extraordinary change in Europe, but which, in the nature of things, also mandated that such change be undertaken slowly if society were to continue and survive.

It was for this reason that the movement for penal reform, which had taken almost a century to succeed in England, achieved wide acceptance in America in less than twenty-five years. By the third decade of the nineteenth century, the American penitentiary was the model for the Western world and the original reason for Tocqueville's visit to the United States.[31] And yet the story is still more complex. The development of the American penitentiary system was very much the product of the Revolution and of the ideas which gave the rebellion form and substance. The institutionalization of penal reform grew naturally from the development of essentially political ideas during the years just preceding the Revolution to the constitution-making era of the late 1780's.

American colonists, like their English forebears, had always understood that a stable social and political system depended, in large measure, upon the ability of the society at large to limit disruptive and deviant behavior among its members. Until the mid-eighteenth century, the prevailing view was that coercion was the only way in which such order might be securely maintained. But beginning in the 1750's, these ideas began to change, as the developing political culture of England came to have a greater impact on the American scene. It is not a coincidence that the clearest

[31] For details of these developments, see David J. Rothman, *The Discovery of the Asylum: Social Order and Disorder in the New Republic* (Boston, 1971); W. David Lewis, *From Newgate to Dannemora: The Rise of the Penitentiary in New York, 1796–1848* (Ithaca, 1965); David Brion Davis, "The Movement to Abolish Capital Punishment in America, 1787–1861," *American Historical Review,* 63 (1957), 23–46; and M. J. Heale, "Humanitarianism in the Early Republic: The Moral Reformers of New York, 1776–1825," *Journal of American Studies,* 2 (1968), 161–175.

articulation of these changes came from the most unstable and politically factious colony—New York. The publication of William Livingston's *The Independent Reflector* marks the earliest and fullest exposition of ideas which were later to become central to the Revolutionary cause. Livingston was not a libertarian in the Jeffersonian mode. Far from it. But he understood, as Madison later did, that individual liberty might be channeled to ensure social stability. Thus he argued for religious tolerance in the belief that by allowing and institutionalizing the broadest kinds of religious conviction, society would be able to prevent the domination of any single religious sect.[32] Only by such counterbalancing of individual interests could what Livingston called the "God-like virtue of Public Spirit" be encouraged among the members of society.[33]

Livingston was little concerned with crime *per se,* although the *Reflector* did publish complaints about the British policy of transporting felons and about a set of proper qualifications for justices of the peace.[34] Similarly, theorists of the Revolutionary generation had little to say about crime, but, like Livingston, they were concerned with public spirit and private virtue. Gordon Wood has brilliantly explicated the development of these ideas and brought into sharp focus their transformation during the period that followed the Revolution.[35] For Wood and, if he is correct, for the Revolutionaries themselves, the rhetoric of virtue acquired special significance in the context of a democratic revolution because it established such high standards for rulers and ruled alike. Their reading of history and the force of contemporary opinion convinced the men who made the Revolution that nothing less than a "republic of pure virtue" could achieve stability and success.

[32] William Livingston, *et al., The Independent Reflector . . . ,* esp. 171–207.

[33] *Ibid.,* 219.

[34] See *ibid.,* 164–170, 352–358.

[35] Gordon Wood, *The Creation of the American Republic, 1776–1787* (Chapel Hill, 1969).

Federalism and ultimately the Constitution embodied mechanisms to secure a virtuous citizenry through satisfactory institutional arrangements rather than coercion.

These ideas related primarily to politics, to the performance of duty by public officials, and to the encouragement of strong community spirit and loyalty in the populace at large. But a political language whose vocabulary was strewn with "licentiousness," "vice," and "immorality" inevitably spilled over into other areas of public life. Thus, in the 1780's—and again New York was a leader —John Jay organized the Society for the Suppression of Vice and Immorality in conjunction with several other humanitarian projects.[36] The Revolution had crystallized and reinforced the absolute necessity of virtue at every level of social intercourse. Beccaria's *Essay on Crimes and Punishments* had been published in New York in 1773—the first and only publication of that central work in America before the Revolution,[37] and it was natural that, as the new nation began to seek institutional means to encourage political virtue without force, its eyes would also turn to the serious problems of crime and law enforcement which, in New York at least, had been increasingly vexing as the Revolution began.

Once again, the ideas were there; and the new republic, unburdened by the weight of its own history, seized the opportunity to reform its mechanisms for the prevention of crime and the enforcement of law. Thus, the constitutional guarantee in the Bill of Rights against "cruel and unusual punishment," which had a long history in England and America, took on new meaning in the con-

[36] The initial proposal made by Jay may be found in the John Jay Papers, Box IV, Bundle 4, in the manuscript collections of the New-York Historical Society. See also Heale, "Humanitarianism in the Early Republic," which suggests, although not explicitly, a connection between the rhetoric of public virtue and the language of reform. For a different view, see William E. Nelson, "Emerging Notions of Modern Criminal Law in the Revolutionary Era: An Historical Perspective," *New York University Law Review,* 42 (1967), 450–482.

[37] See Clifford K. Shipton and James E. Mooney, comps., *National Index of American Imprints through 1800: The Short Title Evans,* Volume One: A-M (1969), 68.

text of this new society. And it was a New York reformer, Thomas Eddy, who became the "John Howard of America," leading and personally supervising the revamping of New York's criminal law and penal institutions in the 1790's.[38] In the early national period men realized that virtue might be instilled in criminals without whipping or branding them. Deterrence need not be based upon fear but might be the natural result of proper "treatment" and humane methods of correction.

America's lack of history, which allowed these changes to take place as quickly as they did, also made them more important in America than they were elsewhere. Without the justification of history to legitimize their new governments, Americans could only rely upon their own virtue and that of their leaders. This is why George Washington so quickly acquired mythic stature, and it is also why the reformist zeal which continued to sweep America during the first half of the nineteeth century held such pivotal significance. In the early years of the nation's history, Americans were driven to prove themselves worthy of their own institutions, and penal reform was nurtured by this need. If social stability was important in the colonial period, it was also vital, albeit in a different way, to the "priesthood of democratic believers" of the early nineteenth century.[39] The Revolution, therefore, allowed Americans to bridge the gap in their own historical consciousness and thus was truly revolutionary, for it permitted an entire people to alter their most fundamental institutions and ideas rapidly and without disastrously rending the social fabric.

The ultimate effect was to bring institutions into closer contact with social reality, but strong imperatives for conservatism were also established. Because the changes of the postrevolutionary era occurred with such startling rapidity, and because they touched the

[38] Lewis, *Newgate to Dannemora,* ch. 1; and Heale, "Humanitarianism in the Early Republic." John Howard was the leading English penal reformer of the period.

[39] This phrase is borrowed from Fred Somkin, *Unquiet Eagle: Memory and Desire in the Idea of American Freedom, 1815–1860* (Ithaca, 1967).

national consciousness where it was most sensitive, they acquired, almost instantaneously, an inertia born of myth rather than history —and myths have profound psychological implications for any people. This is one reason why many of the nineteenth-century reformers so easily and quickly adopted abolitionism. If brutal whippings of criminals conflicted with the encouragement of democratic virtue, how much more discordant was slavery, which destroyed virtue and democracy in a single blow? Racism and abolition were not necessarily contradictory for the ante-bellum reformer because both could be justified by the need for a virtuous citizenry in a republic. But slavery was a blot on the American conscience because, as Tocqueville realized, it contrasted so starkly with the ideology of virtuous republicanism.[40]

Thus, one of the reasons American attitudes toward crime and law enforcement have changed so little, and even regressed over the years, is that they were formed in the postrevolutionary generation, whose mythic sensibilities continue to shape our own notions of our past, present, and future. Over the past 175 years, the American penal system has lost much of its resilience and originality. The penitentiary system began with hopes of moral reformation but soon became a "lock-up" or, rather, a "lock-out"—a way to punish criminals by locking them out of society rather than giving them the tools to re-enter it.[41] George Bernard Shaw called it the "crime of imprisonment"; and he understood, as Thomas Eddy did, that it need not be so.[42] Our own wardens and commissioners of correction, therefore, could do worse than study the original motivations for the development of the penitentiary system.

In sum, there is a sense in which Jonathan Edwards' metaphor

[40] For the political implications of the rhetoric of virtue in the new republic, see Perry M. Goldman, "The Republic of Virtue and Other Essays on the Politics of the Early National Period" (Ph.D. diss., Columbia University, 1970).

[41] See Rothman, *Discovery of the Asylum;* and Michel Foucault, *Madness and Civilization: A History of Insanity in the Age of Reason,* Richard Howard, trans. (New York, 1965).

[42] George Bernard Shaw, *The Crime of Imprisonment* (New York, 1946).

of the spider suspended over the fires of hell was extraordinarily appropriate to the American eighteenth century, but not quite in the way that Edwards used it. Social institutions are often disrupted by extraordinary economic and social changes, and there is no question that such changes were proceeding with great speed in England, much as in the American colonies at mid-century. But until the Revolution, American society lacked what might be termed the resilience of history. That is to say, most societies have a kind of build-in strength imparted to them by the simple fact of their long existence. This was certainly true of England, which had weathered a terrifying degree of social, political, and economic change in the sixteenth and seventeenth centuries. Americans—and indeed these *were* Americans—were more severely affected by such alterations because, in a real sense, their society had no memory or self-confidence entirely its own. (One of the reasons that revivalism had such an enormous impact on American life in the eighteenth and nineteenth centuries was that it provided an outlet for anxieties and fears of social collapse which Americans suffered for want of an historical consciousness of past success to reassure them.) If Americans in later years have been complacent in their belief that their society could weather any storm and exorcise any devil, it is partly because, in the early years of the nation's history, success had seemed doubtful and there had been no history to inspire confidence in the stability of social institutions. It is for this reason that the early success of the nation and the period of the Revolution have exercised such a pervasive influence on the national psyche. Our confidence in the unassailability of our own virtue is very much the product of that myth-making era. The possibility of failure in the early years was, in short, so real and so immanent in the revolutionary situation that it created irresistible imperatives for success.

Today that success often seems very much in doubt, and these reflections may seem somehow too cosmic a conclusion for a study in microhistory. New York was, after all, but one of thirteen colonies; and it may be fanciful to extract such grand conclusions from so particularistic a study. Perhaps so. I hold no brief for New York's typicality; it was not the quintessential American colony—if ever there was such a thing. But I do believe that the experience of the colony with crime and law enforcement had far-reaching implications both for New York and the nation of which it was to become a part. The problems that the New York colonists faced—political divisiveness, intense urbanization, rapid demographic and economic growth, diminished confidence in the viability of government, rising crime, and declining law enforcement—are with us still, and there is no prospect that a new revolution will wipe our slate clean and provide us with the terrifying opportunity and responsibility to remake our world as the generation of the Revolution did theirs. American society is infinitely more complex now than it was then; it is heavier with weighty institutions and established traditions. We have, as our forebears did not, a national memory and mythic sensibilities to justify and rationalize our failure to remake our public life on those principles of equality, humanity, and justice, principles which are, and must be, perfectly consistent with law, order, and stability. Perhaps Scott Fitzgerald was on to something when he wrote that "we beat on, boats against the current, borne back ceaselessly into the past." If Fitzgerald was correct, as I believe he was, there may be considerable value in knowing where the current is taking us, for the waters ahead are surely treacherous and the rapids are filled wtih hazards.

Bibliography

PRIMARY SOURCES

Criminal Court Records

Supreme Court of Judicature

Hamlin, Paul, and Charles E. Baker, eds. *Supreme Court of Judicature of New York, 1691–1704* in *Collections of the New-York Historical Society,* vols. 78–80 (New York, 1945–1947).

"Minutes of the Supreme Court of Judicature" (1693–1701) in *Collections of the New-York Historical Society,* vol. 45 (New York, 1912), 41–214.

"Minute Books of the Supreme Court of Judicature" (1704–1740; 1750–1781). Microfilm copy in Queens College Historical Documents Collection. Rolls SC1–SC8.

Circuit Court of Oyer and Terminer and General Gaol Delivery

"Minutes of the Court of Oyer and Terminer and Gaol Delivery" (1716–1717). Microfilm copy in Queens College Historical Documents Collection. Roll MC27.

"Minutes of the Circuit Court of Oyer and Terminer and General Gaol Delivery" (1721–1749). Two bound folio volumes copied from the original manuscript. Library of the Association of the Bar of the City of New York.

City and County of New York

"Minutes of the Mayor, Deputy Mayor, and Aldermen of New York City" (1733–1742). Microfilm copy in Queens College Historical Documents Collection. Roll MC27.

"Minutes of the Court of General Quarter Sessions of the Peace" (1691–1776). Microfilm copy in Queens College Historical Documents Collection. Rolls CMS1–CMS2.

Horsmanden, Daniel. *The New York Conspiracy,* Thomas J. Davis, ed. (New York, 1971). Contains a list of all those tried in the slave conspiracy trials of 1741 including, as well, the disposition of each case (pp. 467–474).

Kings County

"Court and Road Records Mss., Kings County" (1668–1776). Two bound volumes copied from the original manuscript. Court records are sketchy and incomplete after the first decade of the eighteenth century. St. Francis College Archives, Brooklyn, N.Y.

Queens County

"Minutes of the Courts of General Sessions and Common Pleas" (1722–1787). One bound volume. Sessions records terminate in 1773. Queens County Courthouse, Clerk's Office (Basement Record Room), Jamaica, N.Y.

Richmond County

"Minutes of the Court of General Sessions and Common Pleas" (1711–1745; 1745–1812). Two bound manuscript volumes labeled "Common Pleas." Chronological gap in the second book between 1747 and 1761. Richmond County Courthouse, Clerk's Office (stored in Deed Room vault), St. George, Staten Island, N.Y.

Westchester County

Fox, Dixon Ryan, ed. "Minutes of the Court of Sessions (1657–1696), Westchester County" in *Publications of the Westchester Historical Society,* II (White Plains, N.Y., 1924).

"Minutes of the Courts of General Sessions and Common Pleas" (1710–1723). Typescript copy in Westchester County Office Building, Clerk's Office (Liber D. of Deeds), White Plains, N.Y.

Suffolk County

"Minutes of the Suffolk County Court of General Sessions of the Peace" (1723–1751; 1760–1775). Two bound manuscript volumes, Suffolk County Office Building, Clerks Office (stored in vault), Riverhead, N.Y.

Dutchess County

"Minutes of Dutchess County Court of Common Pleas and General Sessions of the Peace" (1721–1775). Original minutes in dead storage. Microfilm copy on rolls 125, 126, 127 in Dutchess County Office Building, Clerk's Office, Poughkeepsie, N.Y.

Ulster County

"A true Estreat of all the Issues, Fines, Forfeitures, Amercements that have happened . . . in the Court of General Sessions of the Peace . . . for the County of Ulster . . ." (1695–1763), Miscellaneous Court Papers, Ulster County, nos. 7460–7461, New York State Library, Albany, N.Y.

Miscellaneous recognizances and other records, including records of Ulster County Court of General Sessions for 1703. Microfilm copy on exposure 495 in Queens College Historical Documents Collection. Roll UC28.

"Minutes of the Court of General Sessions of the Peace" (1731–1750). Microfilm copy in Queens College Historical Documents Collection. Roll UC50.

"Minutes of the Court of General Sessions" (1711–1720). New York State Library, Albany, N.Y.

Orange County

"Minutes of the Orange County Court of General Sessions of the Peace" (1727–1779). One bound manuscript volume. Orange County Office Building, Clerk's Office (basement storage area), Goshen, N.Y.

Charlotte County

"Minutes of the Court of General Sessions" (1773–1776). New York State Library, Albany, N.Y.

Albany County

"Minutes of the Court of General Sessions of the Peace" (1685–1689; 1717–1723; 1763–1782). Three bound manuscript volumes of different sizes. Albany County Courthouse, Clerk's Office (stored in vault in room 128), Albany, N.Y.

Manuscripts

New-York Historical Society (New York City)

James Alexander, Supreme Court Register (1721–1742).

Richard Bradley Papers.

Miscellaneous Manuscripts, Brooklyn.

George Clarke Papers.

Debating Society Papers (1768–1774).
James Duane, Legal Papers.
John Jay Papers.
Kempe Papers.
McKesson Papers, Register of Cases (1764–1786).
Miscellaneous Manuscripts, New York City.
Miscellaneous Manuscripts, Orange County.
David Provoost Papers.
Miscellaneous Manuscripts, Queens County.
Miscellaneous Manuscripts, Suffolk County.
Miscellaneous Manuscripts, Ulster County.
Peter Van Schaack Papers.
Evert Wendell Papers, Docket of Cases (1723–1749).
Miscellaneous Manuscripts, Westchester County.

New York Public Library (New York City)

William Smith Papers, Supreme Court Register "A," on microfilm (Cornell University Library).

Columbia University Library, Rare Book Room (New York City)

Minutes of the Coroner's Proceedings in the City and County of New York (1747–1758).

Queens College Historical Documents Collection (New York City)

Miscellaneous Manuscripts containing documents concerning Colonial New York from around 1698–1712 from Bodleian Library, Oxford, England, on microfilm. Roll CL2.

New York State Library (Albany, New York)

One hundred and one volumes of miscellaneous colonial documents.

Published Sources

Anonymous. "Journal of a French Traveller in the Colonies, 1765; part II," *American Historical Review,* 27 (1921), 70–90.

Beccaria, Cesare. *An Essay on Crimes and Punishments with a Commentary Attributed to Mons. De Voltaire* (Dublin, 1767).

Benson, Adolph B., ed. *Peter Kalm's Travels in North America: The English Version of 1770,* 2 vols. (New York, 1937).

Bobin, Isaac. *Letters of Isaac Bobin, Esq. Private Secretary of Hon. George Clarke, Secretary of the Province of New-York, 1718–1730* (Albany, 1872).

Burnaby, Reverend Andrew. *Travels through the Middle Settlements in North-America in the Years 1759 and 1760: With Observations upon the State of the Colonies* (reprinted: Ithaca, 1960).

Catterall, Helen, ed. *Judicial Cases Concerning American Slavery and the Negro,* 5 vols. (Washington, D.C., 1926–1937).

Colden, Cadwallader. "Cadwallader Colden Papers," in *Collections of the New-York Historical Society for the Years 1917–1923* (New York, 1917–1923).

——. "The Colden Letter Books, 1760–1775," in *Collections of the New-York Historical Society for the Years 1876–1877* (New York, 1876–1877).

The Colonial Laws of New York from the Year 1664 to the Revolution, 5 vols. (Albany, 1894).

Crevecoeur, Hector St. John de. *Letters from an American Farmer* (reprinted: London, 1912).

——. *Sketches of Eighteenth Century America: More Letters from an American Farmer,* Henri L. Bordin, *et al.,* eds. (New Haven, 1925).

Defoe, Daniel. *An Effectual Scheme for the Immediate Preventing of Street Robberies . . .* (London, 1731).

Eddis, William. *Letters from America,* Aubrey C. Land, ed. (Cambridge, 1969).

"Eighteenth Century Slaves as Advertised by their Masters," *Journal of Negro History,* 1 (April, 1916), 163–216.

Fernow, Berthold, ed. "Calendar of Council Minutes," *New York State Library Bulletin,* 58 (March, 1902; History 6).

Fielding, Henry. *An Enquiry into the Late Increase in Robbers . . .* (London, 1751).

Hamilton, Alexander. *Gentleman's Progress: The Itinerarium of Dr. Alexander Hamilton, 1744,* Carl Bridenbaugh, ed. (Chapel Hill, 1948).

Horsmanden, Daniel. *The New York Conspiracy,* Thomas J. Davis, ed. (Boston, 1971).

Hough, Charles M., ed. *Reports of Cases in the Vice Admiralty Court of the Province of New York* (New Haven, 1925).

Journal of the Legislative Council of the Colony of New York, 2 vols. (Albany, 1861).

"Journal of Reverend John Sharpe," *Pennsylvania Magazine of History and Biography,* 40 (1916), 256–297, 412–425.

Kincaid, Margaret, ed. "John Usher's Report on the Northern Colonies, 1698," *William and Mary Quarterly,* Series 3, 7 (January, 1950), 95–106.

Livingston, William, *et al.*, *The Independent Reflector . . . By William Livingston and Others,* Milton M. Klein, ed. (Cambridge, 1963).

M'Robert, Patrick. *A Tour through Part of the North Provinces of America,* Carl Bridenbaugh, ed. (New York, 1968).

Mereness, Newton D., ed. *Travels in the American Colonies* (New York, 1916).

Miller, Reverend John. *A Description of the Province and City of New York . . . in the Year 1695* (reprinted: London, 1847).

Morris, Richard B., ed. *Select Cases of the Mayor's Court of New York City, 1674–1784* (Washington, D.C., 1935).

Munsell, Joel, ed. *The Annals of Albany,* 10 vols. (Albany, 1850–1859).

——. *Collections on the History of Albany,* 4 vols. (Albany, 1865–1871).

O'Callaghan, Edmund B., ed. *Calendar of Historical Manuscripts in the Office of the Secretary of State, Part II, English Manuscripts* (Albany, 1866).

——. *Calendar of New York Colonial Commissions, 1680–1770* (New York, 1929).

——. *The Documentary History of the State of New York,* 4 vols. (Albany, 1849–1851).

——. *Documents Relative to the Colonial History of the State of New York,* 15 vols. (Albany, 1853–1887).

Old Miscellaneous Records of Dutchess County (Poughkeepsie, 1902).

"Old New York and Trinity Church," in *Collections of the New-York Historical Society for the Year 1870* (New York, 1870), 147–408.

Osgood, Herbert L., *et al.*, eds. *Minutes of the Common Council of the City of New York, 1675–1776,* 8 vols. (New York, 1905).

Padelford, Philip, ed. *Colonial Panorama, 1775: Dr. Robert Honyman's Journal for March and April* (San Marino, Cal., 1939).

Report of the State Historian of New York, Colonial Series I and II (Albany, 1897–1898).

"Reverend John Sharpe's Proposals, Etc.," in *Collections of the New-York Historical Society for the Year 1880* (New York, 1880), 339–364.

Reynolds, Cuyler, comp. *Albany Chronicles: A History of the City Arranged Chronologically from the Earliest Settlement to the Present Time* (Albany, 1906).

Schwartz, Bernard. *The Bill of Rights: A Documentary History,* 2 vols. (New York, 1971).

Smith, William, Jr. *The History of the Province of New York,* Michael G. Kammen, ed., 2 vols. (Cambridge, 1972).

Watson, John F., comp. *Annals and Occurrences of New York City and State in the Olden Times . . .* (Philadelphia, 1846).

Early American Imprints

All of the following titles are catalogued in Charles Evans' *American Bibliography,* 14 vols. (Chicago, 1903) and are available on the American Antiquarian Society's microprint series, edited by Clifford Shipton. Each title is followed by its "Evans Number."

Andrews, Joseph. *The last dying speech and confession of Joseph Andrews who was executed at New-York, on Tuesday, the 23d day of May, 1769, For Piracy and Murder . . .* (New York, 1769). #11152. See also #'s 11149–51.

Campbell, John. *A Short Account of the Life and Character of John Campbell, Now Under Sentence of Death, for Robbery . . .* (New York, 1769). #11463.

The Charge given by the Chief Justice of the Province of New-York, to the Grand Jury of the City of New-York, in March term, 1726–1727 . . . (New York, 1727). #2933.

Clarkwright, John. *The Last Speech and dying words of John Clarkwright who was executed . . . for horse stealing . . .* (New York, 1770). #11602.

Coe, Daniel. *An Address to Mr. Thomas Shreeve, coroner for the city of New York . . .* [ridiculing him for his failings] (New York, 1772). #12356.

Graham, Chauncey. *God will trouble the troublers of his people. A sermon preached . . . July 14th, 1758. Being the day of the execution of Hugh Gillaspie for Felony . . .* (New York, 1759). #8356.

Jubeart, John. *The Confession and dying statement of John Jubeart, who was executed . . . for coining and passing counterfeit dollars . . .* (New York, 1769). #11303.

Parker, Joseph-Bill. *A Journal of the life of and travels of Joseph-Bill Parker, now under sentence of death in the City-Hall of Albany, for counterfeiting the currency . . .* (New York, 1773). #12914.

Personel, Francis Burdet. *An Authentic and particular account of the life of Francis Burdet Personel . . . Who was executed at New-York, September 10th, 1773, in the twenty-sixth year of his age, for the murder of Robert White* (New York, 1773). #12936.

Rum, Sir Richard (pseudonym). *At a Court held at Punch-Hall in the Colony of Bacchus. The Indictment and Tryal of Sr. Richard Rum, a person of noble birth and extraction, well known to both rich and poor throughout all America who was accused of several misdemeanors against his Majesty's liege people, viz. Killing some, wounding others, bringing thousands to poverty, and many good families to utter ruin* . . . (1724). #2582.

Smith, John. *The Last speech, confession and dying words of John Smith, who was executed at Albany . . . for counterfeiting . . .* (Albany, 1773). #13019. See also #13020.

Sullivan, Owen. *Narrative of the wicked Life and surprising adventures of that notorious money maker and cheat, Owen Sullivan . . . hanged in the City of New-York, May 10, 1756 . . .* (Boston, 1756). #7796.

Newspapers

The New-York Gazette, 1725–1744.
The New-York Gazette or *Weekly Post Boy,* 1747–1773.
The New-York Journal or *General Advertiser,* 1766–1776.
The New-York Weekly Journal, 1733–1751.

SECONDARY SOURCES

Early American Society

Blumenthal, Walter H. *Brides from the Bridewell: Female Felons Sent to Colonial America* (Rutland, Vt., 1962).

Bridenbaugh, Carl. *Cities in Revolt: Urban Life in America, 1743–1776* (New York, 1955; reprinted: New York, 1964).

——. *Cities in the Wilderness: The First Century of Urban Life in America, 1625–1742* (New York, 1938).

Bushman, Richard L. *From Puritan to Yankee: Character and the Social Order in Connecticut, 1690–1765* (Cambridge, 1967).

Butler, James. "British Convicts Shipped to the American Colonies," *American Historical Review,* 2 (1896), 12–33.

Curtin, Philip D. *The Atlantic Slave Trade: A Census* (Madison, 1969).

Demos, John. *A Little Commonwealth: Family Life in Plymouth Colony* (New York, 1970).

——. "Underlying Themes in the Witchcraft of Seventeenth Century New England," *American Historical Review,* 75 (1970), 1311–1326.

Flaherty, David H. *Privacy in Colonial New England* (Charlottesville, Va., 1972).

Genovese, Eugene. *Roll, Jordan, Roll: The World the Slaves Made* (New York, 1974).

Greene, Evarts B., and Virginia D. Harrington. *American Population before the Census of 1790* (New York, 1932; reprinted: New York, 1966).

Greven, Philip J. *Four Generations: Population, Land, and Family in Colonial Andover, Massachusetts* (Ithaca, 1970).

Historical Statistics of the United States: Colonial Times to 1957, Series Z (Washington, D.C., 1960).

Jernegan, Marcus W. *Laboring and Dependent Classes in Colonial America, 1607–1783* (Chicago, 1931).

Kammen, Michael G. *People of Paradox: An Inquiry Concerning the Origins of American Civilization* (New York, 1972).

Kurtz, Stephen G., and James H. Hutson, eds. *Essays on the American Revolution* (Chapel Hill, N.C., 1973).

Lauber, Almon W. *Indian Slavery in Colonial Times within the Present Limits of the United States* (New York, 1913).

Lockridge, Kenneth A. "Land, Population, and the Evolution of New England Society, 1630–1790," *Past and Present,* 39 (1965), 62–80.

——. *A New England Town, The First Hundred Years: Dedham, Massachusetts, 1636–1736* (New York, 1970).

Main, Jackson Turner. *The Social Structure of Revolutionary America* (Princeton, 1965).

Morris, Richard B. *Government and Labor in Early America* (New York, 1946).

Mullin, Gerald W. *Flight and Rebellion: Slave Resistance in Eighteenth-Century Virginia* (New York, 1972).

Murrin, John M. "Anglicizing an American Colony: The Transformation of Provincial Massachusetts" (Ph.D. diss., Yale University, 1966).

——. "Review Essay [of books by John Demos, Philip Greven, Kenneth Lockridge, Robert Pope, and Michael Zuckerman]," *History and Theory,* 11 (1972), 226–275.

Nash, Gary. *Red, White and Black: The Peoples of Early America* (Englewood Cliffs, N.J., 1974).

Norton, Mary Beth. *The British Americans: The Loyalist Exiles in England, 1774–1789* (Boston, 1972).

Potter, J. "The Growth of Population in America, 1700–1860," in D. V. Glass and D. E. C. Eversley, eds., *Population in History: Essays in Historical Demography* (Chicago, 1965), 631–679.

Rossiter, W. S. *A Century of Population Growth* (Washington, D.C., 1909).

Smith, Abbot E. *Colonists in Bondage: White Servitude and Convict Labor in America, 1607–1776* (Durham, N.C., 1947).

Sutherland, Stella H. *Population Distribution in Colonial America* (New York, 1936).

Wood, Peter H. *Black Majority: Negroes in Colonial South Carolina from 1670 through the Stono Rebellion* (New York, 1974).

Zuckerman, Michael. *Peaceable Kingdoms: New England Towns in the Eighteenth Century* (New York, 1970).

Colonial New York

Abbott, Carl. "The Neighborhoods of New York City, 1760–1775," *New York History,* 55 (1974), 35–54.

Aiken, John R. "Utopianism and the Emergence of the Colonial Legal Profession: New York, 1664–1710, A Test Case" (Ph.D. diss., University of Rochester, 1967).

Archdeacon, Thomas. "The Age of Leisler—New York City, 1689–1710: A Social and Demographic Interpretation," in Jacob Judd and Irwin H. Polishook, *Aspects of Early New York Society and Politics* (Tarrytown, N.Y., 1974).

——. *New York City, 1664–1710: Conquest and Change* (Ithaca, 1976).

Bonomi, Patricia U. *A Factious People: Politics and Society in Colonial New York* (New York, 1971).

——. "The Middle Colonies: Embryo of the New Political Order," in Alden T. Vaughan and George A. Billias, eds., *Perspectives on Early American History: Essays in Honor of Richard B. Morris* (New York, 1973), 63–92.

Chester, Alden. *The Legal and Judicial History of New York,* 3 vols. (New York, 1911).

Clarke, T. Wood. "The Negro Plot of 1741," *New York History,* 25 (1944), 167–181.

Crary, Catherine Snell. "The American Dream: John Tabor Kempe's Rise from Poverty to Riches," *William and Mary Quarterly,* Series 3, 14 (1957), 176–195.

Earle, Alice M. *Colonial Days in Old New York* (New York, 1896).

Edwards, George W. *New York as an Eighteenth-Century Municipality, 1731–1776* (New York, 1917).

Ehrlich, Jessica K. "A Town Study in Colonial New York: Newtown, Queens County (1642–1790)" (Ph.D. diss., University of Michigan, 1974).

Ellis, David M., *et al. A Short History of New York State* (Ithaca, 1957).

Flick, Alexander C., ed. *History of the State of New York,* 10 vols. (New York, 1933).

Goebel, Julius N., Jr., and T. Raymond Naughton. *Law Enforcement in Colonial New York: A Study in Criminal Procedure, 1664–1776* (New York, 1944; reprinted: Montclair, N.J., 1970).

Hamlin, Paul M. "The First Grievance Committee in New York," *Anglo-American Legal History Series,* Series I, Number 3, (1939), Paul M. Hamlin, ed.

Hamlin, Paul M., and Charles E. Baker. "Supreme Court of Judicature of the Province of New York, 1691–1704: An Introduction," in *Collections of the New-York Historical Society for the Year 1945* (New York, 1945).

Hershkowitz, Leo, ed. "Tom's Case: An Incident, 1741," *New York History,* 52 (1971), 63–71.

——. "The Troublesome Turk: An Illustration of Judicial Process in New Amsterdam," *New York History,* 46 (1965), 299–310.

Houghtaling, Earle H., Jr. "Administration of Justice in New Amsterdam," *de Halve Maen,* 43 (January, 1969), 17–19; 43 (October, 1968), 9–10.

Johnson, Herbert A. "Civil Procedure in John Jay's New York," *American Journal of Legal History,* 11 (1967), 69–80.

——. "George Harrison's Protest: New Light on Forsey *vs.* Cunningham," *New York History,* 50 (1969), 61–82.

Kammen, Michael. *Colonial New York: A History* (New York, 1975).

Kenney, Alice P. "Patricians and Plebeians in Colonial Albany: Part I —Historical Demography and the Hudson Valley Dutch," *de Halve Maen,* 45 (April, 1970), 7–8, 14; "Part II—Aggregation," *de Halve Maen,* 45 (July, 1970), 9–11, 13; Part III—Family Reconstitution," *de Halve Maen,* 45 (October, 1970), 14–15; "Part IV—Community Analysis," *de Halve Maen,* 45 (January, 1971), 13–14; "Part V— The Silent Tradition," *de Halve Maen,* 46 (April, 1971), 13–15.

Kim, Sung Bok. "The Manor of Cortlandt and Its Tenants, 1697–1783" (Ph.D. diss., Michigan State University, 1966).

——. "A New Look at the Great Landlords of Eighteenth-Century New York," *William and Mary Quarterly,* Ser. 3, 28 (1970), 581–614.

Klein, Milton M. "New York in the American Colonies: A New Look," *New York History,* 53 (1972), 132–156.

——. "Prelude to Revolution in New York: Jury Trials and Judicial

Tenure," *William and Mary Quarterly,* Series 3, 17 (1960), 439–462.

——. "The Rise of the New York Bar: The Legal Career of William Livingston," *William and Mary Quarterly,* Series 3, 15 (1958), 334–358.

Levy, Leonard W., and Lawrence H. Leder. " 'Exotic Fruit': The Right Against Self-Incrimination in Colonial New York," *William and Mary Quarterly,* Series 3, 20 (1963), 3–32.

Lewis, Elizabeth D. "Old Prisons and Punishments," in Maude W. Goodwin, ed., *Historic New York,* II (New York, 1899), 83–120.

McAnear, Beverly. "Politics in Provincial New York, 1689–1761" (Ph.D. diss., Stanford University, 1935).

McKee, Samuel. *Labor in Colonial New York, 1664–1776* (New York, 1935).

McManus, Edgar J. *A History of Negro Slavery in New York* (Syracuse, 1966).

Mackey, Philip E. "Capital Punishment in New Netherland," *de Halve Maen,* 47 (July, 1972), 7–8, 14.

Mark, Irving. *Agrarian Conflicts in Colonial New York, 1711–1775* (New York, 1940).

Mohl, Raymond A. "Poverty in Early America, a Reappraisal: The Case of Eighteenth-Century New York City," *New York History* (1969), 5–28.

——. *Poverty in New York, 1783–1825* (New York, 1971).

Nelson, William E. *Americanization of the Common Law: The Impact of Legal Change on Massachusetts Society, 1760–1830* (Cambridge, 1975).

——. "Emerging Notions of Modern Criminal Law: An Historical Perspective," *New York University Law Review,* 42 (1967), 450–482.

Peterson, Arthur E. *New York as an Eighteenth-Century Municipality Prior to 1731* (New York, 1917).

Peyer, Jean B. "Jamaica, Long Island, 1656–1776: A Study of the Roots of American Urbanism" (Ph.D. diss., City University of New York, 1974).

Richardson, James F. *The New York Police: Colonial Times to 1901* (New York, 1970).

Rosenwaike, Ira. *The Population History of New York City* (Syracuse, 1972).

Rothman, David J. *The Discovery of the Asylum: Social Order and Disorder in the New Republic* (Boston, 1971).

Schneider, David M. *The History of Public Welfare in New York State, 1609–1866* (Chicago, 1938).

Scott, Kenneth. *Counterfeiting in Colonial New York* (New York, 1953).

——. "The Slave Insurrection in New York in 1712," *New-York Historical Society Quarterly,* 45 (1961), 43–74.

Still, Bayrd. *Mirror for Gotham* (New York, 1956).

Stoker, Herman M. "Wholesale Prices at New York City, 1720–1800," *Cornell University Agricultural Experiment Station Memoir,* 142 (November, 1932), Part II.

Summers, Robert. "Law in Colonial New York: The Legal System of 1691," *Harvard Law Review,* 80 (1967), 1757–1772.

Szasz, Ferenc M. "The New York Slave Revolt of 1741: A Re-Examination," *New York History,* 48 (1967), 215–230.

Werner, Edgar A. *Civil List and Constitutional History of the Colony and State of New York* (Albany, 1888).

Wright, Langdon G. "Local Government and Central Authority in New Netherland," *New-York Historical Society Quarterly,* 57 (1973), 7–29.

——. "Local Government in Colonial New York, 1640–1710" (Ph.D. diss., Cornell University, 1974).

Crime and Law in Early America

Billias, George A., ed. *Law and Authority in Colonial America* (Barre, Mass., 1965).

Dalzell, George W. *Benefit of Clergy and Related Matters* (Winston-Salem, N.C., 1955).

Erickson, Kai T. *Wayward Puritans: A Study in the Sociology of Deviance* (New York, 1966).

Fitzroy, Herbert W. K. "The Punishment of Crime in Provincial Pennsylvania," *The Pennsylvania Magazine of History and Biography,* 60 (1936), 242–269.

Flaherty, David H., ed. *Essays in the History of Early American Law* (Chapel Hill, N.C., 1969).

——. "Law and the Enforcement of Morals in Early America," *Perspectives in American History,* 5 (1971), 209–253.

Friedman, Lawrence M. "Some Problems and Possibilities of American Legal History," in Herbert J. Bass, ed., *The State of American History* (Chicago, 1970), 3–22.

Gipson, Lawrence H. "Crime and Its Punishment in Provincial Pennsylvania," *Pennsylvania History,* 2 (1935), 3–16.

Hammonds, Oliver W. "The Attorney-General in the American Colonies," *Anglo-American Legal History Series,* Series I, Number 2 (1939), Paul M. Hamlin, ed.

Hartdagen, Gerald E. "The Vestries and Morals in Colonial Maryland," *Maryland Historical Magazine,* 63 (1968), 360–378.

Haskins, George Lee. "Ecclesiastical Antecedents of Criminal Punishment in Early Massachusetts," *Massachusetts Historical Society Collections,* 72 (1957–1960), 21–35.

——. *Law and Authority in Early Massachusetts: A Study in Tradition and Design* (New York, 1960).

Hurst, James W. *Law and Social Process in United States History* (Ann Arbor, 1960).

Minnick, Wayne C. "The New England Execution Sermon, 1639–1800," *Speech Monographs,* 35 (March, 1968), 77–89.

Morris, Richard B. *Studies in the History of American Law* (Second edition; New York, 1959).

Oberholzer, Emil, Jr. *Delinquent Saints: Disciplinary Action in the Early Congregational Churches of Massachusetts* (New York, 1956).

Powers, Edwin, ed. *Crime and Punishment in Early Massachusetts, 1620–1692: A Documentary History* (Boston, 1966).

Rankin, Hugh. *Criminal Trial Proceedings in the General Court of Colonial Virginia* (Williamsburg, 1965).

Scott, Arthur P. *Criminal Law in Colonial Virginia* (Chicago, 1930).

Scott, Kenneth. *Counterfeiting in Colonial America* (New York, 1957).

Semmes, Raphael. *Crime and Punishment in Early Maryland* (Baltimore, 1938).

Smith, Joseph H., ed. *Colonial Justice in Western Massachusetts (1639–1702): The Pynchon Court Record . . .* (Cambridge, 1961).

Weiss, Harry B., and Grace M. Weiss. *An Introduction to Crime and Punishment in Colonial New Jersey* (Trenton, 1960).

Williams, Oscar R. "Blacks and Colonial Legislation in the Middle Colonies" (Ph.D. diss., Ohio State University, 1969).

Crime and Social History: Some Sources of Comparison

Beattie, John M. "The Pattern of Crime in England, 1660–1800," *Past and Present,* 62 (1974), 47–95.

——. "Towards a Study of Crime in Eighteenth-Century England: A Note on Indictments," in Paul Fritz and David Williams, eds., *The Triumph of Culture: Eighteenth-Century Perspectives* (Toronto, 1972), 299–314.

——. "Trends in Crime against Property and Its Punishment in England, 1660–1800" (paper delivered at the meeting of the American Historical Association, New Orleans, December 29, 1972).

Bellamy, John. *Crime and Public Order in England in the Later Middle Ages* (Toronto, 1973).

Blassingame, John W. *The Slave Community: Plantation Life in the Ante-Bellum South* (New York, 1972).

Chevalier, Louis. *Classes Laboreurs et classes dangereuses à Paris pendant la première moitié de 19ème siècle,* Frank Jellinek, trans. (New York, 1973).

Cockburn, J. S. *A History of English Assizes, 1558–1714* (Cambridge, England, 1972).

Davis, David B. "The Movement to Abolish Capital Punishment in America, 1787–1861," *American Historical Review,* 63 (1957), 23–46.

Foucault, Michel. *Madness and Civilization: A History of Insanity in the Age of Reason,* Richard Howard, trans. (New York, 1965).

Gundersheimer, Werner L. "Crime and Punishment in Ferrara," in Lauro Martines, ed., *Violence and Civil Disorder in Italian Cities, 1200–1500* (Los Angeles, 1972).

Heale, M. J. "Humanitarianism in the Early Republic: The Moral Reformers of New York, 1776–1825," *Journal of American Studies,* 2 (1968), 161–175.

Heath, James, ed. *Eighteenth Century Penal Theory* (Glasgow, 1963).

Hibbert, Christopher. *The Roots of Evil: A Social History of Crime and Punishment* (Boston, 1963).

Hobsbawm, Eric. *Bandits* (London, 1969).

Journal of Social History (Summer, 1975).

Lane, Roger. "Crime and Criminal Statistics in Nineteenth Century Massachusetts," *Journal of Social History,* 2 (1968), 156–163.

——. *Policing the City: Boston, 1822–1855* (New York, 1971).

Langbein, John H. *Prosecuting Crime in the Renaissance* (Cambridge, Mass., 1974).

Lewis, W. David. *From Newgate to Dannemora: The Rise of the Penitentiary in New York, 1796–1848* (Ithaca, 1965).

Nelson, William E. "Emerging Notions of Modern Criminal Law in the Revolutionary Era: An Historical Perspective," *New York University Law Review,* 42 (1967), 450–482.

Radzinowicz, Leon. *A History of English Criminal Law and Its Administration from 1750,* 2 vols. (New York, 1948–1957).

Rothman, David J. *The Discovery of the Asylum: Social Order and Disorder in the New Republic* (Boston, 1971).

Rudé, George. *The Crowd in History, 1730–1848* (New York, 1964).

——. *Hanoverian London, 1714–1808* (Los Angeles, 1971).

Samaha, Joel B. *Law and Order in Historical Perspective: The Case of Elizabethan Essex* (New York, 1974).

Shaw, A. G. L. *Convicts and the Colonies: A Study of Penal Transportation from Great Britain and Ireland to Australia and Other Parts of the British Empire* (London, 1966).

Shaw, George Bernard. *The Crime of Imprisonment* (New York, 1946).

Somkin, Fred. *Unquiet Eagle: Memory and Desire in the Idea of American Freedom, 1815–1860* (Ithaca, 1967).

Thompson, E. P. "The Moral Economy of the English Crowd in the Eighteenth Century," *Past and Present,* 50 (1971), 76–136.

Tobias, J. J. *Crime and Industrial Society in the Nineteenth Century* (London, 1967).

Theory and Method: A Select Listing

Barnes, Harry Elmer, and Negley K. Teeters. *New Horizons in Criminology* (New York, 1933).

Clinard, Marshall B., ed. *Anomie and Deviant Behavior: A Discussion and Critique* (New York, 1964).

——. *Crime in Developing Countries: A Comparative Perspective* (New York, 1973).

——. "The Process of Urbanization and Criminal Behavior," *American Journal of Sociology,* 43 (1942), 202–213.

Elliott, Mabel A. "Crime and Frontier Mores," *American Sociological Review,* 9 (1944), 185–192.

Hay, Douglas, *et al., Albion's Fatal Tree: Crime and Society in Eighteenth-Century England* (London, 1976).

Quinney, Richard. *The Social Reality of Crime* (Boston, 1970).

Rusche, George, and Otto Kircheimer, *Punishment and Social Structure* (New York, 1939).

Schafer, Stephen. *Theories of Criminology: Past and Present Philosophers of the Crime Problem* (New York, 1969).

Walker, Nigel. *Crime and Punishment in Britain* (Edinburgh, 1965).

Index

Crime and Law Enforcement in the Colony of New York, 1691–1776

Designed by R. E. Rosenbaum.
Composed by York Composition Company, Inc.,
in 10 point Linotype Times Roman, 3 points leaded,
with display lines in Bulmer.
Printed letterpress from type by York Composition Company
on Warren's Number 66 text, 50 pound basis.
Bound by John H. Dekker & Sons, Inc.
in Joanna book cloth
and stamped in All Purpose foil.

Library of Congress Cataloging in Publication Data

Greenberg, Douglas.
Crime and law enforcement in the Colony of New York, 1691–1776.

Bibliography: p.
Includes index.
1. Crime and criminals—New York (State)—History.
2. Law enforcement—New York (State)—History. 3. New York (State)—History—Colonial period, ca. 1600–1775.
I. Title.
HV6793.N5G74 1974 364'.9747 76-13658
ISBN 0-8014-1020-7